Dr Belcher has been teaching o
five years, and it shows. Belch
Systematic Theology and the l
of each of the Covenants. Th
Reformed view, including both
Covenant of Works, in addition to looking at the details of each of the
individual covenants within the Covenant of Grace. Another strength
of this book is that Belcher irenically interacts with several minority
views, e.g., confessional Baptists, aspects of Meredith Kline. Finally,
Belcher concludes the study by reviewing three important aspects that
are emphasized to varying degrees within the Covenants; that is, the
Covenants show that there are legal, personal, and corporate aspects to
our glorious full salvation. I highly recommend this book.

ROBERT CARA
Hugh and Sallie Reaves Professor of New Testament,
Reformed Theological Seminary, Charlotte, North Carolina

While some think that 'covenant theology' is an outdated theological
innovation belonging to a bygone era, others have more recently
discovered that it is a central doctrine of the Christian faith unfolded
progressively in the biblical text. Richard Belcher belongs to this latter
group. He believes that 'covenant theology' provides the God-given
framework that safeguards the Scriptural message of salvation by grace
and promises spiritual renewal, forgiveness of sin, perfect righteousness
and deep assurance of faith. Thus 'covenant theology' offers the only
secure basis for joyful and fruitful Christian living.

He writes in the attractive and simple style of a biblical theologian
who nevertheless makes systematic theological sense of a complex
subject. This important book offers a comprehensive theology of the
covenant that is grounded in a historical and contextual analysis of
Scripture that is both irenic and fair-minded and will be of significant
appeal to the wider Evangelical/Reformed community. This book is a
tour de force on the subject.

PETER HASTIE
Principal, Presbyterian Theological College, Melbourne, Victoria

Dr Belcher offers a clear explanation of the covenants in their biblical context. In addition to covering the classic Westminster formulation of covenant theology, he addresses varying views of the covenants, including those of reformed Baptists. One of the strengths of the book is that he has taken time to understand the views of those with whom he differs and presents them with kindness and accuracy. His summaries are most helpful. People who are new to the reformed faith will benefit from this easy to read summary of covenant theology which is rooted in Scripture and saturated with the gospel.

JIM NEWHEISER
Executive Director,
The Institute For Biblical Counseling and Discipleship

Richard Belcher has given us a welcomed survey and analysis of divine covenants in the Scriptures. His commitment to traditional Reformed Theology is evident as he explains and evaluates a variety of outlooks on biblical covenants. His explanations are clear and insightful. This volume will help many theological students and lay people alike as they explore the contours of Covenant Theology today.

RICHARD PRATT
President, Third Millennium Ministries, Orlando, Florida

Dick Belcher's *The Fulfillment of the Promises of God* is now the introduction to covenant theology. It will join the syllabus of my Covenant Theology course, and will be the first book that I recommend to seminarians not only for introducing the subject, but providing assessment of the main alternatives to classic Reformed covenant theology. This is now the starting point for those looking for a confessional Reformed presentation.

LIGON DUNCAN
Chancellor and CEO, Reformed Theological Seminary

MENTOR

The FULFILLMENT of the PROMISES of GOD

An Explanation of Covenant Theology

RICHARD P. BELCHER, JR.

ⅢENTOR
Encouraging Christians to Think

CONTENTS

Acknowledgements

A book written on covenant theology later in life enables one to pause and reflect on the goodness of God's promises. I grew up in the home of a Southern Baptist preacher and walked the aisle at a revival meeting when I was six years old. I was truly converted, for I had a consciousness of my sin before a holy God and trusted in Christ for my salvation.

Several years later, before I went to college, my father had a 'conversion' from Arminianism to the doctrines of grace. It totally changed his approach to pastoral ministry. We lived near St. Louis, Missouri, so he attended Covenant Seminary and then received his Th.D. at Concordia Seminary on A. W. Pink's view of Predestination. He ended up teaching at Columbia Bible College (now Columbia International University) in Columbia, South Carolina, for almost thirty years. He was involved in the Founder's Movement and attended the Southern Baptist convention faithfully to vote for the conservative candidates.

Back in those days, Calvinism was not very prominent among Baptists and my father encouraged me to go Covenant College. In one sense, the die was cast and eventually I went over to the 'other side'. This was never a point of contention between us and he was very supportive of my pursuit of a Ph.D. at Westminster Seminary and was happy to have us close by when I took the job of teaching the Old Testament at Reformed Theological Seminary (RTS) in Charlotte, North Carolina.

After my father retired, eventually my parents moved in with us. My mother died several years ago of Alzheimer's and my father now has that dreadful disease. He is living in a memory care unit and does not know who I am because his mind is gone. Having heard him preach many sermons on the sovereignty of God, I know he would say that God has His purpose in these events, even if we do not know what His purposes are, and that we must seek to be faithful to the God who ordains all things for our good and His glory.

I am very thankful for RTS and the privilege of teaching OT at the Charlotte campus. I was hired in 1995, soon after the campus started. Ric Cannada had moved to Charlotte to be the President of the Campus and the faculty when I arrived was Robert (Bob) Cara (NT), Doug Kelly (ST), Will Norton (Missions) and Frank Kik (PT). Bob and I had a lot in common. Both of us were pastor's kids and grew up in relatively poor areas of the country. He became an engineer and I a pastor, but we both ended up at Westminster Theological Seminary for our Ph.Ds (although I came later, so we did not know each other at WTS). In the early days of the Charlotte campus we spent a lot of time discussing how to teach the different sections of the canon. I have greatly benefited from his friendship and the many hours of discussing theology with him, including covenant theology. In fact, the idea to write a book on basic covenant theology, as represented in the Westminster Confession of Faith, was his idea. Perhaps it would have been better if he had written the book! However, I take full responsibility for the contents of it.

Several years later another NT professor was hired, Mike Kruger. He fit right in with the ethos of the Charlotte campus and the three of us spent a lot of time together discussing the Bible and theology. Those were good days. Other professors added along the way included Don Fortson, Ken McMullen, Harold O. J. Brown, John Oliver, and John Currid. With deaths and retirements, other professors were hired, including Rod Culbertson, James Anderson, Jim Newheiser, Blair Smith, Kevin DeYoung, and William Ross. Bob Cara become Chief Academic Officer of RTS and then Provost. Mike Kruger became President of the Charlotte campus, and I have had the privilege of being the Academic Dean of the campuses of RTS Charlotte and Atlanta. I have been thankful for the unity and the humility of my colleagues, and the joy we have serving together. I have been blessed by each of them.

I would also like to thank my family who have been a great blessing to my life. My wife Lu is a wonderful companion and is multi-talented, using her gifts at home and at church for the Lord. We are blessed with three daughters and five grandchildren, all who live close by, so we have the privilege of seeing them regularly. I would also like to thank Robert

Hertha, my teaching assistant, for his help in this project and the other projects he has worked on for me. The library staff at RTS Charlotte has been wonderful in tracking down books and references. Thank you, Ken McMullen, Jessica Hudson, and Emily Haggar.

The God that we serve is a sovereign and loving God. He planned our salvation from eternity past and worked out that salvation in redemptive history through the unfolding of His promises by means of covenants. He has been and will be faithful to those covenant promises. Thus, we face the future with the confidence that He will work out His purposes for our individual lives and for His people to His glory for all eternity.

RICHARD P. BELCHER, JR.
Charlotte, NC
July 2019

Abbreviations

1LCF	First London Confession of Faith (1646)
2LCF	Second London Confession of Faith (1689)
AB	Anchor Bible
ANE	Ancient Near East
AOTC	Apollos Old Testament Commentary
ARP	Associate Reformed Presbyterian Church
BBR	*Bulletin for Biblical Research*
BDAG	*A Greek-English Lexicon of the New Testament and other Early Christian Literature*, rev. and ed. Frederick William Danker. 3rd ed. University of Chicago Press, 2000.
BECNT	Baker Exegetical Commentary on the New Testament
CBQ	*Catholic Biblical Quarterly*
CTJ	*Calvin Theological Journal*
EQ	*Evangelical Quarterly*
FV	Federal Vision
GKC	*Gesenius Hebrew Grammar*, eds. E. Kautzsch and A. E. Cowley. Oxford: Clarendon Press, 1910.
ICC	International Critical Commentary
JAOS	*Journal of the American Oriental Society*
JBL	*Journal of Biblical Literature*
JETS	*Journal of the Evangelical Theological Society*
KTC	*Kingdom Through Covenant*
NAC	New American Commentary

NAS	New American Standard Version
NCB	New Century Bible Commentary
NCT	New Covenant Theology
NIBC	New International Bible Commentary
NICOT	New International Commentary on the Old Testament
NIDOTTE	*New International Dictionary of Old Testament Theology and Exegesis*, ed. W. A. VanGemeren, 5 vols., Grand Rapid: Zondervan, 1997
NIVAC	NIV Application Commentary
NSBT	New Studies in Biblical Theology
NTC	New Testament Commentary
OTL	Old Testament Library
OPC	Orthodox Presbyterian Church
PC	Progressive Covenantalism
PCA	Presbyterian Church of America
PNTC	Pillar New Testament Commentary
RB	*Revue Biblique*
RBAP	Reformed Baptist Academic Press
SJT	*Scottish Journal of Theology*
THOTC	Two Horizons Old Testament Commentary
TOTC	Tyndale Old Testament Commentary
TWOT	*Theological Wordbook of the Old Testament*, eds., R. Laird Harris, Gleason L. Archer, Jr., and Bruce K. Waltke, 2 vols., Chicago: Moody Press, 1980
TynBul	*Tyndale Bulletin*
VT	*Vestus Testamentum*
WBC	Word Biblical Commentary
WCF	Westminster Confession of Faith
WLC	Westminster Larger Catechism
WSC	Westminster Shorter Catechism
WTJ	*Westminster Theological Journal*

CHAPTER 1

Introduction to Covenant Theology

❋ ❋ ❋

The Difficult Nature of Covenant Theology

COVENANT theology is a vast and complex topic. It is easy to get lost in the various approaches and the different emphases of covenant theologians. Part of the confusion comes from the fact that scholars who approach the topic from similar viewpoints use different terminology to describe the components of covenant theology. Is there a covenant in Genesis 1–2 and what should it be called (Covenant of Works, Covenant of Life, Covenant of Creation)? Are there two basic overarching covenants in Scripture (bi-covenantal) or is there only one (mono-covenantal)? How should the Mosaic Covenant be understood? Is it part of the Covenant of Grace? Is it a republication of the Covenant of Works? How does the principle of works operate in the Mosaic Covenant (Lev. 18:5)? Major players in covenant theology have not always agreed on these questions. Various emphases within covenant theology have developed associated with certain individuals – it is not unusual to find those who follow John Murray or Meredith Kline.

The work of such men is greatly appreciated, but there is a need for a book that explains covenant theology according to the Westminster

Confession of Faith (WCF). This confession is the standard for several denominations and so it makes sense to begin with what the WCF has to say about covenant theology. The goal of this book is to explain covenant theology as it is presented in the WCF. This approach will not solve all the questions related to covenant theology, but it hopes to give clarity to some contested issues. Covenant theology, as presented in the Westminster Standards, is the starting point for understanding reformed covenant theology. This confession is the culmination of reformed thinking going back to the Reformation. The doctrine of the covenant is one of the distinctive features of the Westminster Standards because it is not merely a peripheral issue but is central to the system of doctrine taught in the confession.[1] In fact, it was the first confessional standard to use the terms Covenant of Works and Covenant of Grace.[2] In addition, this confessional standard is the creed used by conservative Presbyterian denominations all over the world.[3] Many who read this book will have taken vows to uphold the Westminster Standards. Thus, one of the purposes of this book is to help seminary students, elders, and lay people understand covenant theology and to navigate the various approaches to it that are prominent today. Then, other approaches will be compared to the viewpoint of the Westminster Standards.

---

1. Geerhardus Vos, 'The Doctrine of the Covenant in Reformed Theology,' in *Redemptive History and Biblical Interpretation, The Shorter Writings of Geerhardus Vos*, ed. Richard B. Gaffin, Jr. (Phillipsburg, NJ: Presbyterian and Reformed Publishing Co., 1980), p. 239. He comments, 'The Westminster Confession is the first Reformed confession in which the doctrine of the covenant is not merely brought in from the side, but it is placed in the foreground and has been able to permeate at almost every point.'

2. Morton H. Smith, 'Federal Theology and the Westminster Standards,' in *The Covenant*, eds. Joseph A. Pipa, Jr. and C. N. Willborn (Taylors, SC: Presbyterian Press, 2005), p. 18. Cornelius P. Venema argues that there is no substantive difference between the Westminster Standards and the Three Forms of Unity on the doctrine of Christ and the covenants (*Christ and Covenant Theology: Essays on Election, Republication, and the Covenants* [Phillipsburg: P&R, 2017], p. 16, n. 21).

3. Besides the ARP, PCA, and OPC in the U.S.A., the Free Church of Scotland, the International Presbyterian Church (a family of churches spread across Great Britain, Europe and Korea since 1954 that affirm belief in either the WCF or the Three Forms of Unity), the Evangelical Presbyterian Church of England and Wales, the Presbyterian Church of Australia, The Presbyterian Church of Brazil, and the National Presbyterian Church in Mexico, among others.

The Importance of Covenant Theology

John Stek has questioned whether the concept of 'covenant' has been too heavily overloaded with an enormous weight of theological importance. Covenant is used so much that it comes to have a life of its own outside the Scriptural data.[4] There may be some truth to this in circles where the word 'covenant' becomes an adjective appended to almost anything. Yet one cannot read Scripture for very long before it becomes obvious that covenant is a key concept in the Bible.[5] The central place of covenant theology in the Bible is expressed well by Packer when he calls covenant theology a hermeneutic, 'a way of reading the whole Bible that is itself part of the overall interpretation of the Bible that it undergirds.'[6] Horton calls covenant the architectural structure of the Bible that holds together biblical faith and practice. Like the architecture of a building, the covenant is largely hidden from view.[7] Thus the covenant structure is always there even if it is not recognized or noticed.

Packer shows how covenant theology undergirds the structure of Scripture by the story it tells, by the place it gives to Jesus Christ, by the specific parallel between Christ and Adam, and by explicitly declaring the Covenant of Redemption in John's Gospel (He has come to do the Father's will and is given a particular people to save).[8] There are many concepts in Scripture that cannot be understood properly without understanding the covenant. Jesus used covenant terminology

---

4. John H. Stek, 'Covenant Overload in Reformed Theology,' *CTJ* 29 (1994): pp. 12-41. For other objections to covenant theology, see Ligon Duncan, 'Recent Objections to Covenant Theology: A Description, Evaluation and Response,' in *The Westminster Confession of Faith into the 21st Century, Volume Three*, ed. Ligon Duncan (Ross-shire: Christian Focus, 2009).

5. Craig G. Bartholomew, 'Covenant and Creation: Covenant Overload or Covenantal Deconstruction?' *CTJ* 30 (1995): pp. 11-33. He seeks to answer the arguments of Stek. See also John Bolt, 'Why the Covenant of Works is a Necessary Doctrine,' in *By Faith Alone: Answering the Challenges to the Doctrine of Justification*, eds. Gary L. W. Johnson and Guy P. Waters (Wheaton, IL: Crossway, 2006), pp. 171-90. He interacts with both John Stek and Anthony Hoekema.

6. J. I. Packer, 'Introduction: On Covenant Theology,' in Herman Witsius, *The Economy of the Covenants between God and Man* (2 vols.; Phillipsburg, NJ: P&R, 1990), n.p.

7. Michael Horton, *God of Promise: Introducing Covenant Theology* (Grand Rapids: Baker Books, 2006), pp. 13-14.

8. Packer, 'Introduction,' n.p.

at a Passover to explain the significance of His death (Luke 22:20). Paul uses the language of covenant curse in explaining the importance of participating in the Lord's Supper in a worthy manner (1 Cor. 11:25, 29). The book of Hebrews speaks of a covenant mediator in reference to the high priestly work of Christ (Heb. 8:6). Covenant is so central to the outworking of God's plan of salvation that the gospel needs the framework of covenant theology.[9] Covenant explains the work of Christ on the cross, the administration of salvation in the Old Testament, the administration of salvation in the New Testament in the covenant signs of baptism and the Lord's Supper, and the relationship established between God and His people. Covenants give assurance to God's people that a relationship with God is secure through covenant promises (see God's response to Abraham in Genesis 15 and 17).[10]

The Definition of Covenant

The word 'covenant' (*bĕr'ṯ*) refers to a legal agreement between two parties that is ratified by certain rituals that emphasize the binding nature of the agreement. The phrase in the Old Testament that is used to establish a covenant is 'to cut a covenant'. This phrase highlights the rituals of sacrifices and oaths that are at the heart of establishing a covenant (Gen. 15:7-18).[11] Covenants are made in a variety of situations. There are covenants between human parties who are equal (Gen. 21:27, 26:26-31, 31:44-50; 1 Sam. 18:3), between human parties who are not equal (Josh. 9:3-21; 1 Sam. 11:1; 1 Kings 20:34), and between God and humans (Gen. 6:18; 15:18; 17:2; Exod. 19:5; 2 Sam. 7; Ps. 89:3).[12]

Common elements in covenants include promises made and oaths taken to ensure the promises will be carried out. They include stipulations or laws that must be kept. There are blessings for keeping the covenant, and curses for breaking the covenant. Covenants also include descendants. Covenants are ratified by blood. Not every mention of a covenant includes the rituals that establish the covenant, but the importance of sacrifices

---

9. Packer, 'Introduction,' n.p.
10. Duncan, 'Recent Objections to Covenant Theology', pp. 498-500.
11. Elmer B. Smick, ברה, [ברית], *TWOT*, p. 1:128.
12. Gordon J. McConville, ברית, *NIDOTTE*, p. 1:748.

is seen in the covenant with Abraham (Gen. 15:7-18). The importance of the oath is seen in the covenant between Israel and the Gibeonites (Josh. 9).[13] Many times witnesses are a testimony to the covenant that has been ratified (c.f. Gen. 31:44-47). The importance of the stipulations (laws) and the sanctions (penalties for breaking the covenant) are seen in the Mosaic Covenant (Deut. 27–28; Lev. 26). Covenants also produced written documents where the promises, stipulations, and sanctions are spelled out (Deuteronomy).[14] Signs are also important in covenants, as seen in the rainbow (Gen. 9:12-13), circumcision (Gen. 17:11), and the Sabbath (Exod. 31:16-17).

The Covenant of Redemption

The Covenant of Redemption, also called the *pactum salutis* (a counsel of peace), is a pre-temporal agreement between the members of the Trinity concerning the different roles each member would perform to bring about the salvation of God's people. The Father promises to redeem an elect people. The Son promises to earn the salvation of His people by becoming a human being in order to be a mediator for them. In this role Christ fulfills the conditions of the covenant through His perfect obedience to the Law of God and His substitutionary death on the cross. The Holy Spirit applies the work of the Son to God's people through the means of grace. This covenant is foundational for the outworking of the historical covenants. When Christ kept the law, He was fulfilling both the historical Covenant of Works made with Adam and the pre-temporal covenant He made with the Father and the Spirit. This covenant was also the basis upon which the Covenant of Grace rested because salvation is applied to the elect based on the work of Christ.[15]

---

13. The Gibeonites lived within the land of Canaan and should have been destroyed, but they presented themselves to Israel as living outside the land and coming from a distance to make a treaty with Israel. Once the covenant was made, Israel was bound to keep the covenant even when they found out that the Gibeonites lived in the land. The importance of the oath is seen in Israel's later history in 2 Samuel 21:1-9.

14. Smick, ברה, [ברית], *TWOT*, pp. 1:128-29. See also Michael J. Kruger, *Canon Revisited* (Wheaton: Crossway, 2012), pp. 160-94.

15. David VanDrunen and R. Scott Clark, 'The Covenant before the Covenants,' in *Covenant, Justification, and Pastoral Ministry*, ed. R. Scott Clark (Phillipsburg, NJ:

The biblical basis for the Covenant of Redemption is found in passages that describe the relationship between the Father and the Son as conditioned on the obedience of the Son with the promise of reward (John 10:18; 12:49; 14:31: 15:10; 17:4; Phil. 2:8; Heb. 5:8; 10:5-10). Covenantal language of being bound by oath is used to describe this relationship (Isa. 45:23 used in Phil. 2:10-11; Ps. 110:1, 4). Many early Reformed confessions did not explicitly refer to the Covenant of Redemption but they contained ideas that were foundational for understanding it.[16] This covenant is not explicitly referred to in the WCF but many who attended the Westminster Assembly affirmed it.[17] The Trinitarian Covenant of Redemption facilitated the distinction that the Covenant of Grace was made with Christ and with His elect in Him.[18] The ideas behind it are expressed in comments concerning Christ fulfilling the stipulations of the covenant as the mediator of His people (WCF 8).[19]

Covenant in Historical Perspective

There are many questions concerning covenant theology that will not be addressed in this book, particularly questions related to the development of covenant theology in church history. What role did the covenant play in the early church fathers? What is the relationship between the understanding of the covenant in the Reformation and

P&R, 2007), p. 168. See also Scott R. Swain, 'Covenant of Redemption,' in *Christian Dogmatics: Reformed Theology for the Church Catholic*, eds. Michael Allen and Scott R. Swain (Grand Rapids, MI: Baker Academic, 2016), pp. 107-25. For an analysis of the Covenant of Redemption from historical, exegetical, and theological perspectives, see J. V. Fesko, *The Trinity and the Covenant of Redemption* (Ross-shire: Christian Focus, 2016). For a negative view of this covenant, see Paul R. Williamson, 'The "Pactum Salutis": A Scriptural Concept or Scholastic Mythology?' *TynBul* 69.2 (2018): pp. 259-82.

16. VanDrunen and Clark, 'Covenant before the Covenants,' pp. 171-72. They discuss the Belgic Confession, the Heidelberg Catechism, the Canons of Dort, and the WCF.

17. Andrew A. Woolsey, *Unity and Continuity in Covenantal Thought: A Study in the Reformed Tradition to the Westminster Assembly* (Grand Rapids: Reformation Heritage Books, 2012), pp. 58-59.

18. Woolsey, *Unity and Continuity*, p. 59. For the importance of the Covenant of Redemption concerning union with Christ, see Donald Macleod, 'Covenant Theology,' in *Dictionary of Scottish Church History and Theology*, ed. Nigel M. de S. Cameron (Downers Grove, IL: InterVarsity Press, 1993), p. 215.

19. VanDrunen and Clark, 'Covenant before the Covenants,' pp. 172-73.

the early church fathers? What was Calvin's view of the covenant? What is the relationship between the Reformers' view of the covenant and the view of seventeenth century reformed scholars? These are important questions and there are answers to them. The concept of the covenant was not a foreign concept in the early church fathers.[20] The views of the covenant in the Reformation did not develop out of thin air. Calvin expresses all the major ideas related to covenant theology.[21] The seventeenth century reformed scholars build upon the covenant theology of the Reformation to develop it. They should not be seen as taking the idea of the covenant in completely new directions.[22]

The aim of this book will be to set forth standard reformed covenant theology as exemplified in the Scriptures and explained in the WCF. The first eight chapters discuss the major covenants in Scripture. There will also be an attempt to show where scholars have deviated from the standard of the WCF. Some of these deviations will be minor, but others will hit at the heart of covenant theology and will have implications for other important doctrines that are related to it. Meredith Kline has had such a significant impact on how people understand covenant theology that two chapters focus on his views. A chapter is devoted to the confessional Baptists, and then a chapter discusses the recent, magisterial work *Kingdom Through Covenant*, which represents a prominent view among Baptists today.

20.　J. Ligon Duncan, 'The Covenant Idea in Ante-Nicene Theology,' PhD Dissertation, University of Edinburgh, 1995. For a historical review of the concept of covenant in different periods of church history, see Peter Golding, *Covenant Theology: The Key of Theology in Reformed Thought and Tradition* (Ross-shire: Christian Focus, 2004).

21.　Anthony A. Hoekema, 'Calvin's Doctrine of the Covenant of Grace', *Reformed Review* 15.4 (1962): p. 1-12; Peter A. Lillback, 'The Continuing Conundrum: Calvin and the Conditionality of the Covenant,' *CTJ* 29 (1994): pp. 42-74; and Lillback, *The Binding of God: Calvin's Role in the Development of Covenant Theology* (Grand Rapids: Baker, 2001).

22.　Hoekema, 'Calvin's Doctrine of the Covenant of Grace,' pp. 1-12. For a general discussion of the relationship of the Reformation to seventeenth century Reformed theology, including the covenant, see Richard A. Muller, *After Calvin: Studies in the Development of a Theological Tradition* (Oxford: Oxford University Press, 2003); for the relationship between Calvin and the covenant theology of the WCF, see Paul Helm, 'Calvin and the Covenant: Unity and Continuity,' *EQ* 55 (1983): pp. 65-82.

CHAPTER 2

The Covenant of Works

❋ ❋ ❋

ONE of the perceived weak links of covenant theology is the Covenant of
Works. Many argue that there is no evidence of a covenant between God and
Adam in Genesis 1–3.[1] Without the Covenant of Works the bi-covenantal
nature of covenant theology crashes to the ground, leaving one covenant to
define the relationship between God and humanity. A 'mono-covenantal'
approach does not see a difference between the way God dealt with Adam
before the Fall and the way God deals with human beings after the Fall.
The implications of denying the Covenant of Works can be monumental
for theology because the Covenant of Works lays a foundation for other key
doctrines of Scripture, including the obedience of Christ, the relationship

---

1. Some examples include Karl Barth, *Church Dogmatics* (Edinburgh: T & T Clark,
1958), III/1, pp. 231-32 and IV/1, pp. 56-65; Holmes Rolston III, *John Calvin versus the
Westminster Confession* (Richmond, VA: John Knox, 1972); T. F. Torrance, 'From John
Knox to John McLeod Campbell: A Reading of Scottish Theology,' in *Disruption to
Diversity: Edinburgh Divinity 1846–1996*, eds., David F. Wright and Gary D. Babcock
(Edinburgh: T & T Clark, 1996); J. B. Torrance, 'Covenant or Contract? A Study of the
Theological Background of Worship in Seventeenth-Century Scotland,' *SJT*, 23.1 (1970):
pp. 51-76; and G. C. Berkouwer, *Sin* (Grand Rapids: Eerdmans, 1971). For an analysis of
some of these authors, see Venema, *Christ and Covenant Theology*, pp. 6-17 and Mark I.
McDowell, 'Covenant in the Theology of Karl Barth, T. F. & J. B. Torrance,' in *Covenant
Theology*, eds. Guy Waters, J. Nicholas Reid, and John Muether (Wheaton, IL: Crossway,
forthcoming November 2020).

between Adam and Christ, and the concept of Christ as a mediator. These ideas are important for a correct view of justification by faith and the imputation of Adam's sin and Christ's righteousness.[2] This chapter seeks to set forth the basic teachings of Scripture and the WCF on the Covenant of Works and to show the importance of this covenant to the work of Christ and the nature of salvation.

The Evidence for the Covenant of Works in Genesis 1–3

The word 'covenant' does not occur in Scripture until the Flood account in Genesis 6:18. If the word 'covenant' does not occur in Genesis 1–3, what is the evidence that the relationship between God and Adam is a covenant relationship? The absence of the word 'covenant' does not necessarily mean that there is no covenant in Genesis 1–3. The word 'covenant' does not occur in 2 Samuel 7 or 1 Chronicles 17 where God makes certain promises to David, but other passages refer to this relationship as a covenant (2 Sam. 23:5; Pss. 89:3, 28; 132:11-12). A similar situation occurs with Genesis 1–3. The term 'covenant' is not used in the early chapters of Genesis, but later Scripture refers back to Genesis 1–3 and uses the word (see the discussion of Hosea 6:7 below). The key is not whether the word 'covenant 'occurs in Genesis 1–3 but whether the elements of a covenant are present.

The Elements of a Covenant in Genesis 1–3

Several elements commonly associated with covenants are present in Genesis 1–3.[3] First, the parties to the covenant are clearly identified. Genesis 1:1 assumes the existence of God who is 'in the beginning'. He is the sovereign ruler of the universe as demonstrated in His creation of the world. Special attention is given to His creation of mankind in His image and who have a special place in God's creation under His

---

2. The importance of covenant theology in general is stated by Duncan, 'Covenant theology explains the meaning of the death of Christ … undergirds our understanding of the nature and use of the sacraments, and provides the fullest possible explanations of the grounds of our assurance' (Duncan, 'Recent Objections to Covenant Theology,' p. 467).

3. The following elements of the Covenant of Works are discussed in L. Berkhof, *Systematic Theology* (Grand Rapids: Eerdmans, 1941), pp. 213-17 and, more substantially, in Herman Witsius, *The Economy of the Covenants Between God and Man* (Escondido, CA: The den Dulk Christian Foundation, 1990), pp. 50-103.

authority (Gen. 1:26-28). In Genesis 1 the generic term for humanity is used (*'ādām*) and in Genesis 2 the specific partner in this covenant is identified as Adam (*'ādām*). God takes the initiative in creating the world and in entering into a covenant relationship with the first man.

Second, covenants have conditions. The condition to this covenant relationship is set forth in the commandment that God gave to Adam not to eat of the tree of the knowledge of good and evil (Gen. 2:16-17). God provided everything that Adam needed for life in the garden, including water, work, and companionship in marriage. His abundant goodness was shown in allowing Adam to eat from most of the trees in the garden, but He prohibited him from eating the fruit of one tree. God tested Adam to see if he would disdain God's beneficent provision of food and eat from the prohibited tree. No reason is given why Adam could not eat from the tree of the knowledge of good and evil. This commandment with a penalty attached to it focuses on the importance of the requirement of Adam obeying God in everything.[4] It presents Adam with a clear choice of obedience or disobedience to God, and Adam could keep this divine commandment.

Third, covenants have blessings and curses. The relationship between God and Adam also includes blessings and curses. In Genesis 1:28 God blesses mankind and commands them to multiply and fill the earth, to subdue it, and to have dominion over every living thing that moves on it. God's blessings are experienced in the fulfillment of God's commands. God's blessings are also seen in how God provides everything that Adam needs in the garden for a full and productive life (Gen. 2). The curse is connected to the prohibition that Adam should not eat from the tree of the knowledge of good and evil, 'for in the day that you eat of it you shall surely die' (Gen. 2:17). The penalty for breaking God's commandment

---

4. Francis Turretin saw the tree of knowledge of good and evil as a sacrament of trial (*Institutes of Elenctic Theology: Volume One*, ed. James T. Dennison, Jr (Phillipsburg: P&R, 1992), pp. 580-82. G. K. Beale understands the tree of knowledge of good and evil as a probationary, judgment tree where Adam should have gone to discern between good and evil. He should have judged the serpent as evil and pronounced judgment on it (*A New Testament Biblical Theology: The Unfolding of the Old Testament in the New* [Grand Rapids: Baker Academic, 2011], p. 35; see also Meredith G. Kline, *Kingdom Prologue: Genesis Foundations for a Covenantal Worldview* [Overland Park, KS: Two Age Press, 2000], p. 103-07).

is death. If Adam disobeys God, there will be momentous changes in his relationship with God, his relationship with Eve, his relationship with creation, and his perception of himself. Death will include physical death, but it will also have immediate spiritual implications.

Fourth, covenants operate on the basis of a representative principle so that the actions of the covenant representative impacts others who are part of the covenant relationship. In every covenant this principle includes descendants (Gen. 17:7; Deut. 5:2-3; 2 Sam. 7:12-16). The penalty clearly states that if Adam eats from the fruit of the tree of the knowledge of good and evil, he will die. The entrance of sin and death into the world not only impacts Adam, and his descendants, but also creation (Gen. 3:17-18). The triumph of sin is shown in the children of Adam and Eve when Cain murders Abel. There is a separation of the ungodly line from the godly line with the intensification of sin in the boast of Lamech (Gen. 4:23-24). Not even the godly line is exempt from the result of sin as the genealogy of Adam in Genesis 5 highlights the refrain 'and he died'. Adam was the covenant head of the human race and his sin negatively impacted all of his natural descendants. Theologically, sin was imputed to every natural descendant of Adam because of his transgression (Rom. 5:12). The implication is that if Adam had obeyed God's commandment and had passed the test, then he would have experienced further blessings. If disobedience brings death, then it is reasonable to conclude that obedience would mean life enjoyed with greater blessing.[5] Adam was created in a state of positive holiness and was not subject to the law of death, but the possibility of sinning still existed. He did not yet enjoy life in its fullness to the highest degree of perfection.[6]

Fifth, covenants have signs that point to the blessings of the covenant relationship. Scholars have debated how many signs there are in Genesis

---

5. Woolsey, *Unity and Continuity in Covenantal Thought*, p. 49. See also Beale, *A New Testament Biblical Theology*, pp. 29-45, who lays out the evidence from Genesis 1–3 that if Adam had been obedient, he would have experienced even greater blessings than he had before his sin. He argues on the basis of 1 Corinthians 15:45, where Paul appeals to Adam in his pre-fall and sinless condition, that even if Adam had never sinned, his pre-fall existence still needed to be transformed at some climactic point into an irreversible glorious existence. He concludes that '... Adam would have been rewarded with a transformed, incorruptible body if he had remained faithful' (p. 45).

6. Berkhof, *Systematic Theology*, p. 217.

1–3 but most agree that the tree of life is a sign of the covenant.[7] The tree of life was a pledge of the covenant of life (WLC 20), the promised reward for obedience. The fruit of this tree should not be regarded as having an innate power to prolong life.[8] Rather, the tree symbolized life so that when Adam forfeited the promise he was kept from the sign (Gen. 3:22).

Hosea 6:7: A Reference to a Covenant with Adam?

It is also significant that another passage in the Old Testament refers to God's relationship with Adam in Genesis 1–3 and uses the term 'covenant'. Hosea 6:7 states, 'But like Adam they transgressed the covenant; there they dealt faithlessly with me.' Much discussion centers on whether 'Adam' is a personal name, a generic use referring to humanity, or a place name. Support for the place name 'Adam' comes from the use of the preposition 'there' ($\check{sam}$) in the next clause. This would refer to some transgression of the covenant that took place at Adam. Yet, no Scriptural evidence of covenant breaking at Adam exists.[9] Also, this view requires that the preposition before 'Adam' be amended from 'like' (k^e) to 'at' (b^e). The preposition 'like' supports the view that 'Adam' is either a reference to the first human being who broke the covenant through his disobedience[10] or to human beings who 'show themselves to be men in violating the covenant'.[11] The generic view of 'human beings' takes

---

7. Berkhof, *Systematic Theology*, p. 217. Kline understands both the tree of life and the Sabbath as covenantal signs (*Kingdom Prologue*, p. 96). Witsius discusses paradise, the tree of life, the tree of knowledge of good and evil, and the Sabbath as sacraments of the Covenant of Works, showing what good they signified and sealed to mankind with respect to God (*Economy of the Covenants*, pp. 104-17).

8. Turretin, *Institutes: Volume One*, p. 580. He saw the tree of knowledge of good and evil as a sacrament of trial and the tree of life as a symbol of the reward (p. 582).

9. James L. Mays argues that this verse refers to a geography of sin in Israel at the three cities of Adam, Gilead, and Shechem (*Hosea*, [OTL; Philadelphia: Westminster Press, 1969], pp. 100-01). Yet, Adam is only mentioned in Joshua 3:16 as the place where the waters of the Jordan heaped up prior to Israel's invasion of Canaan. Otherwise, it seems to have no significance (Duane A. Garrett, *Hosea, Joel*, NAC [Nashville: B&H, 1997], p. 162).

10. John L. MacKay, *Hosea* (Ross-shire: Christian Focus, 2012), p. 196. He argues that the preposition 'there' may function in poetry as an exclamatory particle that means 'look' (Pss. 14:5; 36:13; 48:7; 66:5; Zeph. 1:14).

11. John Calvin, 'Hosea,' in *Calvin's Commentaries*, vol. 13 (Grand Rapids: Baker, 1996), pp. 234-35. He understands the word 'there' to refer to their sacrifices. Robertson

away from the forceful comparison between the Israelites and Adam as covenant breakers.[12] In the context of Hosea 6:6-10, the preposition 'there' could be referring to the false worship at Bethel.[13]

Others are swayed that the preposition 'there' is referring to a place name but also believe that Adam is referring to a personal name. In this view the prophet makes a pun on the name of the town and the name of the first transgressor so that the reference is to both.[14] Hosea is well known for his use of wordplays and metaphors.[15] He also refers many times to the stories of Genesis.[16] The least likely view is that Hosea 6:7 is only referring to a geographical location where Israel broke a covenant. Whether 'Adam' only refers to the first man or is a pun that refers to both a person and a place, Hosea 6:7 identifies Adam as a covenant breaker to make the point that the Israelites are also covenant breakers and will experience the consequences of breaking the covenant.

Major Issues related to the Covenant of Works
The Name of the Covenant

There are several questions that arise in discussing the Covenant of Works. The first question concerns the appropriate name for this covenant. Turretin uses the term 'covenant of nature'. It is considered

---

argues for either Adam or mankind but understands Genesis 1–3 as a covenant (*Christ of the Covenants*, pp. 22-25).

12.   B. B. Warfield, 'Hosea 6:7: Adam or Man?' in *Collected Shorter Writings*, ed. John E. Meeter, 2 vols. (Phillipsburg: Presbyterian and Reformed, 2001), p. 1:127.

13.   C. F. Keil and F. Delitzsch, *Commentary on the Old Testament*, vol. 10 [Grand Rapids: Eerdmans, 1978], p. 100). Hosea 6:6 mentions burnt offerings and 6:10 refers to Ephraim's whoredom which are a direct cause of the false worship at Bethel and is a violation of a specific covenant prohibition (Deut. 12:5).

14.   Garrett, *Hosea, Joel*, pp. 162-63 and Bryon G. Curtis, 'Hosea 6:7 and Covenant-Breaking Like/At Adam,' in *The Law is not of Faith: Essays on Works and Grace in the Mosaic Covenant*, eds. Bryan D. Estelle, J. V. Fesko, and David VanDrunen (Phillipsburg, NJ: P&R, 2009), pp. 197-99.

15.   J. Andrew Dearman, *The Book of Hosea* (NICOT; Grand Rapids: Eerdmans, 2010), pp. 9-16.

16.   Curtis, 'Hosea 6:7.' He has an extensive discussion of the wordplays in Hosea (pp. 198-207) and the many references that Hosea makes to Genesis and to the Pentateuch (pp. 188-94).

a natural relationship because it is founded on the nature of mankind as first created by God. Adam was created in a state of innocence and liberty without the need of a mediator. This relationship was also a legal relationship because the condition was the observance of the law of nature engraved within him. The relationship depended on the obedience that he ought to render to God. Turretin also uses the term 'Covenant of Works' to refer to this relationship.[17]

Vos speaks of a natural relationship in which Adam stood to God to which a Covenant of Works was added by God. The distinction between a natural relationship and a covenant relationship is logical and juridical, not temporal. Adam did not for a single moment exist outside of the Covenant of Works. It is through this covenant that Adam received the right to eternal life if he fulfilled its conditions. When the Covenant of Works served its purpose the natural relationship stayed in force in all circumstances, including the demands that stem from it.[18]

The discussion of the natural relationship of humanity to God at creation explains to some extent the statement in the WCF 7.1:

> The distance between God and the creature is so great, that although reasonable creatures do owe obedience unto Him as their Creator, yet they could never have any fruition of Him as their blessedness and reward, but by some voluntary condescension on God's part, which He hath been pleased to express by way of covenant.

The natural relationship refers to the Creator/creature relationship, to which obedience is required, but for there to be a special relationship that offered mankind a reward for obedience, a covenant relationship was needed. Mankind could not merit anything before God based on the natural relationship alone. In light of this, it seems best not to call Adam's relationship with God the covenant of nature.[19]

Some have trouble with the name Covenant of Works because of possible misunderstandings associated with the term. It gives the impression that the relationship was a commercial exchange and that

---

17. Turretin, *Institutes: Volume One*, pp. 575-86.

18. Geerhardus Vos, *Reformed Dogmatics, Volume Two: Anthropology*, ed. Richard B. Gaffin, Jr. (Bellingham, WA: Lexham Press, 2012–2014), pp. 31-36.

19. Berkhof, *Systematic Theology*, p. 215.

Adam was entirely left on his own.[20] The term Edenic covenant has been suggested, but it can be confusing because the Covenant of Grace also begins in the garden of Eden (Gen. 3:15). Another term for God's relationship with Adam is the covenant of creation.[21] This term refers to the bond established between God and mankind at creation. It recognizes that there are general aspects of the covenant that relate to the responsibilities of mankind to his Creator and that there are more specific responsibilities of Adam than just the special point of testing instituted by God.[22] This is a useful term that allows a broad discussion of the issues in Genesis 1–3 as long as the significance of the period of testing for Adam is not overlooked as foundational to the covenant.

The Westminster Standards affirm that the relationship between God and Adam is a covenant relationship. WCF 7.2 calls it a Covenant of Works with life offered upon condition of perfect and personal obedience. The Westminster Larger Catechism (WLC) 20 and the Westminster Shorter Catechism (WSC) 12 both state that life and death are set forth in the covenant of life with the tree of life offered as a pledge and the tree of knowledge of good and evil prohibited upon pain of death. The term 'covenant of life' emphasizes that life was the reward for Adam if he had kept the covenant.[23] The term 'Covenant of Works' highlights that the condition of the covenant is perfect obedience. Even after Adam disobeyed God's command, the condition of perfect obedience remains a requirement for human beings to meet even though no one can meet it. The obedience of Christ is necessary for this condition to be fulfilled because He kept the law as a basis for the imputation of His righteousness to those who have faith in Him. The term 'Covenant of Works' may sound cold and legal, but it expresses

---

20. John M. Frame, *Systematic Theology: An Introduction to Christian Belief* (Phillipsburg, NJ: P&R, 2013), pp. 62-66. Frame goes on to affirm that the focus is on what Adam does rather than on God's action as the ground of Adam's blessing or curse and that any blessing he received based on his work he would have deserved. These statements answer the objections Frame himself raises concerning the term 'Covenant of Works'.

21. Robertson, *Christ of the Covenants*, p. 57.

22. Robertson, *Christ of the Covenants*, p. 67.

23. Johannes G. Vos, *The Westminster Larger Catechism: A Commentary*, ed. G. I. Williamson (Phillipsburg, NJ: P&R, 2002), p. 50.

what is necessary for salvation,[24] and in light of the obedience of Christ, the believer in Christ has great assurance.

The Role of Grace in the Covenant of Works

The legal relationship of the Covenant of Works and the fact that God condescended to mankind has raised the question of the role of grace during the period before the Fall. This question depends on the definition of grace and the understanding of merit. Some use the term 'grace' in a redemptive sense for the pre-fall situation,[25] but grace in its fullest redemptive sense of unmerited or demerited favor cannot exist before the entrance of sin into the world.[26] It is true, however, that the condescension of God to mankind overcame a great gulf between the creature and the Creator.[27] God could have required obedience without any promised reward and the covenant relationship does not place God in mankind's debt.[28] God condescends to mankind and enters into a covenant relationship out of 'grace', defined as the favor of freely

---

24. Berkhof calls it the preferred name (*Systematic Theology*, p. 211).

25. An emphasis on redemptive grace in the pre-fall situation that does not recognize the differences between the pre-fall and post-fall condition of mankind tends to confuse the relationship between faith and works in salvation and to deny the law/gospel distinction. The contrast between the law and the gospel leads to a biblical view of justification by faith (as in much Lutheran theology). The results of such denials impact justification where justifying faith is defined as covenant faithfulness and justification ultimately takes place at the final judgment where it will be based on performance (Norman Shepherd, 'Thirty-four Theses on Justification in Relation to Faith, Repentance, and Good Works, presented to the Philadelphia Presbytery of the Orthodox Presbytery of the Orthodox Presbyterian Church', Nov. 18, 1978, Thesis 19 and N. T. Wright, *The Letter to the Romans* in *The Interpreter's Bible*, 12 vols. [Nashville: Abingdon Press, 2002], p. 10:440).

26. Duncan, 'Recent Objections to Covenant Theology', p. 3:487. Duncan notes that 'grace' (*ḥēn*) does not appear in the Bible until Genesis 6:8. Ferguson comments that following *biblical usage,* Puritan theology usually reserved 'grace' for the activity of God towards *fallen* man (Sinclair B. Ferguson, *John Owen on the Christian Life* [Carlisle, PA: Banner of Truth Trust, 1987], p. 23 n. 6; emphasis original). Venema uses 'undeserved favor' to refer to the pre-fall state but clearly distinguishes between the pre-fall and post-fall condition of mankind and argues against obliterating the difference between the two (*Christ and Covenant Theology*, p. 24-28).

27. Turretin (*Institutes: Volume One*, p. 574) and Ball (Woolsey, *Covenantal Thought*, p. 46) use the term 'infinite' to refer to God's condescension to mankind.

28. Turretin, *Institutes: Volume One*, p. 578.

bestowing all kinds of gifts and favors, temporal and eternal, upon Adam in his condition before the Fall.[29]

Some also question if the concept of merit is appropriate to use in reference to Adam's obedience before the Fall.[30] There is nothing wrong with the idea of merit if understood properly. Adam received everything he had from God so that he could not seek anything from God as his own by right. It is not possible for God to be a debtor to Adam because the intrinsic value of Adam's obedience is out of proportion to the infinite reward of life. God sovereignly bound Himself to the arrangement that Adam's obedience would lead to greater life.[31] Perfect and personal obedience is the condition required for receiving the reward of eternal life in the Covenant of Works. If Adam would fulfill the condition of the covenant, he would merit the reward according to the terms of the covenant (called 'covenanted' merit). There is no problem with the concept of merit as defined in this way in relationship to Adam's obedience.[32]

The obedience of Christ as mediator of God's people operates with a stricter concept of merit because of His divine nature. There is no condescension on God's part to Christ because He is fully God. As the divine Son of God, He was able to fully satisfy the demands of God and to earn eternal life for His people through His perfect and personal obedience (called 'strict' or 'proper' merit). This is taught in WCF 8.5

---

29.   See the summary of the views of Ball and Ussher in Woolsey, *Covenantal Thought*, pp. 46, 48. There can be confusion concerning the pre-fall relationship of God and Adam if the term grace is left undefined or if it is not defined properly.

30.   Rich Lusk, 'A Response to "The Biblical Plan of Salvation,"' in *The Auburn Avenue Theology: Pros & Cons*, ed. E. Calvin Beisner (Fort Lauderdale, FL: Knox Theological Seminary, 2004), pp. 136-38. He also does not want to use 'merit' in reference to the work of Christ. Murray does not use merit to refer to Adam's situation, but he does use merit to refer to the work of Christ. It is also possible to avoid the use of 'merit' without denying that the Covenant of Works operates according to a works principle (Guy Prentiss Waters, *The Federal Vision and Covenant Theology: A Comparative Analysis* (Phillipsburg, NJ: P&R, 2006), p. 41.

31.   Turretin, *Institutes: Volume One*, p. 578.

32.   Francis Turretin, *Institutes of Elenctic Theology: Volume Two* (Phillipsburg, NJ: P&R Publishing, 1994), p. 712. Although he denies merit to Adam in the strict sense, he allows it in the broader sense because of the covenant that God entered with Adam under the condition of perfect obedience. For a helpful discussion of merit, see Andrew M. Elam, Robert C. Van Kooten, and Randall A. Bergquist, *Merit and Moses: A Critique of the Klinean Doctrine of Republication* (Eugene, OR: Wipf & Stock, 2014), pp. 49-58.

where the perfect obedience of Christ satisfies and purchases everlasting life and in WLC 38 where the reason is given why the mediator must be God: in order to procure salvation. The typological relationship between Adam and Christ includes their obedience. Although Adam's obedience before the Fall would have been acceptable to God to earn life because of the Covenant of Works, Christ's obedience is even greater because of His divine nature. Once sin entered the world merit was no longer a proper category for fallen human beings who are not able to merit anything before God (WCF 16.5; WLC 193).

The Covenant of Works and the Gospel

The elements of the Covenant of Works are important because they lay a foundation for the gospel.[33] It was a probationary test for Adam to see if he would obey God and keep the terms of the covenant. When Adam broke the covenant, the probationary test came to an end, but the obligation to perfectly fulfill the terms of the covenant remained.[34] This obligation is implied in Genesis 3 and is clearly taught in other passages of Scripture (Gal. 3:10-14). First of all, the punishments of Genesis 3 are passed on to the descendants of Adam. The world of Cain and Abel in Genesis 4 shows the impact of sin that is a result of Adam's transgression. Human beings are held accountable to God and subject to death on the basis of the terms of the original covenant.[35] If the punishment of the broken covenant is extended to all, the covenant and the law are also extended to all.[36] The descendants of Adam are held accountable by God for what Adam did because of the special relationship that Adam had as a representative of his descendants in the Covenant of Works. Paul makes the point in Romans 5:12-14 that even though the law had not yet been given, death reigned from Adam to Moses. Sin was in the

---

33. For a concise analysis of how the Covenant of Works is related to justification by faith, see Morton H. Smith, 'The Biblical Plan of Salvation with Reference to the Covenant of Works, Imputation, and Justification by Faith,' in *The Auburn Avenue Theology Pros and Con: Debating the Federal Vision*, ed. Calvin E. Beisner (Fort Lauderdale, FL: Knox Theological Seminary, 2004), pp. 96-117.

34. Robert L. Reymond, *A New Systematic Theology of the Christian Faith* (Nashville: Thomas Nelson Publishers, 1998), p. 439.

35. Reymond, *Systematic Theology*, p. 439.

36. Turretin, *Elenctic Theology, Volume One*, p. 617.

world before the giving of the law and sin is not counted against anyone without a law. Yet, death reigned because of Adam's transgression. The descendants of Adam were held accountable for Adam's sin because he was their representative. When Adam sinned, his sin was imputed to his descendants (see also 1 Corinthians 15:22, 'in Adam all die').

Second, the continuing obligation to fulfill the covenant require-ments is affirmed later in Scripture in the principle 'Do this and live'. It is found in Leviticus 18:5 and is affirmed in Romans 10:5 when Paul writes about a righteousness based on the law over against a righteous-ness based on faith.[37] Jesus Himself refers to this principle in Matthew 19:16-17. If someone could keep the law perfectly, they could obtain salvation on that basis. The problem is that no human being can keep the law perfectly (James 2:10). All people are condemned because they have not fulfilled their continuing obligation to keep the law.

Third, Christ fulfills the obligations of the covenant for the salvation of His people. The same obligation of personal, perfect, and perpetual obedience that God laid upon Adam as the federal representative by the Covenant of Works is also laid on Christ as the second Man and the last Adam (1 Cor. 15:45, 47), who by his obedience accomplished the salvation of the elect represented by Him.[38] Salvation is by works, not our works, but the works of Christ received by faith. Christ kept the law perfectly on behalf of those He represents (those united to Him). His righteousness is imputed to His descendants through faith in His person and work.[39] Christ kept the law and died on the cross as the sacrifice for sin by taking upon Himself the covenant curse that falls on all those who break the law (Gal. 3:12-14). In this way God can justify sinners through faith in Christ. The Covenant of Works is essential to the work of Christ as the basis for our salvation.

Those who deny the existence of the Covenant of Works also tend to argue that the pre-fall relationship between God and Adam was only of

---

37. Guy Waters, 'Romans 10:5 and the Covenant of Works,' in *The Law is not of Faith: Essays on Works and Grace in the Mosaic Covenant*, eds. Bryan D. Estelle, J. V. Fesko, and David VanDrunen (Phillipsburg, NJ: P&R, 2009), pp. 210-39. Later chapters will cover the Mosaic Covenant and Romans 10:5.

38. Reymond, *Systematic Theology*, pp. 439-40.

39. Turretin, *Elenctic Theology, Volume One*, p. 618. He develops the double imputation of the righteousness of Christ and the imputation of Adam's sin.

grace. This view flattens the differences between the pre-fall relationship between God and Adam and their post-fall relationship. The principle of works is many times rejected as a way to speak of God's relationship to Adam before the Fall and as a way to describe the work of Christ. Sometimes these views also result in a weakening of the use of the law with a denial of the contrast between the law and the gospel. Such ideas can easily lead to a denial of the traditional view of justification by faith, including the imputation of Christ's righteousness, and a conflation of faith and works as the basis of justification.[40]

Not everyone who denies that there is a Covenant of Works gets justification by faith wrong because they affirm certain key Scriptural teachings. These teachings include that there is a major difference between the pre-fall and post-fall condition of Adam so that God's relationship to mankind greatly changes after the Fall because lawbreakers stand condemned by the law. Faith in Christ over against keeping the law is the way of salvation. The contrast between the righteousness of the law and the righteousness of faith, a contrast between the law and the gospel, is foundational for a proper view of the work of Christ (Rom. 10:5-6) and our justification.[41] The Covenant of Works gives the work of Christ a rationale for why He had to come and what He had to accomplish for our salvation (Rom. 5:12-21). The Covenant of Works is important, but more important is a proper understanding of the gospel, and we should rejoice when people get the gospel right even if they reject the Covenant of Works.[42]

---

40. Views that do not recognize the differences between the pre-fall and post-fall condition of mankind tend to confuse the relationship between faith and works in salvation. Justifying faith is defined as covenant faithfulness and justification ultimately takes place at the final judgment where it will be based on performance (Shepherd, 'Thirty-four Theses on Justification', Nov. 18, 1978, Thesis 19 and Wright, *Romans*, p. 10:440).

41. The contrast between the law and the gospel leads to a biblical view of justification by faith even without a recognition of a Covenant of Works, as in much Lutheran theology ('Formula of Concord, Epitome 5', in *The Book of Concord*, trans. and ed. by Theodore G. Tappert (Philadelphia: Fortress Press, 1959), pp. 477-79; John T. Mueller, *Christian Dogmatics* (St. Louis, MO: Concordia Publishing House, 1934), pp. 44-47; and C. F. W. Walther, *The Proper Distinction Between Law and Gospel* (St. Louis, MO: Concordia Publishing House, 1929 reprint).

42. John Murray and Paul R. Williamson are examples (see Chapter 9).

CHAPTER 3

The Initiation of the Covenant of Grace

❀ ❀ ❀

WHEN Adam disobeyed God and broke the Covenant of Works serious consequences followed. Those consequences were a result of the entrance of sin and death into the world. Adam's perception of himself, his relationship with Eve, his relationship with God, and his relationship with creation changed. Sin brought guilt, shame, alienation, and death into the experience of Adam.[1] He felt the need to cover himself because he was naked, he blamed Eve for his sin, and he fled from God. His work became difficult, marriage became a battlefield, and life in general became hard as he faced a continuing struggle with the impact of sin. Adam's response was inadequate because he tried to take care of the situation apart from God. He made coverings for Eve and himself in order to hide the sense of shame that came with the realization of his nakedness. The bad news was that God's requirement of perfect obedience still had to be met. God's claim to the obedience of His creatures was not terminated by their sin. Aspects of the Covenant of Works continue, including the legal burden of fulfilling God's law

---

1. For more on the impact of sin, see Richard P. Belcher, Jr., *Genesis: The Beginning of God's Plan of Salvation* (Ross-shire, Scotland: Christian Focus, 2012), pp. 73-75.

perfectly (James 2:10) and the curse of the conditional promise when the law is not obeyed (Lev. 18:5; Rom. 10:5). The problem for human beings is compounded because there is no longer the ability not to sin due to the imputation of Adam's sin and the impact of sin in people's lives. Adam, Eve, and their descendants face a hopeless situation summarized by WCF 7.3:

> Man, by his fall, having made himself incapable of life by that covenant, the Lord was pleased to make a second, commonly called the covenant of grace wherein he freely offereth unto sinners life and salvation by Jesus Christ (see also WLC 30, WSC 20).

Genesis 3:15: The Protoevangelium (the first gospel)

God does not leave Adam and Eve in their sin and misery but responds with grace in order to redeem them from the curse of the law and its consequences. God's gracious actions toward Adam and Eve in their sinfulness include providing an adequate covering for their shame and guilt (Gen. 3:21). Animal skins foreshadow the necessity of blood to be shed for the forgiveness of sin. God also pronounced a curse on the serpent that ensures that the serpent will be defeated at some point in the future (Gen. 3:15). This is the first revelation of the Covenant of Grace and it has been called the Protoevangelium (the first gospel). When God declared the curse on the serpent, He also gave hope to mankind for the rescue of human beings and creation from the curse and power of sin. God established the Covenant of Grace by declaring 'I will put enmity between you and the woman' (NIV).[2] God makes sure that the continuing relationship between the serpent and the woman is not one of friendship but is a relationship of hostility. Warfare will constantly be at work between the serpent and the woman and will continue to be fought between the seed (offspring) of the woman and the seed of the serpent. The descendants of each will continue the battle throughout history. This is not a struggle that will end in a short period of time.[3]

---

2. Meredith G. Kline argues that the promise of redemptive grace was present in the curse of Satan in Genesis 3:15 as the implicit corollary of that curse (*Kingdom Prologue*, p. 146).

3. T. Desmond Alexander, 'Messianic Ideology in the Book of Genesis,' in *The Lord's Anointed: Interpretation of Old Testament Messianic Texts*, eds. Philip E.

God's pronouncement of the curse for sin on Adam and Eve shows that God does not bring final judgment against them immediately. There is hope for the future. The responsibilities God had given to them, such as marriage (Gen. 2:24), procreation (Gen. 3:16), and labor (Gen. 3:17-19), continue even though it will be more difficult to carry out these tasks. Adam responds in faith to the salvation promise of Genesis 3:15 by naming his wife 'Eve' (Gen. 3:20). There is a wordplay between the name Eve (*ḥawwāh*) and the Hebrew word for life (*ḥayyāh*), as 'she was the mother of all living'. Even though Adam disobeyed God in the Covenant of Works, he and Eve are the first members of the Covenant of Grace.

The word 'seed' (*zeraʿ*) is a collective singular noun that can be used in a corporate sense to refer to a group or in a singular sense to refer to an individual. The corporate idea is clearly manifested in history and starts in Genesis 4 with the triumph of sin and the division of humanity into two communities. When Cain killed Abel he and his family were driven away from the presence of the LORD and from other family members as they became wanderers on the earth (Gen. 4:12-14). Sin escalated in this family when Lamech took two wives and boasted of killing a man (Gen. 4:23-24). The ungodly community follows the evil one (1 John 3:12). The wicked increased until the spread of wickedness on earth was so great that God sent the Flood as judgment against sin. At the end of Genesis 4 the godly community is described as those who call on the name of the LORD.[4] The seed of the woman is traced in the godly community committed to God's ways and the seed of the serpent is traced in the ungodly community that rebels against God. But there is more to the seed of the serpent than human beings. The serpent in the garden was an instrument of Satan that elevates this battle to cosmic dimensions because Satan is an archenemy of God. His seed includes the fallen angels who do his bidding and manifest

---

Satterthwaite, Richard S. Hess, and Gordon J. Wenham (Grand Rapids, MI: Baker Books, 1995), pp. 30-31. He comments that the conflict will last a long time because enmity denotes lengthy hostility, the reference to the seed suggests it will continue for generations, and the verb is imperfect with an iterative sense indicating repeated actions.

4. John D. Currid understands the passive construction of Genesis 4:26b as the seed of the woman is now being called by the name of Yahweh (*A Study Commentary on Genesis, Volume 1: 1:1–25:18* [Darlington: Evangelical Press, 2003], p. 152).

themselves at certain periods of redemptive history culminating in the New Testament (Dan. 10:10-21; Matt. 12:22-32; Rev. 12:7-17). These two groups of the seed of Satan are mentioned together in Jesus' statement to some Jews, '*You* are of your father the *devil*, and your will is to do your father's desire' (John 8:44). Those Jews were opposed to Jesus and so they were on the side of Satan.

Genesis 3:15 also gives an indication of the culmination of this warfare in the phrase, 'he shall bruise your head and you shall bruise his heel.' Although there is debate about whether this can refer to a single individual because the corporate aspect of the seed has been in view,[5] there are good reasons to take this clause as referring to single individuals.[6] The pronouns used with 'seed' determine whether 'seed' has in view one descendant or many descendants. If the pronouns are plural, then seed refers to a plurality of descendants, but if the pronouns are singular, then seed refers to a single individual.[7] In Genesis 3:15 the pronouns are singular so that seed is referring to an individual who will do battle with the seed of the serpent. The victory of the seed of the woman is also highlighted. The same verb is used for the blows that both will give to the other, but one of the blows is fatal. Satan's blow is on the heel but the blow from the seed of the woman is on the head of the serpent. The seed of the woman will triumph over the seed of the serpent by defeating him.

The identity of this descendant is progressively revealed throughout Old Testament history and is fulfilled in the person and work of Christ. Genesis 3:15 speaks ultimately of Christ, the second Adam, the mediator

---

5. Some conservative authors deny that this passage is messianic because of the corporate nature of seed in Genesis 3:15 (see John Calvin, 'Genesis,' in *Calvin's Commentaries, Volume 1* [Grand Rapids: Baker Book House, 1996], pp. 170-171; E. W. Hengstenberg, *Christology of the Old Testament* [Grand Rapids: Kregel, 1970], p. 22; and Geerhardus Vos, *The Eschatology of the Old Testament*, ed. James T. Dennison [Phillipsburg, NJ: P&R, 2001], p. 77.

6. Those who understand Genesis 3:15 as referring to an individual include Walter Kaiser, *The Messiah in the Old Testament* (Grand Rapids: Zondervan, 1995), p. 38, Michael Rydelink, *The Messianic Hope* (Nashville, TN: B&H Publishing, 2010), p. 141, and Kenneth A. Mathews, *Genesis 1–11:26* (Nashville: Broadman & Holman, 1996), p. 248.

7. C. John Collins, 'A Syntactical Note on Genesis 3:15: Is the Woman's Seed Singular or Plural?' *TynBul* 48.1 (1997): pp. 141-48.

of the Covenant of Grace (WLC 36), the redeemer of God's elect (WSC 20). Just as Adam represented his descendants in his actions, so Christ represented those elected to eternal life. Just as the sin of Adam was imputed to his descendants, so the righteousness of Christ's obedience was imputed to those who have faith in Him. Thus, the obligations of the covenant are met in the mediator as an appointed means to obtain eternal life. The obedience of the second Adam in keeping the law is the foundation for justification by faith.

The Covenant of Works and the Covenant of Grace

There are two distinct covenants in Scripture, the Covenant of Works and the Covenant of Grace (bi-covenantal). The Covenant of Grace was historically initiated right after Adam broke the Covenant of Works. Although the two covenants are very different, there are similarities between them. God is the author of both, He initiated both covenants. God entered into both covenants with Adam and they both include his descendants. The promise of both covenants is to receive eternal life and the general aim of the covenants is the glory of God.

There are also major differences between these two covenants. In the Covenant of Works God is the Creator and Lord who condescends to establish the covenant with His innocent creature. In the Covenant of Grace God is the redeemer who graciously pursues the sinner and covenant breaker. In the Covenant of Works the promise of eternal life depends on the perfect, personal obedience of Adam, but in the Covenant of Grace the promise of eternal life depends on the sinner having faith in the person and work of Christ. In the Covenant of Works there was no need of a mediator because there was fellowship between God and Adam, and Adam had the ability to keep the covenant; but in the Covenant of Grace there was the need of a mediator because the fellowship between God and Adam had been broken by sin, and Adam did not have the ability to obey God's law.[8]

There is a principle of works in both covenants. In the Covenant of Works Adam was to obey the stipulation related to the tree of the

---

8. Some of the similarities and differences between the Covenant of Works and the Covenant of Grace are listed in Berkhof, *Systematic Theology*, p. 272.

knowledge of good and evil and in the Covenant of Grace Christ fulfills the works requirement. The Covenant of Grace did not abolish the Covenant of Works because both required that the righteousness of the law be fulfilled. Christ fulfilled this righteousness by meeting the requirement of the Covenant of Works, enabling His righteousness to be offered to those who believe in Him. The Covenant of Grace through Christ accomplishes what the Covenant of Works required.[9]

Issues related to the Covenant of Grace

The Condition of Faith

There are certain questions related to the Covenant of Grace that are important for understanding its nature and historical manifestation. The Covenant of Works had the condition of perfect obedience. The Covenant of Grace also has a condition. How grace is manifested in this covenant is addressed in WLC 32: 'The grace of God is manifested in the second covenant, in that he freely provideth and offereth to sinners a Mediator, and life and salvation by him, and requiring faith as the condition to interest them in him.' WCF 7.3 does not use the word 'condition' but describes the Covenant of Grace as God 'freely offereth unto sinners life and salvation by Jesus Christ, requiring of them faith in Him, that they may be saved.'

Some struggle with the concept of a condition connected to the Covenant of Grace, but it is important how that condition is understood. The Bible requires faith as necessary for someone to experience the blessings of salvation (John 3:16, 36; Acts 8:37; Rom. 10:9). God requires faith but He also gives faith to the elect as a gift (Eph. 2:8). Faith as a condition of the covenant is not meritorious because believers do not merit the blessings of salvation. God fulfills the condition by providing Christ who meets the conditions originally laid down in the Covenant of Works so that the elect can experience the transformation of regeneration.[10] No believer is saved on the basis of his or her own works

---

9. Woolsey, *Unity and Continuity*, p. 66.
10. Herman Witsius, *The Economy of the Covenants between God and Man* (Escondido, CA: The den Dulk Christian Foundation, 1990, orig. 1822), pp. 166, 202-55. He has an extensive discussion of the surety of Christ in satisfying the demands of the covenant.

but is saved through faith in the work of Christ. Faith is a condition met by God and given by God so that salvation is all due to the grace of God.[11]

The Unity of the Covenant

There is only one Covenant of Grace, but it was administered differently in the time of the law and in the time of the gospel. The administration of the covenant in the time of the law was 'by promises, prophecies, sacrifices, circumcision, the paschal lamb, and other types of ordinances delivered to the people of the Jews, all foresignifying Christ to come' (WCF 7.5). The substance of the covenant is the same, even as it was administered in different historical manifestations that include the covenant with Adam (Gen. 3:15), the covenant with Noah (Genesis 6–9), the covenant with Abraham (Genesis 15 and 17), the covenant with Moses (Exodus 19–24), and the covenant with David (2 Sam. 7), which are all fulfilled in the New Covenant in Christ. There are many elements to the one substance, but they can be summarized as the same promise of eternal life, the same mediator Jesus Christ, and the same condition of faith.[12] Each covenant will display these elements in various ways.

The unity can also be seen in the effectiveness of the administration of the covenant in the time of the law, as the WCF states that it was 'for that time, sufficient and efficacious, through the operation of the Spirit, to instruct and build up the elect in faith in the promised Messiah, in whom they had full remission of sins, and eternal salvation; and is called the old Testament' (7.5).[13] These elements are seen in the initiation of the Covenant of Grace with Adam in the garden. The issue of eternal life

---

11. Berkhof, *Systematic Theology*, p. 281. He states that, if there were no conditions of the covenant, God only would be bound by the covenant, and the Covenant of Grace would lose its character as a covenant without two parties involved.

12. Witsius, *The Economy of the Covenants*, p. 292.

13. Turretin, *Institutes: Volume Two*, p. 194. He writes, 'Rather the question is whether they looked to Christ and were saved in the hope of his coming. Whether promises not only temporal, but also spiritual and heavenly concerning eternal life and the Holy Spirit were given to them. And whether the same covenant entered into with us in Christ had already been contracted with them, although more obscurely and reservedly.'

was part of the promise of the Covenant of Works and it continues as a promise in the Covenant of Grace. After Adam broke the covenant, if he would have eaten of the tree of life in the condition of sin, he would live forever in that condition (Gen. 3:22).[14] Part of the reason Adam is driven from the garden is to ensure that the hope of eternal life continues. The tree of life is not destroyed, but the way to it is guarded because the way to it will be more clearly laid out as redemptive history unfolds. The emphasis at this stage is on the continuation of life. The line of the woman will continue, according to the promise of Genesis 3:15, and in response Adam names his wife Eve because she was the mother of all living (Gen. 3:20). The mediator is set forth as the one who will come to bruise the head of the serpent (Gen. 3:15) and His work is foreshadowed in the garments of skin God used to clothe Adam and Eve (Gen. 3:21). The condition of faith in God's promise is exhibited in Adam when he calls his wife Eve, the mother of all living, after God's pronouncement of the results of his disobedience.

The Parties to the Covenant of Grace

There is some debate concerning who the parties are to the Covenant of Grace. God is one of the parties but who is the second party? The Westminster Standards seem to answer this question in two ways. One answer is that the covenant is made with the elect. The answer to the question, 'Did God leave all mankind to perish in the estate of sin and misery?' is 'God having, out of his mere good pleasure, from all eternity, elected some to everlasting life, did enter into a Covenant of Grace, to deliver them out of the estate of sin and misery, and to bring them into an estate of salvation by a Redeemer' (WSC 20). Here the covenant is made with the elect in order to deliver them from their hopeless condition of sin.

But then in WLC 31 the question is asked, 'With whom was the covenant of grace made?' The answer is 'with Christ as the second Adam, and in him with all the elect as his seed.' There is no discrepancy between these two statements. The Covenant of Grace cannot be established with sinful human beings without a mediator who acts on their behalf. The

---

14. Mathews, *Genesis 1:1–11:26*, p. 256.

work of the mediator satisfies the justice of God so that there can be a relationship restored between God and sinners. Thus, there is a close relationship between Christ the mediator and the elect sinners whom He represents. The elect are in Christ, and so it is appropriate that the covenant be made with Christ or with the elect.

Some think that the Westminster Standards reflect the existence of a Covenant of Redemption in the way the parties are identified, particularly in the statement in WCF 8.5 that Christ purchased redemption 'for all those whom the Father hath given unto him'. If this is the case, then the Covenant of Grace is the historical outworking of the Covenant of Redemption.

The Historical Administration of the Covenant

The question concerning who the parties are to the covenant raises the issue of the character of the covenant relationship. For example, if the Covenant of Grace is made between Christ and the elect, then only the elect are in the covenant. Sections of the Westminster Standards emphasize the efficacy of the covenant for the elect who receive the benefits of the covenant (faith, the remission of sins, and eternal salvation) through the work of the Holy Spirit (WCF 7.5; WLC 32, 34; WSC 20). Here the Standards are looking at the Covenant of Grace from God's standpoint and the impact of the covenant on the elect because only the elect receive the benefits of the covenant. Other sections of the Westminster Standards speak of the historical administration of the Covenant of Grace by the sacraments as signs and seals of the covenant which are to be administered to believers and their children. This principle is stated in the Abrahamic Covenant (Gen. 17:7-8) and affirmed in the New Covenant (Acts 2:39; Gal. 3:29).

The historical administration of the Covenant of Grace explains certain distinctions found in Scripture and in the Westminster Standards. There is a visible and invisible church, with the visible church defined as 'all those throughout the world that profess the true religion; together with their children; and of their children: and is the kingdom of our Lord Jesus Christ, the house and family of God' (WCF 25.2). There is no perfect church on this earth for even 'The purest Churches under heaven are subject both to mixture and error' (WCF 25.5). The visible church includes the elect, but it also includes those who may not be the elect, whether children of believers who do not believe or those who make a false profession of faith. The Covenant of Grace has both relationship aspects and legal aspects and a person can be part of the Covenant of Grace legally but not be in a relationship with God. There are legal aspects to covenant administration that continue to operate in the New Covenant. Romans 11:16-24 sets forth a holiness that comes from being engrafted into the tree that is not the inward holiness that is a result of the Spirit's work in the life of a believer. This holiness is shared by the branches that are connected to the root of the tree. The church is depicted in Romans 11 with the same imagery as that of Israel, so that this principle of covenant administration continues in the New Covenant because Gentiles who are grafted in can also be cut off (Rom. 11:21-22).[15] Thus, the church should not be defined only in terms of election (believers) because it also includes believers and their children.[16]

---

15. For further discussion of covenant administration, see Kline, *Kingdom Prologue*, 362-64, Berkhof, *Systematic Theology*, pp. 284-89, and Vos, *Reformed Dogmatics*, pp. 2:104-05.

16. Some of the discussion of covenant administration comes from Belcher, *Genesis*, p. 136; for more discussion of this issue, see Chapter 13.

CHAPTER 4

The Noahic Covenant

✳ ✳ ✳

THE covenant with Noah has several challenges that some of the other covenants in Scripture do not have. One challenge is that the WCF does not say very much about the covenant with Noah and its role in redemptive history.[1] Another is that there has not been agreement on how to fit together the broader, common grace aspects with the redemptive aspects of the covenant. Are there two covenants or just one covenant? There is also debate to what 'my covenant' of Genesis 6:18 refers. Does it look back to a previous covenant or does it look forward to the covenant with Noah? There is general agreement that the covenant with Noah includes both common grace and redemptive sides to it, even if there is not agreement on how they relate to each other. The Noahic Covenant comes in the context of the history of redemption and is God's way of ensuring that the salvation purposes of history will not be hindered by sin.

God's grace was clearly demonstrated in the garden of Eden when Adam sinned and experienced the consequences of sin. God initiated the Covenant of Grace to hold out the hope of redemption for Adam and his descendants. Although Adam and Eve lost the garden, life continued

---

1. See also Aaron Chalmers, 'The Importance of the Noahic Covenant to Biblical Theology,' *TynBul* 60.2 (2009): pp. 207-16; he shows how the Noahic Covenant has been neglected or ignored in discussions of the covenant.

with the expectation that one would come to defeat the serpent, but until that day the enmity between the seed of the woman and the seed of the serpent was displayed in the events that followed. The impact of sin became evident in Genesis 3, but the triumph of sin dominated the next several chapters of Genesis.

The Triumph of Sin

Genesis 4 shows the immediate results of sin in the family of Adam. The enmity of the two seeds becomes evident in the story of Cain and Abel. Cain kills Abel out of anger because God accepted Abel's sacrifice and not Cain's. The result is that the family of Cain is separated from the rest of mankind. God tells Cain that he will be a fugitive and wanderer on the earth. Cain recognizes that he is being driven from the presence of Yahweh and the text explicitly states that Cain went away from the presence of Yahweh (4:14, 16). There is a separation between the godly line and the ungodly line. The ungodly line is represented in the family of Cain where the evidence of the increase of sin is found in Lamech's boast (4:23-24). The progression of moral corruption includes bigamy, pride in boasting to his wives, and a revenge murder. Moral wickedness dominates the ungodly line.

There is also the development of civilization through the ungodly line. Although Cain, his family, and his descendants reject God, they carry out, in a limited way, the mandate that God had given to humanity in Genesis 1–2. Their descendants multiply as children are born and they rule over creation in the development of civilization and culture. Cain built a city (4:17), Jabal developed husbandry (4:20), Jubal developed music (4:21), and Tubal-Cain developed the work of craftsmen (workers in bronze and iron, 4:22). This is a result of common grace, defined as God's benevolence extended to all people by virtue of the fact that they live in God's world and experience common and general blessings.[2] These developments in the ungodly line demonstrate that unbelievers can understand the way God's created world works even when God is not acknowledged by them. And yet, because of the

---

2. See Berkhof, *Systematic Theology*, pp. 434-46 and John Murray, 'Common Grace' in the *Collected Writings of John Murray, Volume Two: Select Lectures in Systematic Theology* (Carlisle, PA: The Banner of Truth Trust, 1977), pp. 93-122 for discussions of common grace.

ultimate commitment of unbelievers, technical advancement cannot hide moral failure. The implication is that believers can learn certain things from unbelievers even if their ultimate commitment is faulty. The appropriate response is not to reject these developments of civilization but to use them within the framework of belief in God and for His glory.

The godly line of Adam is carried on through Seth, who is appointed to take the place of Abel. The word 'seed' occurs again with reference to Seth and at the end of Genesis 4 the activity of the worship of Yahweh is announced in the godly line. The genealogy of Adam (Gen. 5:1-32) carries forward the godly line from Adam to Noah. The emphasis on 'other sons and daughters' shows that the mandate to be fruitful and multiply (Gen. 1:28) is being fulfilled. The other emphasis in the genealogy, 'and he died,' shows the power and impact of sin that now dominates all human life. The hope that sin will not ultimately triumph is expressed in two ways. First, Enoch did not die but God took him. Enoch is characterized as one who walked with God. The refrain 'and he died' does not occur with Enoch, giving hope that death would not have the final word. Also, they are looking for the one who would give them relief from the curse of the painful toil of work. Lamech (not the Lamech of Genesis 4) named his son Noah (*nôaḥ*), which is related to the word for rest (*nûaḥ*) and there is a wordplay with the word translated 'relief' (*nāḥam*). They are looking for the one to be born from the seed of the woman to deliver them from the curse. Although Noah will be used by God to bring relief, he is not the promised one of Genesis 3:15 who will defeat the serpent.

The genealogy of Adam ends with a narrative conclusion (Gen. 6:1-8) that demonstrates the increase of wickedness on the earth as a justification for the judgment of the Flood. Part of the problem is that there are intermarriages between the godly line and the ungodly line leading to wickedness that permeates the earth.[3] The wickedness is described as intense, inward, pervasive, and constant (Gen. 6:5). God's response to the wickedness of humanity is that He is going to destroy man and animals from the earth. Hope is expressed in one named Noah who found favor in the eyes of Yahweh (Gen. 6:8).

---

3. For a discussion of the various views of 'the sons of God', see Belcher, *Genesis*, pp. 87-90.

The Judgment of the Flood

The Common Grace and Redemptive Elements in the Noahic Covenant

The Account of Noah is the story of the Flood and its aftermath (Gen. 6:9–9:29). These chapters can generally be divided into Preparations for the Flood (6:9-22), the Preservation of Noah's Family through the Flood (7:1–8:19), God's Covenant with Noah (8:20–9:17), and the Continuing Problem of Sin after the Flood (9:18-29). The word 'covenant' occurs first in Genesis 6:18 and then in Genesis 9:8, 12, 15-17. Do these two passages refer to the same covenant or to two different covenants? For example, Kline sees a reference to a redemptive covenant in Genesis 6 and a common grace covenant in Genesis 9.[4] Although much of what Kline has to say about the content of these two covenants is helpful, it is better to see one covenant that has both common grace and redemptive elements. Although the Flood separates these two passages that mention the covenant, there is a structural unity to the passage. Wenham presents B. W. Anderson's chart that shows an extended chiastic pattern of 6:9–9:19, with 'God remembers Noah' as the center.

Transitional introduction (6:9-10)
  1. Violence in creation (6:11-12)
    2. First divine speech: resolve to destroy (6:13-22)
      3. Second divine speech: 'enter ark' (7:1-10)
        4. Beginning of Flood (7:11-16)
          5. The rising Flood (7:17-24)
            God remembers Noah
          6. The receding Flood (8:1-5)
        7. Drying of the earth (8:6-14)
      8. Third divine speech: 'leave ark' (8:15-19)
    9. God's resolve to preserve order (8:20-22)
  10. Fourth divine speech (9:1-17)
Transitional conclusion (9:18-19)

---

4. Kline sees a literary structure that unites 6:13–8:22 and argues that the Flood narrative proper ends at 8:22 (*Kingdom Prologue*, p. 213). This fulfills the covenant announced in the opening section (a redemptive covenant). A different, subsequent covenant is covered in 9:1-17 (a common grace covenant). Kline's structure does not begin with 6:9 or 6:11.

The first and fourth divine speeches both contain the word covenant.[5] God announces that He is going to destroy the world with a flood, but He promises that He will save Noah in the ark and establish His covenant with him. After the Flood God enters into a covenant with Noah. The two uses of 'covenant' are not referring to two covenants but to one covenant.[6] The redemptive and common grace elements are found throughout the account, with the common grace elements taking a primary role and the redemptive elements a secondary role.[7]

The Use of 'My Covenant' in Genesis 6:18

There is also debate about the use of 'my covenant' in Genesis 6:18. This is the first time in Scripture that the term 'covenant' appears. The question is complicated because the normal phrase for initiating a covenant ('to cut a covenant' with the verb *kārat*) does not occur here. The phrase that is used (*qûm* in the hifil) means to establish a covenant and it is used many times to confirm a pre-existing commitment (Gen. 17:7, 19, 21; Exod. 6:4; Lev. 26:9; Deut. 8:18).[8] If that is the meaning here, then God is confirming His prior commitment to creation. There are clear connections between the creation account and the Flood, as well as between directives God gives to Adam and to Noah (see below), but the covenant with Noah should not be regarded as the same covenant that God made with Adam in the garden of Eden. The Covenant of Works was a probationary covenant and when Adam, as our representative, broke the covenant, it formally came to an end. It is true, however, that the requirement of the Covenant of Works to live a perfect life is still operative, but since no one can meet that requirement every human

---

5. Wenham, *Genesis 1–15* (WBC; Dallas: Word Books, 1994), pp. 157-158.

6. The unity of the covenant with Noah can also be supported with parallels to the Abrahamic Covenant. Just as Noah was given a promise of life (Gen. 6:17-18), so Abraham was given the promise of offspring and land (Gen. 12:1-3), ratified by a covenant (Gen. 15:1-6, 17-21). Then a crisis associated with those promises occurred, a catastrophic flood for Noah (Gen. 7:1–8:12) and an illegitimate heir for Abraham. Finally, a covenant sign sealed the promises in Genesis 9:8-17 and 17:1-14 (unpublished paper by Christopher M. Diebold, 'New Covenant Fulfillment of the Noahic Covenant: Re-creative Life with God through De-creative Judgment').

7. Geerhardus Vos, *Biblical Theology* (Grand Rapids: Eerdmans, 1948), pp. 56-59.

8. Mathews, *Genesis 1–11:26*, p. 367.

being stands condemned by it. The use of 'establish my covenant' should not be used to identify the Noahic Covenant with a previous covenant in the sense that there is only one covenant (mono-covenantal)[9] instead of two covenants (bi-covenantal).[10]

It is clear that when sin entered the world the order of creation did not come to an end. Although sin impacted creation, the sun kept rising and setting. The work that God gave to Adam and Eve continued even if the curse of sin made that work difficult. God initiated the Covenant of Grace and there is clear evidence of redemption in Genesis 3. The progress of sin is what brings about the crisis of the Flood (Gen. 6:1-8). Because the whole world is going to be destroyed, except one family, there needed to be confirmation on God's part that He was committed to creation and to the mandate He had given humanity to fulfill. In this general way the phrase 'establish my covenant' can be referring back to creation and to God's purposes for human beings. These connections will become clear in the account of the Flood and the covenant with Noah. But the phrase 'I will establish my covenant' is also looking to what is going to transpire in the next couple of chapters culminating in Genesis 9. Thus, it anticipates the formal initiation of the covenant in Genesis 9.[11] God commits Himself to the regular order of creation so that His program of salvation can be fulfilled. Both aspects are found in the covenant with Noah.

Preparations for the Flood

The account of Noah and the Flood begins with an introduction about Noah, and then reminds the reader why the Flood is necessary, what Noah needs to do to get ready for it, what God's purposes are in the Flood, and how their preparations will provide for them when the Flood is over. There is an emphasis on how the Flood will further God's redemptive purposes, but there is also provision for life in general to continue after the Flood. Noah is introduced as a man of unassailable character who has a close relationship with God. He walked with

---

9. Dumbrell, *Covenant and Creation*, pp. 41-46.

10. For a discussion of the bi-covenantal framework, see Chapter 2 on the Covenant of Works.

11. Matthews, *Genesis 1–11:26*, p. 367.

God and lived his life in demonstration of his relationship with God. He exemplified a wholeness of character (blameless) that exhibited a practical righteousness in his life. Noah is clearly of the line of Seth, both by physical descent and moral conduct. His life stands over against the wicked lives of his generation who are described as corrupt and full of violence (Gen. 6:12-13). God is going to destroy the world but save the family of Noah as well as two of every kind of animal in the ark (Gen. 6:13-17). Noah does everything that God asked him to do to get ready for the Flood.

The Preservation of the Godly Line through the Flood

The Flood destroys all living things on the earth. The ungodly line, the seed of the serpent, perishes but God saves Noah and his family in the ark. The Flood brings the earth into a state of chaos that resembles the state of the earth as formless and void at the beginning of Genesis 1. In fact, there are clear parallels to the creation account throughout this section of Genesis. Instead of the declaration that God saw that everything was good, as in Genesis 1, God saw that the wickedness of mankind was great on the earth and that their hearts were only evil continually (Gen. 6:5). In Genesis 1 the Spirit of God was hovering over the face of the waters before the earth became a place where mankind can live. In Genesis 6:3 God's Spirit is mentioned again but this time in a context of judgment that is going to fall upon the earth, bringing to an end the life of mankind. In Genesis 1 there is a movement from chaos (the formless and void state of the earth) to order by the separation and gathering together of the waters (Gen. 1:6-10). In the Flood the disorder of judgment is brought about by the unleashing of waters that cover the earth (Gen. 7:17-23). The Flood brings the earth into a state of not being habitable for humanity or any other life that existed on the earth (Gen. 7:21-23). Although all life outside the ark perished, God saved Noah and his family from destruction. God protected Noah by shutting him in the ark (7:16) and God remembered Noah by causing the Flood waters to recede (8:1). God then brought the earth into a state where it was habitable again for human beings. There are further parallels with the creation account. A wind (*rûaḥ*) blew over the earth and the waters of the Flood subsided (Gen. 8:1), just like the Spirit (*rûaḥ*) was hovering over the waters in Genesis 1:2. There is a renewed separation of the land and sea (Gen. 1:7 and 8:3, 7, 13) with the appearance of dry land again (Gen. 1:9 and 8:14).

God's Covenant with Noah

Although there are redemptive elements in this section (8:20–9:17), there is an emphasis on the continuation of the common grace elements in the operation of creation. When Noah left the ark, he built an altar to Yahweh and offered burnt offerings on the altar. This act of worship was pleasing to God and He promises never again to destroy every living creature on the earth. The rationale for never cursing the ground this way again is stated in verse 21, 'for the intention of man's heart is evil from his youth.' This seems like a strange rationale, but it recognizes that the sinfulness of the human race will continue and that the sin-problem will never be cured by judgment and curse. The earth must be preserved so that God's plan of salvation can be fulfilled.[12]

God promises to continue the order of creation so that seedtime and harvest, cold and heat, summer and winter, day and night shall not cease (Gen. 1:14 and 8:22). God also promises to continue the mandate that God had given Adam and Eve to be fruitful, multiply, and fill the earth. Noah is presented as a second Adam as he and his family are given the same commands that Adam and Eve were given. They are to be fruitful and multiply on the earth (Gen. 8:17), which is repeated in Genesis 9:1 with the addition that they were to fill the earth (Gen. 1:28). This assumes that the institution of marriage given in Genesis 2:24 is still relevant. Human dominion over creation is also affirmed but with the recognition that animals will fear human beings as God gives animals to human beings for food (Gen. 9:3).[13] In Genesis 1:26-28 human beings are made in God's image and the implication of the sanctity of life is affirmed in Genesis 9:6. Human life is so significant that the taking of human life by one person requires their life be taken in return, 'for God made man in his own image.' This lays the foundation of government and establishes capital punishment as an appropriate response to murder. God starts

---

12. Robertson, *Christ of the Covenants*, p. 114.
13. In Genesis 1:30 God gives to everything that has life on the earth plants for food.

over with the family of Noah to see if this second opportunity to carry out His purposes for creation will be any more successful.

God confirms His commitment to creation and to Noah, as the representative of the human race, by means of a covenant. This covenant is established not only with Noah and his offspring after him, but with every living creature that came out of the ark. Never again will God destroy the earth by the waters of a flood (9:11). The sign of this covenant is a rainbow and it primarily stands as a reminder to God of His covenant commitments (Gen. 9:15-16).[14] Twice God states, 'I will remember' when He sees the rainbow in the clouds. For God to remember the covenant does not mean that He just thinks about it, but that He acts to fulfill His covenant promise to never destroy the world again with a flood.[15] The rainbow is a universal sign that all can see because the covenant with Noah is a covenant made with all creation. It is fitting that the sign would be manifested in creation. The term for 'rainbow' (*qešeṭ*) also refers to the bow used as a weapon. Instead of a symbol of combat it is a symbol of peace.[16]

The Continuing Problem of Sin (Gen. 9:18-29)

The judgment of the Flood did not eradicate the problem of sin in the human race. An incident in the family of Noah will lead to another division between the godly and ungodly lines. The sons of Noah who went out from the ark were Shem, Ham and Japheth, with a parenthetical note that Ham is the father of Canaan. After the Flood Noah planted a vineyard, became drunk on too much wine, and lay uncovered in his tent. Ham saw the nakedness of his father and told his two brothers. They took

---

14. Chalmers, 'Noahic Covenant', p. 210.

15. Michael V. Fox, 'The Sign of the Covenant: Circumcision in the Light of the Priestly *'ôt* Etiologies', *RB* 81.4 (October 1974): pp. 572-73. Although he works with critical terminology, like J, E, and P, the categories he uses to talk about the various signs in Scripture are perceptive, including the sign of the covenant with Noah.

16. V. P. Hamilton, *The Book of Genesis 1–17* (NICOT; Grand Rapids: Eerdmans, 1990), p. 317. This view has been challenged because Yahweh is not presented as a warrior in the early chapters of Genesis. An alternate view is that the rainbow is a representation of the firmament that guarantees the cosmological structure of the world so that the waters above the firmament will never again be unleashed on the earth as in the Flood (see Laurence A. Turner, 'The Rainbow as a Sign of the Covenant in Genesis ix 11-13,' *VT* 43.1 [1993]: pp. 119-24).

a garment and walked backwards into the tent, so they did not see their father's nakedness (Gen. 9:22-23). There is debate about what it means that Ham saw the nakedness of his father.[17] The best understanding of this in the context of the story is that Ham saw his father naked in the tent and disrespected his father by making it known to his brothers.[18] Noah's response to this incident is to offer a curse and a blessing that have implications for the future descendants of the three brothers. The curse of being a servant to his brothers does not fall on Ham but on his descendant Canaan and is fulfilled in the Israelite conquest of the land of Canaan. The descendants of Ham become like Ham in their disobedience and become subject to Israel when Joshua leads Israel into the land.[19]

The blessing of Shem and Japheth gives priority to Shem who will be the godly line that will lead to Abram. Yahweh, the God of Shem, is blessed and the blessing of Japheth includes God enlarging Japheth so that he will dwell in the tents of Shem. This phrase refers to a peaceful harmony that will take place between the descendants of Shem and Japheth. In the table of nations that follows in Genesis 10, the descendants of Japheth are those who dwell in the areas of Anatolia and Greece. Through the line of Shem, God promises to bless all the families of the earth (Gen. 12:1-3). This peaceful coexistence is fulfilled in Jesus Christ and the mission He gives to His people to go into the world with the gospel (Matt. 28:19-20). Paul takes the gospel to the Gentiles in the area of Greece and many of the descendants of Japheth came to dwell peacefully in the tents of Shem when they were united to Christ. Genesis 9:26-27 is a foreshadowing of the salvation that will come to the world and is the reason that there needed to be the covenant of Noah to ensure history would continue to carry out this plan of God's salvation.

The Noahic Covenant and the Covenant of Grace

The Covenant of Noah is also called the covenant of nature or the common grace covenant because of its general characteristics and its emphasis on natural blessings. In this way it differs from some of the

---

17. See Belcher, *Genesis*, pp. 100-01 for a brief discussion of the options.

18. Mathews, *Genesis 1–11:26*, p. 420; Hamilton *Genesis 1–17*, p. 323; and Bruce K. Waltke, *Genesis: A Commentary* (Grand Rapids, MI: Zondervan, 2001), p. 149.

19. For issues related to this curse on Ham, see Belcher, *Genesis*, pp. 100-01.

emphases in the Covenant of Grace. The Noahic Covenant focuses on earthly and temporal blessings and the Covenant of Grace focuses primarily on spiritual blessings. The Noahic Covenant deals with all the creation order, including human beings and animals, while the Covenant of Grace deals with believers and their seed. Although there are certain obligations for human beings in the covenant with Noah, there are no conditions to be met for the covenant to continue. Although there are differences between the two covenants, there is also an intimate connection between them as the Noahic Covenant rests upon the Covenant of Grace. The temporal blessings of life in God's creation were forfeited by sin and thus granted by God's grace. There was evidence in Noah of the impact of the Covenant of Grace in the way he lived his life and in his relationship with God.

The primary purpose of the covenant with Noah was to provide for the continuation of creation so God's redemptive program of salvation under the Covenant of Grace could be carried out. Thus one is not surprised to see elements that relate to both God's common grace to humanity and to God's redemptive purposes for His people. The common grace aspects include the preservation of the created order, the institution of family and state, and the continuation of dominion. The redemptive aspects include the evidence in Noah's life of divine grace, the fact that God works through the family of Noah as the godly line, the worship of God through the offering of sacrifices, and the separation of the godly from the ungodly line after the Flood. It is appropriate to view the Noahic Covenant as an outworking of God's Covenant of Grace initiated in Genesis 3:15.

The universal aspect of the Noahic Covenant means that the elements that are integral to the unity of the Covenant of Grace are highlighted in different ways. The covenant with Noah promises the continuation of life so that the promise of eternal life can be fulfilled. It also preserves the godly line so that the mediator promised in Genesis 3:15 can come. The response of faith is foundational to the continuation of the Covenant of Grace in the godly line as Noah found favor with God.

The Typological Elements of the Flood

The events associated with Noah's Flood are used to explain both judgment and redemptive aspects of salvation. The global judgment of the undoing of creation makes the Flood a fitting picture of the end of the world. The people of Noah's day carried on their normal lives of eating, drinking, and marriage without any awareness of the coming Flood of judgment until suddenly the Flood came and their lives were swept away (Matt. 24:38; Luke 17:27). The people who are alive when the Son of Man comes will experience the same thing. They will not be aware of the coming of Christ until, suddenly, He comes, and it will be too late. Such a pattern is typical of unbelievers who live their lives without understanding the danger they are in apart from Christ. This example is used by Jesus to warn people of His coming.

Peter uses Noah and the Flood to support his teaching of the perseverance and suffering of Christians. He warns against the danger of false teachers in 2 Peter and encourages Christians with the reality that God will destroy such teachers. He uses Noah and the Flood twice to show that their coming destruction is certain (2 Pet. 2:5; 3:6). Just like in the Flood, none of the wicked will be able to escape the judgment, except this time it will be by fire. God not only judged the wickedness of the ancient world, but He also preserved Noah, along with seven others, from the destruction of the Flood. God will save His people even if they are outnumbered.[20]

Peter had already used the deliverance of Noah in the Flood to speak of salvation (1 Pet. 3:18-22). He encouraged the Christians who were suffering because of their good behavior in Christ by reminding them that Christ also suffered unjustly for their salvation and that God brought Noah and his family safely through the Flood waters. The reference to salvation through water brought to Peter's mind baptism, which corresponds to the Flood, and 'now saves you'. There is a typological relationship between the waters of the Flood and the waters of baptism,[21] but what the correspondence involves is debated because the waters of the Flood brought destruction for the wicked but salvation

---

20. Thomas R. Schreiner, *1, 2 Peter, Jude* (NAC; Nashville, TN: Broadman & Holman, 2003), p. 338.

21. Karen H. Jobes, *1 Peter* (BECNT; Baker Academic, 2005), p. 251. She comments that the typological correspondence of the Flood waters to the water of baptism would suggest taking the prepositional phrase 'through water' (*dia*) as instrumental rather than locative because Peter uses the instrumental sense that 'baptism now saves you'.

for Noah and his family.[22] The focus of Peter is more on salvation because he specifically mentions the cleansing nature of baptism. It is not the ritual of baptism that saves because water can only remove dirt from the body,[23] but it is the inner renewal that comes from the work of Christ. There is 'an appeal to God for a good conscience' which comes from the heart. Whether the word 'appeal' refers to asking God to help us or the pledge we make toward God, it can only occur 'through the resurrection of Christ'.[24] The work of Christ is the basis for the renewal of the believer, with the water of baptism pointing to that reality.

22.   Patrick Fairbairn, *Typology of Scripture* (Grand Rapids: Kregel Publications, 1989), pp. 272-73.

23.   See Jobes (1 Peter, pp. 254-55) for the view that a ritual of outward cleansing is not in view, but the moral filth characteristic of a carnal existence is what Peter has in mind (based on the two words *sarx* and *rhypos*). Peter's point is that, since baptism does not remove moral filth once for all, Christians should be concerned about how they live after their baptism.

24.   Simon J. Kistemaker, *Exposition of the Epistles of Peter and of the Epistle of Jude* (Grand Rapids: Baker, 1987), p. 148 and Jobes, *1 Peter*, p. 253.

CHAPTER 5

The Abrahamic Covenant

THE Flood was a major judgment of God against sin and a way to start anew with Noah and his family. Of course, the problem of sin continued within the family of Noah (Gen. 9:20-27) and in his descendants at the Tower of Babel. This incident is a clear case of rebellion against God and a refusal to fill the earth by staying in one place to make a name for themselves (Gen. 11:1-9). Babel expressed total confidence in human achievement apart from God. This is the logical end of Genesis 4–11 which is an account of human failure and the continuing problem of sin. The call of Abram is God's response to the growth of sin because through Abram and his descendants God will bless the nations and restore creation. Everything that went before was preparation for the revelation of the promises to Abram and everything that came afterwards in redemptive history is a fulfillment of God's promises to Abram.[1]

Genesis 12: The Promises of God

The call of Abram (Gen. 11:27–12:9) can be divided into the background of the call (Gen. 11:27-32), the promises of God's call (12:1-3),

---

1. Reymond, *Systematic Theology*, p. 513.

and Abram's obedience to the call (12:4-9). The call itself and the promises are given in Genesis 12:1-3. Terah and the family had settled in Haran in Mesopotamia. God called Abram to leave his country, his family, and the security of his father's house and go to a land he had not seen. God promised to bless Abram in several ways. God was going to give Abram a land, but He was also going to make him into a great nation.[2] For the latter promise to be fulfilled at least one descendant will have to be born to Abram and Sarai. The two promises of land and seed dominate the narrative account. God also promises to make the name of Abram great in direct contrast to the Tower of Babel episode where people tried to make a name for themselves (Gen. 11:4).

The word blessing occurs five times in Genesis 12:1-3. This matches the five times the word curse (*'ārar*) occurs in Genesis 1–11 (Gen. 3:14, 17; 4:11; 5:29; 9:25). God will use the blessing of Abram to counter the curse of sin prominent in the first eleven chapters of Genesis. He promises not only to bless Abram but also to bless all those who are a blessing to him, and to curse anyone who seeks to dishonor or harm him. The blessing of God will come to all the families of the earth through Abram and his descendants.[3] God moves from the universal setting of Genesis 1–11 to focus on one man and his family with the purpose to bring blessing to the whole world.[4]

---

2. Wenham comments on the significance of the use of *gôy* as a political unit with a common land, language, and government. This promise is closely paralleled in the offer made to Moses that his descendants would become a great nation in Exodus 32:10. The promise 'make your name great' also parallels the promise to David in 2 Samuel 7:9 (Gordon J. Wenham, *Genesis 16–50* [WBC; Dallas: Word Books, 1994], p. 275). These connections show the foundational nature of God's promises to Abram in the rest of the covenants.

3. Not everyone understands Genesis 12:3 as affirming that Abram is the instrument of blessing for the nations. Some argue that Abram is a model of blessing for the nations in the sense that they will appeal to the blessing Abram has received as an example of the way they can be blessed (J. Skinner, *A Critical and Exegetical Commentary on Genesis* [ICC; 2d. ed., Edinburgh: T&T Clark, 1910], pp. 244-45). For a discussion of why this view should be rejected and reasons for accepting the view that Abram will be an instrument of blessing to the nations, see Belcher, *Genesis*, pp. 113-14, Mathews, *Genesis 11:27–50:26*, p. 117, and Hamilton, *Genesis 1–17*, pp. 374-75.

4. Mathews, *Genesis 11:27–50:26*, p. 105.

Genesis 15: The Establishment of the Covenant

God makes promises to Abram in Genesis 12 concerning land and seed. Genesis 12–14 focuses on the promise of land and Genesis 16–22 focuses on the promise of seed. Both promises concerning land and seed come together in Genesis 15 which culminates in God's covenant with Abram. After Abram rescues Lot and honors God with his wealth in Genesis 14, God appears to him in a vision in Genesis 15, assuring him that God is the one who gives protection and security ('I am your shield') and that his reward shall be very great (15:1). Abram responds by reminding God that the promise of an offspring has not yet been fulfilled and suggests that his servant Eliezer should become his heir. God rejects Abram's proposal and emphasizes that Abram's own son will be his heir. He shows Abram the innumerable stars of heaven and proclaims, 'So shall your offspring be' (15:5 NIV). Abram believes God's promise and 'he counted it to him as righteousness' (15:6).[5] This is not the first time that Abram has trusted Yahweh's word (12:1-3), but his faith is mentioned here because of the significance of the promise of innumerable descendants in light of Abram's continuing childlessness.[6]

God also raises the issue of land by stating, 'I am the LORD who brought you out of the Ur of the Chaldeans to give you this land to possess' (15:7 CSB). Abram responds with a question concerning how he is to know that he will possess the land. God secures the promises He has made to Abram with a covenant ceremony (15:9-21). Abram is told to bring several animals, to cut them in half, and to lay the halves over against each other (15:9-10). As the sun goes down, he falls into a deep sleep[7] and 'a dreadful and great darkness fell upon him' (15:12). These events signify that something ominous is about to be revealed. God informs Abram that his descendants will be afflicted for four hundred years in a land that is not their own. However, God will bring judgment on that nation, bring his descendants out of that land, and give them the land of Canaan in the fourth generation when the iniquity of the

---

5. In Romans 4, Paul uses Abram as an example of one who is not justified by his works but who is justified by his faith.

6. Hamilton, *Genesis 1–17*, 423 and Wenham, *Genesis 1–15*, p. 329.

7. The term for 'deep sleep' (*tardēmāh*) is associated with divine revelations in dreams and visions (Job 4:13; 33:15; Isa. 29:10).

Amorites is complete. The covenant ceremony includes a statement of these promises (15:13-16), as well as a description of the boundaries of the land and its occupants (15:18-21). The promise of land will be fulfilled even though that fulfillment is in the distant future.

God confirms the covenant promises to Abram by taking upon Himself the responsibility to fulfill those promises. The smoking firepot and the flaming torch symbolize the presence of God as they pass between the slain animals. Normally, both parties of the covenant would walk through the animals, but here God is the only party to pass between them. He places Himself under covenant curse if He does not keep the promises. In other words, the curse would fall on God, and He would become like the slain animals if He is not faithful to the covenant (a self-maledictory oath).[8] Support for understanding this ceremony as involving a self-maledictory oath is found in ancient Near Eastern texts[9] and in a similar covenant ceremony described in Jeremiah 34:17-20. Those who pass through the slain animal, the officials of Judah and Jerusalem, the court officers, the priests, and all the people of the land, are the ones who will experience the judgment of being given into the hand of their enemies. On the one hand, it is difficult to conceive of God undergoing covenant curse, but He allows Himself to be bound by covenant obligation to show that He is serious about keeping the covenant promises. On the other hand, we know that God did take upon Himself a covenant curse, not because He failed to keep the covenant promises, but because the descendants of Abram failed to keep them (Exod. 24:7; Deut. 27–28). Thus, God in the person of Jesus Christ took upon Himself the curse of the covenant that should have fallen on those who were covenant breakers.[10]

There is some debate whether Genesis 15 is the establishment of the covenant with Abram. Some argue that the covenant was

---

8. Kline, *Kingdom Prologue*, pp. 297-98. Dumbrell argues that imprecation is not necessarily at the heart of the ceremony in Genesis 15, but it is a theophanic assurance of God's protection (*Covenant and Creation,* pp. 48-49); see also Wenham, *Genesis 1-15,* p. 335. Those who understand the covenant ceremony as involving a self-maledictory oath include Murray (*The Covenant of Grace* [Phillipsburg, NJ: P&R, 1953/1988], p. 16), Kline (*Kingdom Prologue,* p. 296), and Robertson (*The Christ of the Covenants,* pp. 130-31).

9. Hamilton, *Genesis 1–17,* pp. 430-34.

10. Belcher, *Genesis,* pp. 125-126.

established in Genesis 12. Dumbrell argues that Genesis 15 cannot be the inauguration of the covenant because both parts of the chapter are bound by the common theme of divine assurance concerning promises already given in Genesis 12.[11] Thus, the covenant ritual of Genesis 15 functions as confirmation of a relationship previously established in Genesis 12.[12] Yet, although Abram already has a relationship with God, Genesis 15 is best understood as the establishment of God's covenant with Abram. The typical terminology to establish a covenant is used in Genesis 15:18: 'On that day the LORD made a covenant with Abram' (CSB, NIV). The phrase 'made a covenant' is the expression 'cut a covenant' (*karāt*) which is the technical expression for entering a covenant relationship.[13] Dumbrell acknowledges that 'to cut a covenant' is the normal covenant terminology.[14] The proclamation 'I am Yahweh' in verse 7 is a declaration of self-identification that is commonly found in the preamble to covenants. Kings would commence treaties with self-identification,[15] as Yahweh also does in Exodus 20:2. The promises of Genesis 12 set forth the provisions of the covenant that are authenticated in the establishment of the covenant in Genesis 15, particularly land and seed (15:18).[16]

---

11.   Dumbrell argues, based on the preterite verb (past aspect) 'I have given' in 15:18, that the land that will be given to Abram's descendants has *already* been given. Also, the verb 'give' must bear the same sense it does in Genesis 17:2 of bringing into effect an arrangement already concluded (Dumbrell, *Covenant and Creation*, p. 49).

12.   Dumbrell, *Covenant and Creation*, p. 55. He comments that Genesis 12:1-3 is a summary of the relationship begun by God with Abram to which the title 'covenant' is later given in Genesis 15.

13.   Mathews, *Genesis 11:27–50:26*, p. 176. He comments that this expression is usually attributed to the practice of cutting an animal in a symbolic rite associated with the making of a treaty. He lists all the places in the Pentateuch where this phrase occurs.

14.   Dumbrell, *Covenant and Creation*, p. 25. He also notes that the normal covenant terminology 'to cut a covenant' is not prominent in Genesis, except for 15:8. Perhaps he is referring to God's relationship with human beings because 'to cut a covenant' does occur several times to refer to the making of a covenant between human parties (Gen. 21:27, 32; 26:28; 31:44). This would make 15:8 all the more significant.

15.   Currid, *Genesis 1:1–25:18*, p. 294.

16.   Mathews, *Genesis 11:27–50:26*, p. 106. Part of Dumbrell's argument that the covenant is not established in Genesis 15 is that the verb in 15:18 is in the 'perfect aspect', translated 'to your offspring I have given this land' (see footnote 11). The use of this type of verb emphasizes the certainty of God's promise to Abram. The promise is so certain

Genesis 17: The Confirmation of the Covenant

The fact that God alone walks through the slain animals in Genesis 15 shows that He obligates Himself to make sure that the promises of the covenant are fulfilled. On one level, this means that the covenant promises will come to pass regardless of whether Abram and his descendants continue to trust God. And yet, it is important how Abram and his descendants respond to God and His promises. Abram is in a relationship with God and has already shown loyalty to Him by trust in His word and obedience (Gen. 12:1-3). Although not perfect (Gen. 12:10-20), he has consistently lived a life of faith up to this point, and he responds with faith in God's assurance that He will fulfill His promises (Gen. 15:6). Plus, each of the patriarchs commit themselves to the covenant promises (Isaac in 26:1-5, 23-25 and Jacob in 28:10-22). The importance of how Abram and his descendants respond is demonstrated in Genesis 16–17.

The theme of land dominated Genesis 12–15 and the theme of seed dominates Genesis 16–22, even framing this section (16:1; 22:17). These chapters show how God fulfilled His promise of a seed. The statement at the beginning of Genesis 16 that Sarai had not produced any children stands in sharp contrast to the promise of Genesis 15 that their descendants would be innumerable as the stars of heaven. Sarai becomes impatient and comes up with a plan of her own to produce an heir. She offers her Egyptian servant Hagar to Abram so that 'it may be that I shall obtain children by her' (16:1-2). Although such a practice may have been common in the culture of the day, it stands sharply opposed to God's promise that Abram and Sarah's son would be the heir (15:4). Not only did this plan go against the promise of God, but the results of this plan bring negative consequences into the household of Abram.[17]

---

that God can say that He has already given the land to Abram's offspring. This is called a prophetic perfect (Wenham, *Genesis 1–15*, p. 325; GKC, 106m) or rhetorical perfect (Bill T. Arnold and John H. Choi, *A Guide to Biblical Hebrew Syntax* [Cambridge: Cambridge University Press, 2003], pp. 55-56) or a perfect of certitude (Ronald J. Williams, [Third ed.; Toronto: University of Toronto Press, 2007], pp. 68-69). This would give further assurance to Abram that God's promises would be fulfilled.

17. There are parallels between Adam and Eve in Genesis 3 and Abram and Sarai in Genesis 16. Like Eve, Sarai took and gave to her husband (16:3), except Sarai is not giving fruit from a tree but a servant to raise up a seed. Like Adam, Abram listened to the voice of his wife and disobeyed God (Belcher, *Genesis*, p. 126)). It is important to

When Hagar conceived, she 'looked with contempt' on Sarai (16:4). Sarai perceives that Hagar is a threat to her place in the house and she blames Abram for the situation even though it was her idea (16:5). She regrets her decision and is looking for vindication of her place in the household.[18] Abram confirms Sarai's place but also relieves himself of responsibility by giving her the power to treat Hagar however she wanted (16:6). She treats Hagar harshly, and Hagar decides the best option for her is to flee. The whole household loses: Sarai loses respect, Hagar loses a home, and Abram is caught in the middle of a quarrel between two women.

There is a clear contrast between the human plan to produce an heir and God's promise of an heir. The latter required faith in God's power to bring life out of a barren womb that was past the normal age of bearing children. Sarai became impatient and devised a human plan to produce the heir. Abram and Sarai tried to solve the problem through their own efforts rather than faith in God's promise. It was important that Abram should have responded with faith in order to avoid disastrous consequences.

The significance of responding appropriately is highlighted in Genesis 17 when God confirms the covenant promise of an heir through a covenant sign that Abram and his descendants must keep. Genesis 16 ends with the age of Abram at the time of the birth of Ishmael as eighty-six years old. Genesis 17 begins by stating that he is ninety-nine years old when the LORD appeared to him. There are thirteen years of silence between Ishmael's birth and God's appearance to Abram. Failure to bring about the promised heir through human, natural means does not destroy the covenant promise. This fits the unilateral nature of the ceremony in Genesis 15 where God takes upon Himself the responsibility to fulfill the promises of the covenant. The LORD identifies Himself as 'God Almighty'[19] (17:1), showing that He has the power to fulfill the promise of an heir through Abram and Sarai. He then exhorts

---

note that later God tells Abraham to listen to the voice of Sarah when she suggests that Ishmael should be sent away (21:12).

18. Mathews, *Genesis 11:27–50:26*, p. 186.

19. The name God Almighty is 'El Shaddai' in Hebrew. The meaning and etymology of Shaddai is uncertain (see Hamilton, *Genesis 1–17*, p. 462, for the different possibilities). The name is regularly used in connection with the promise of descendants evoking the idea that God has the power to fulfill His promises (Wenham, *Genesis 16–50*, p. 20).

Abram with two imperatives, 'walk before me and be blameless' (NKJV), which emphasize Abram's faithfulness and obedience.

Genesis 17 should be understood as the confirmation of the covenant promises and not as a second covenant. The promises of blessing, seed, and land (17:5-8) are the same promises as in Genesis 12 and 15. The need for a covenant sign to confirm God's promises is demonstrated by the lack of faith in Genesis 16. The terminology used in Genesis 17 supports the view that it is not a new covenant but the confirmation of promises already given. The characteristic phrase for entering a covenant relationship ('to cut a covenant') is not used in Genesis 17. The phrase 'that I may make my covenant between me and you' (17:2 NKJV) uses the verb *nāṭan* ('to give, set'), which is the verb used in Genesis 9:12-13 for the appointment of the rainbow as the sign of the covenant with Noah. The statement 'my covenant is with you' (17:4 NKJV) refers to an ongoing covenant relationship, the confirmation of which will have significant implications for Abram and his descendants. The phrase 'I will establish my covenant' (17:7 NIV, NKJV) is used to confirm a covenant already established.[20] God confirms that He will bring about what He has already promised. The sign of circumcision will testify to the reality of a covenant relationship already established.

Genesis 17 can be divided into four sections with the first three sections setting forth the responsibilities that each party has to the covenant (17:4-8; 17:9-14; 17:15-21), and the fourth section shows Abraham's obedience in carrying out the covenant sign of circumcision (17:22-27). Genesis 17:4-8 begins with 'I', translated by some versions with 'as for me' (NAS, NKJV). These verses set forth what God promises to accomplish through this covenant confirmation. He promises to make Abram 'exceedingly fruitful' and the evidence of this fruitfulness will

---

20. Leonard J. Coppes, קוּם (*qûm*), *TWOT*, 2:793. The question is whether the use of this verb refers only to the confirmation of the covenant or whether it can also refer to the initiation of a covenant (Paul R. Williamson, *Sealed with an Oath: Covenant in God's Unfolding Purpose* [NSBT; Downers Grove, IL: Inter-Varsity Press, 2007], p. 73-74). Williamson argues that the use of the verb *qûm* cannot be limited to the confirmation of a covenant, but he also emphasizes that context is the determinative factor. Although he argues for two covenants in Genesis 15 and 17, the terminology and context favor one covenant (the initiation of the covenant in chapter 15 and the confirmation of the covenant in chapter 17).

be that nations and kings will come from him (17:6). God reinforces this promise by changing Abram's name to Abraham. Abram means 'exalted father' and Abraham means 'father of a multitude'.[21] Every time Abraham hears his new name he will be reminded of this promise of God. Confirmation of God's promises also comes in 17:7 where His commitment includes the promise that He will be a God to Abraham and his descendants, who will one day inherit the land of Canaan.

In Genesis 17:9-14 God tells Abraham ('as for you' CSB, NIV) that he and his offspring shall keep the covenant by circumcising every male infant when he is eight days old. This is the sign of the covenant and is so important that it is identified with the covenant itself: 'this is my covenant' (17:10 CSB, NIV, NKJV). To fail to circumcise an eight-day-old male child is to break the covenant which will lead to very serious consequences: 'any uncircumcised male ... shall be cut off from his people' (17:14 NKJV). God then addresses Abraham concerning Sarai his wife ('as for Sarai') in 17:15-21. She is also given a new name, Sarah, as evidence that God will bless her and give Abraham a son by her who will be the beginning of a multitude of descendants. The exact meaning of this name change is not as clear as Abraham's name change. Both Sarai and Sarah may be dialectical variants that mean 'princess'. It is possible that her birth name 'Sarai' looks back on her noble descent and the new name 'Sarah' looks forward to her noble descendants.[22] This fits God's promise that her descendants will become nations, with kings of peoples coming from her (17:16). The chapter ends by showing Abraham's faith in the covenant promise by being obedient to the covenant.[23] He is circumcised, Ishmael is circumcised, and all the men of his household are circumcised.

The Meaning of Circumcision

Circumcision is a ritual act performed on a male infant when he is eight days old that has spiritual implications. Circumcision was practiced

---

21. There is a wordplay involved in this name change with the word 'father' (*'ab*) and 'many' (*hamôn*) sounding very similar to Abraham (Mathews, *Genesis 11:1-50:26*, p. 202, along with many other commentaries).

22. Waltke, *Genesis*, p. 262.

23. Abraham circumcised his household 'on that very day'. Wenham (*Genesis 16– 50*, p. 27) points out that this phrase is used for significant events in redemptive history, such as the day the Flood came (Gen. 7:13) and the day Israel left Egypt (Exod. 12:17).

by other nations, but they associated it more with puberty or a rite of passage into manhood.[24] For Israel circumcision was a sign of the covenant, but who was it a sign for and what did it signify? First, it was a sign of the covenant that only applied to male infants. Does this mean that females were not considered part of the covenant? Several reasons have been given to explain why a sign of God's covenant would only be applied to males, such as it shows the necessity for males to be involved in the religion of Israel (Exod. 23:17; 34:23; Deut. 16:16),[25] or that the one flesh relationship of male and female would include females in the sign.[26] A better explanation relates circumcision to the struggle of Abraham to believe in the promise of God that a son would be born to him through Sarah. By performing circumcision on his household Abraham demonstrated that he believed in God's promise of a seed who will be produced through a physical relationship with Sarah.[27] The sign testifies that Abraham himself will be the progenitor of a seed. Also, the sign of the covenant does not exclude females from being covenant members because covenants operate by a principle of representation.[28] Both males and females born into a covenant household become members of the covenant and come under the requirements of the covenant, including the blessings and curses of the covenant.[29]

Circumcision as the sign of the covenant also pointed to the true meaning of the covenant relationship. Each person who was a member

---

24. Waltke, *Genesis*, p. 261.

25. Wenham, *Genesis 16–50*, p. 24.

26. Hamilton, *Genesis 1–17*, p. 470.

27. Allen P. Ross, *Creation and Blessing* (Grand Rapids, MI: Baker Book House, 1988), p. 333.

28. The principle of representation works differently in the covenant with Abraham than it does in the covenant with Adam (Berkhof, *Systematic Theology*, p. 296). Abraham cannot be considered the head of the Covenant of Grace as Adam was in the Covenant of Works. The Abrahamic Covenant did not include the believers who preceded him who were in the Covenant of Grace. Abraham could not accept the promises for us or believe in our stead. The representative head in the Covenant of Grace who acts on our behalf can only be Christ. Abraham can be called head only in the sense that he received the promise of its continuance in the line of his natural and spiritual descendants (Rom 4:11).

29. Not only males born into one's household are circumcised but any non-Israelite males brought into the household are to be circumcised (Gen. 17:12-13) because they also become part of the covenant community and so are under the authority of God.

of the covenant had the privileges and responsibilities that came with being a member of it. There were both blessings and curses associated with the covenant. The physical act of cutting the foreskin showed the importance of the covenant relationship and any male who was not 'cut' in this way would be cut off from God's people because he had broken the covenant (Gen. 17:14). The blessings of the covenant included a spiritual relationship with God and the promise of descendants and land. The two imperatives to Abraham in Genesis 17:1 to walk before God and to be blameless emphasized the importance of a spiritual relationship with God. The result would be that God would grant to Abram descendants and land (17:4, 7-8). The physical sign of the covenant was meant to lead to a spiritual relationship, the kind of relationship that Abraham already had with God. Later passages in Scripture will emphasize the circumcision of the heart (Deut. 10:16; 30:6), a fitting phrase to show that the physical sign of circumcision pointed to a spiritual relationship. Such a relationship only came about through faith in God and His promises.

Even though the sign of circumcision pointed to a spiritual relationship with God, the covenant with Abraham also had a legal side to it. Not everyone who was a member of the covenant had a spiritual relationship with God, but they enjoyed the temporal blessings of the covenant. The promise of land, numerous descendants, and protection against enemies were temporal blessings that all of God's covenant people enjoyed. These earthly and temporal blessings had a higher purpose because they were a type of the benefits that God would one day grant to His people in the consummation.[30] When God told Abraham that He would give him a son by Sarah, Abraham fell on his face and laughed because they were too old, humanly speaking, to have children (17:17).[31] Abraham pleaded with

---

30. Vos, *Reformed Dogmatics*, 2:128. The land of Canaan and the blessings associated with it are a type of the new heavens and earth (Vern S. Poythress, *The Shadow of Christ in the Law of Moses* [Phillipsburg, NJ: P&R Publishing, 1991], pp. 69-73).

31. There is debate among commentators whether the laughter by Abraham is incredulous laughter, like Sarah in Genesis 18:9-15, or the laughter of joy or amazement. John H. Sailhamer understands the laughter as an expression of a limited faith rather than a lack of faith ('Genesis' in *The Expositor's Bible Commentary*, eds. Tremper Longman III and David Garland [13 vols.; rev. ed.; Grand Rapids, MI: Zondervan, 2008], p. 1:182). It is likely that Abraham's emotions here are mixed (Currid, *Genesis 1:1–25:18*, p. 317). Sailhamer also shows how 'laughter' is a key word throughout these narratives.

God that Ishmael would be the promised heir (17:18). God responded by emphasizing that Abraham and Sarah would have a son and that his name would be called Isaac. He was the one through whom the covenant would be established (17:19). God then addressed Abraham's concern for Ishmael and assured him that He has blessed Ishmael and would make him fruitful. There were temporal blessings associated with being in the covenant. Twelve princes would come from him and his descendants would become a great nation (17:20). Yet, the covenant promises would continue through the line of Isaac. With this information about Ishmael, Abraham circumcised him along with the rest of the males of his household. The circumcision of Ishmael is emphasized by being mentioned three times in 17:22-27. He received the sign of the covenant and was a member of the covenant community even though the promises of the covenant would continue with Isaac. The descendants of Ishmael settled outside the boundaries of the promised land (Gen. 25:12-18) and were not part of the community of God's people. It was possible to be in the covenant legally by receiving the sign of the covenant and not to develop a spiritual relationship with God. This distinction becomes important for later theological developments, such as the distinction between the visible and invisible church and the administration of the covenant under the New Covenant (Rom. 11:16-24).

The Emphasis on Offspring

For God's promises to Abraham to come to pass, there must be a son born to Abraham and Sarah. For many years this promise was not fulfilled. Genesis 16–22 shows the struggles of Abraham and Sarah's faith in relationship to this promise culminating in Abraham believing God's promise even when he is told to offer Isaac as a sacrifice to God (22:1-5, 9-11). The emphasis on offspring, or seed (*zera*ʿ), is a common theme going back to Genesis 3:15 where God promises that one from the seed of the woman will come to bruise the head of the seed of the serpent. The godly community is looking for the seed (Gen. 5:28-30) and Noah and his family are used by God to save humanity from complete destruction. After the Flood, the line goes through Shem to Abraham. The future fulfillment of the promises of the Abrahamic Covenant is confirmed in Genesis 17 with circumcision, the sign of covenant. and the statement that Abraham and Sarah will have a son. Isaac will be the promised seed through whose descendants the promises of the covenant will continue.[32] There is an emphasis in Genesis 17 on one seed (one heir) and many descendants. The covenant will be established with Isaac (17:19), but it also includes the descendants of Abraham because the promise to give them the land is included (17:8). This is the normal way that covenants operate. The promises include the descendants and are passed down from generation to generation. It is also significant that the word for 'offspring' is a collective singular that can refer to one offspring or many descendants. These principles become important for later discussions of the covenant (Acts 2:39; Gal. 3:29) and show the primacy of the Abrahamic Covenant for the New Covenant as fulfilled in the one seed, Jesus Christ (Gal. 3:16).[33] In fact, the Abrahamic Covenant can be considered the primary revelation of the Covenant of Grace. Paul connects the promise to Abraham that 'In you shall all the nations be blessed' as being fulfilled in the New Covenant in the preaching of the gospel to the Gentiles (Gal. 3:8).[34]

---

32. Peter Golding comments that 'The grand purpose, then, of the Abrahamic covenant was to reveal the line from which the seed of the woman would come' (*Covenant Theology*), p. 154.

33. Golding, *Covenant Theology*, p. 153. Berkhof considers the Abrahamic Covenant as the formal establishment of the Covenant of Grace even though it was initiated in Genesis 3:15 (*Systematic Theology*, p. 295).

34. Kline, *Kingdom Prologue*, p. 193. For a discussion of the unity of the covenant, see Chapter 3 above.

CHAPTER 6

The Mosaic Covenant

THE Mosaic Covenant is the most difficult covenant to understand. Prominent reformed scholars have disagreed on its nature and character. Questions abound concerning its relationship to the Covenant of Grace, the role that the law plays in the covenant, the purposes of the curses of the covenant in relationship to Israel's inheritance of the land, and the relationship of this covenant to Christ and the New Covenant. The Mosaic Covenant has many aspects to it, and it is difficult to incorporate all the parts into one explanation. Minor differences of nuance can make a big difference in one's understanding and explanation of this covenant. The aim of this chapter is to explain the meaning of the Mosaic Covenant, its relationship to the Covenant of Grace, and its role in redemptive history.

The Historical Context of the Mosaic Covenant

God's Promises to Abraham

God had made certain promises to Abraham that He was committed to fulfill. Those promises are part of His plan to restore humanity's relationship with Him and their role in creation. The goal is that all creation will one day experience restoration. By the end of Genesis, it is clear that God is at work to fulfill His promises. The promise of a seed who would come (Gen. 3:15) narrows from the line of Abraham to the family of Judah with an emphasis on royal terminology and victory (Gen. 49:8-12). The promise of innumerable descendants (Gen. 15:5; 17:6) begins to be fulfilled in the land of Egypt as the sons of Israel transition from a family of seventy to a nation (Exod. 1:1-7). The multiplication of the sons of Israel, even in the midst of oppression, uses language from the creation account. Genesis 1:28 states that God blessed them (Adam and Eve) and said to them, 'Be fruitful, multiply, and fill the earth.' Exodus 1:7 uses the same language to describe Israel in Egypt: 'But the people of Israel were fruitful, and increased greatly; they multiplied and grew exceedingly strong, so that the land was filled with them.' God had promised to make Abraham's name great and the rise of Joseph to power as the second in command in Egypt is a partial fulfillment of this promise. Joseph was also a blessing to the nations by providing food for them during the seven years of famine. Other descendants of Abraham were used by God to bless others, including Jacob's relationship with Laban (Gen. 30:27) and Joseph's relationship with Potiphar (Gen. 39:3). God's promise of curse to those who mistreat Abraham's descendants will be demonstrated by God delivering Israel from Egypt by means of the judgment of the plagues. Finally, the promise of land is still future, but God will deliver His people in order to bring them to the land He had promised them (Gen. 50:24).

God Remembered His Covenant with Abraham

Exodus 1–18 sets the stage for God's redemption of His people. Exodus 1:1-7 shows the transition from the focus on the family of the sons of Abraham in the patriarchal period to the focus on the sons of Abraham as a nation. Seventy people went down to Egypt, but while in Egypt they multiplied. There is also a transition from a Pharaoh who knew Joseph to a Pharaoh who did not know Joseph (Exod. 1:8) and from a situation of prosperity to a situation of bondage (Exod. 1:9-22). Out of the situation of oppression Moses, the deliverer of God's people, is born and raised as an Egyptian. Being torn between his Jewishness and his Egyptian upbringing he tried to help his people by slaying an Egyptian taskmaster, but had to flee when Pharaoh heard of it. He settled in Midian and while shepherding the sheep of his father-in-law in the wilderness, where he will later lead the Israelites, God appeared to him to press upon him the oppression of God's people and that God had chosen him to lead them out of Egypt. God's determination to deliver His people out of Egypt goes back to the covenant He had made with Abraham, Isaac, and Jacob (Exod. 2:23-25).

After Moses' failure to help his people and his flight to Midian, Exodus 2:23-25 offers a summary conclusion of the story setting the stage for God to confront Moses with the need for someone to lead God's people out of Egypt. The time was right because the king who sought Moses' life had died. The situation of God's people was desperate with no relief in sight. They cried out to God and He heard their groaning and He remembered His covenant. The fact that God remembered His covenant does not mean He had forgotten His promises, but that the time had come to act on behalf of His people because of those promises. This covenant is the one made with Abraham, but also Isaac and Jacob are mentioned to remind the reader that the covenant with Abraham is applicable to the generations of Israelites that come after him, including those suffering in Egypt.[1] The promises of the Abrahamic Covenant provide the historical impetus for the deliverance of God's people from Egyptian bondage and the institution of the Mosaic Covenant.

The Setting of the Covenant (Exodus 19)

In Exodus 19 the Israelites arrive at Mt. Sinai where they will enter into a covenant with God to become a nation, receive His law (Exodus 19–24), and a system of worship that will lead to the presence of God dwelling with them (Exodus 25–40). Exodus 19 prepares the people to receive the Law of God and to enter the covenant. The people need to be reminded of certain things concerning His character. He is a God who has been faithful to His covenant promises. The people have seen what He did to the Egyptians in the plagues and the deliverance at the Red Sea. He brought them to Himself by bearing them up on eagle's wings (19:4). This metaphorical description of the deliverance from Egypt emphasizes God's presence and reminds the people of the various

---

1. Douglas K. Stuart, *Exodus* (NAC; Nashville, TN: B&H Publishing Group, 2006), pp. 102-04.

ways He was with them in the Exodus from Egypt and the crossing of the Red Sea. God's presence with them brought great blessings, but He is also a God who is holy, demonstrated in the manifestation of His presence on Mt. Sinai. God appeared to Moses in a thick cloud so that the people will listen to God through Moses (19:9). Moses was to help the people prepare themselves for God's appearance by consecrating them (19:10). The people were to be set apart and cleansed, represented by the washing of their garments, in preparation for God's appearing. God's presence made the whole mountain holy so that the people were prohibited from even touching it lest they die (19:12-13). They were also to avoid sexual relationships (19:15). On the third day the people took their stand at the foot of the mountain. God appeared in smoke and fire so that the whole mountain trembled (19:18).[2] The seriousness of entering a relationship with God is emphasized. A holy God must be approached in the right way. The boundary around the mountain shows the distance between a holy God and the people and that He must not be approached through human initiative.[3] There is danger in not taking seriously what He demands.

The manifestation of God's holy presence to His people had important implications for their relationship. The people needed a mediator to intercede for them and to speak to them the Word of God. Part of the reason for the manifestation of God's presence in the thick cloud was that the people will have confidence in Moses as their mediator and believe what he says (19:9). When God descended on the mountain in smoke and fire Moses spoke and God answered him in thunder (19:19). Second, the people must be willing to obey God's voice and keep the covenant He will make with them (19:5). This obedience is a response to what God has done for them (19:4) and will flow from a heart that properly fears God (20:20). Moses tells the people, 'Do not fear, for God has come to test you that the fear of him may be before you, that you may not sin.' The same word is used for 'fear' (the verb is $y\bar{a}r\bar{a}$' and the noun $yir'\bar{a}h$). The people of God do not need to be terrified of God even

---

2. Vern S. Poythress, *Theophany: A Biblical Theology of God's Appearing* (Wheaton, IL: Crossway, 2018), pp. 34, 273-74. He identifies this as a thunderstorm theophany.

3. John N. Oswalt, 'Exodus,' in *Cornerstone Bible Commentary*, ed. Philip W. Comfort (Carol Stream, IL: Tyndale House, 2008), p. 434.

as they see His mighty power displayed at Mt. Sinai (20:18-19), but they do need to have the proper respect for God that leads to a heart willing to obey His commands and to keep them from sin.

If the people respond appropriately to God, they will not only experience the benefit of a relationship with God, but they also will fulfill His purposes for them (Exod. 19:5-6).[4] Three terms are used to describe Israel's unique covenant relationship with God. They will be a treasured possession. The word *sᵉgullāh* refers to a king's personal treasure and shows that Israel will be Yahweh's unique, prized possession.[5] The other two terms describe the mediatorial role that Israel will have toward the nations. As a kingdom of priests, Israel will seek to extend the worship and presence of God. As a holy nation, Israel will demonstrate the blessings that come with being in a relationship with God. He promises to pour out abundant blessings on his people (Deut. 7:8-16; 28:1-14) so that she can influence the nations. By living in obedience to God in the land He is going to give them, Israel will draw the nations to the God she worships.[6]

The Ratification of the Covenant (Exodus 24)

Already in Exodus 19:8 the people commit themselves to do all that Yahweh has spoken to them. God moves forward with His covenant purposes by giving to Israel His law (Exod. 20:1–23:19), reminding them of the promise to conquer the land of Canaan (Exod. 23:20-33), and ratifying the covenant through a covenant ceremony (Exod. 24:1-18). These matters are important for understanding the covenant that God makes with Israel.

---

4.   Stuart highlights the importance of 19:4-6 by calling it a summary of the covenant that will be spelled out more formally in Exodus 20–Leviticus 27 (*Exodus*, p. 421).

5.   John I. Durham, *Exodus* (WBC; Waco, TX: Word Books, 1987), p. 263.

6.   This mission was partially fulfilled in the early reign of Solomon (1 Kings 11), but he fell away from the Lord, and the kingdom divided. For how this mission is kept alive in the Old Testament and is eventually fulfilled, see Belcher, *Prophet, Priest, and King* (Philipsburg, NJ: P&R Publishing, 2016), pp. 14-16. For other discussions of Israel's mission, see Walter C. Kaiser, *Mission in the Old Testament* (Grand Rapids: Baker, 2000) and Christopher J. H. Wright, *The Mission of God* (Downers Grove, IL: InterVarsity Press, 2006). For a discussion of how Israel was to attract the nations, see Christopher J. H. Wright, *The Mission of God's People* (Grand Rapids: Zondervan, 2010), pp. 128-47.

The Giving of the Law (Exod. 20:1–23:19)

The distinctive element of the Mosaic Covenant is the Law of God. It is important to understand how the law functions in the covenant. The law is given in a context of an awe-inspiring demonstration of God's holiness in thundering, lightnings, and thick darkness. The giving of the Ten Commandments is framed by the manifestations of God's holiness (Exod. 19:16-20; 20:18-21). The people hear the voice of God[7] and must respond in the right way to avoid judgment. As Moses drew near to the thick darkness where God's presence was, the people stood far off. But blessings will also be associated with God's law because the law is given to God's people in the context of redemption. Exodus 20:2 identifies the parties to the covenant and tells how they came to be related.[8] Yahweh is identified as the giver of the covenant and Israel is the recipient.[9] The context of the giving of the law is redemption from the slavery of Egypt. A relationship has already been established between God and Israel and now that relationship is formalized in a covenant that will make the people into a nation. The covenant relationship between God and Israel is primary and the law will regulate that relationship.

The Law of God is composed of two different types of law identified as the Ten Words and the covenant code. The Ten Words are absolute statements of what should or should not be done (Exod. 20:1-17). There is no social context or penalties associated with them. They are closely identified with the covenant itself (Deut. 4:13) and were uniquely written by the finger of God on two tablets of stone (Exod. 31:18). The Ten Words, also called commandments in the New Testament (Matt. 19:17; Mark 10:19; Luke 18:20; Rom. 7:7-8; 13:9), come from God to Israel directly and personally. These characteristics set them apart from the other laws in the Old Testament and give them priority. The

---

7. Stuart, *Exodus*, p. 445.

8. Stuart shows how the legal portion of Exodus is patterned after a suzerainty treaty. He identifies Exodus 20:2 with the preamble and the prologue (*Exodus*, pp. 439, 445). The self-identification 'I am Yahweh' is royal speech emphasizing God's kingship as their suzerain (John D. Currid, *A Study Commentary on Exodus; Volume 2: Chapters 19–40* [Darlington: Evangelical Press, 2001], p. 35).

9. The second person singular pronoun 'you' is used to emphasize that Israel as a united people respond as one to God's commands (Currid, *Exodus Chapters 19–40*, p. 34).

other laws are case laws written in response to various situations where the law must be applied (Exod. 20:22–23:19). These laws give insight into Israel's social relationships and the penalties that accompany the breaking of them. The case law is mediated through Moses to the people. The decalogue is primary and the case law is derivative with a focus on the application of the law to Israel.

The Conquest of the Land (Exod. 23:20-33)

Israel is reminded of the purpose for which God has redeemed her. She is to take the land of Canaan in order to serve God in the midst of the nations (and so fulfil Exodus 19:5-6). God's presence is represented by an angel that God will send before them to lead them to the place He has prepared for them. This angel must be obeyed; in fact, the voice of this angel is identified with God's instructions ('do all that I say'). Israel at Mt. Sinai stood far off from the presence of God in the thick darkness and this angel is God's presence among the people in a form that allows Him to come near to them in order to lead them.[10] If the people are obedient, God will be an enemy to their enemy (23:22). If the people destroy the idols of the nations, God will drive out the nations before them until they have possessed the land. He will also greatly bless everything they do. Redemption from Egypt and entering a covenant relationship with God will empower them to fulfil God's purposes.

The Covenant Ceremony (Exodus 24)

Israel enters into a covenant relationship with God through a commitment to keep the terms of the covenant that is ratified by blood. There is a formal acceptance of the terms of the covenant represented in a ceremonial meal between the covenant parties (introduced in 24:1-2 and described in 24:9-11), the taking of an oath before witnesses (24:3-8), and receiving the official text of the covenant (24:12-18).[11] Several important ideas are emphasized in this chapter. The people

---

10. Stuart identifies this angel with Yahweh (*Exodus*, p. 542) and Currid with a pre-incarnate appearance of the Messiah (*Exodus Chapters 19–40*, p. 125). Isaiah 63:9 identifies this angel as 'the angel of his presence'. The next verse in Isaiah describes the people's rebellion as grieving the 'Holy Spirit' (Oswalt, 'Exodus', p. 479).

11. Oswalt, 'Exodus,' p. 482.

should exercise caution when coming into the presence of such a glorious God. The chapter is framed by two passages where only Moses is allowed to come before God (24:1-2; 12-18). The people are not allowed to ascend the mountain and although the elders, along with Aaron and his sons, can come up the mountain, they must worship God from afar (vv. 1-2). The glory of Yahweh covers the mountain in a cloud, with its appearance like a devouring fire, so that only Moses enters the cloud (vv. 15-18).[12] The powerful appearance of the glory of Yahweh shows that He is a holy God and that to enter into a covenant with Him is serious.

There is also an emphasis on the importance of the Law of God as the focus of this covenant. Several times the people agree to do all that Yahweh has spoken, including Exodus 19:8, which occurs before the giving of the law. Once the law is given to the people they again agree to do all the words that Yahweh has spoken (Exod. 24:3).[13] At that point Moses makes preparation for the formal acceptance of the covenant by the people where the Book of the Covenant would be read as part of the covenant ceremony (24:4-8). After the covenant is ratified, God calls Moses up to the mountain again to receive the law written by God on tablets of stone (Exod. 24:12-14). This time he is accompanied by Joshua, but only Moses enters the cloud on the mountain. Moses' presence with God on the mountain continues through Exodus 32 when Moses must come down from the mountain because of the golden calf incident. While on the mountain he receives the Law of God and the instructions for the proper worship of God.[14]

The formal ratification of the covenant is described in Exodus 24:4-8. The main elements of the covenant ceremony included the building of an altar, erecting twelve stone pillars, offering animal sacrifices, applying blood to the people, and the reading of the covenant. These elements prepared the people to commit themselves

---

12. Currid comments that before Exodus 24 God had addressed Israel, but in Exodus 24 God only speaks to Moses, the covenant mediator. This shift demonstrates his important role (*Exodus Chapters 19–40*, p. 134).

13. Stuart comments that the 'words' and 'rules' in Exodus 24:3 are likely a reference to the Ten Commandments and the Book of the Covenant which God has just given to Israel through Moses (*Exodus*, p. 553).

14. Stuart, *Exodus*, p. 558.

to the covenant. The altar was needed for the animal sacrifices and represents Yahweh as a party to the covenant. Throwing half of the blood on the altar (24:6) commits Yahweh as a covenant partner to keep His part of the covenant.[15] The twelve stone pillars served as witnesses to remind the people of their commitment.[16] Animal sacrifices were common in covenant ceremonies emphasizing death if the covenant is broken. The terms of the covenant were put into writing as part of its ratification. When Moses read the Book of the Covenant to the people they verbally committed themselves to keep it through obedience to the law.[17] At that point Moses sprinkled the blood from the animal sacrifices on the people declaring, 'Behold, the blood of the covenant that the LORD has made with you in accordance with all these words' (24:8). The people were bound by oath to honor God by keeping the covenant. The use of blood shows that the extremes of life and death were in view. Keeping the covenant would ensure life but breaking the covenant would lead to death.[18]

Covenant ceremonies typically ended with a meal to confirm that both parties agreed to the terms of the covenant and were bound together by them (Exod. 24:9-11). To eat a meal with someone signified an alliance, kinship, or friendship.[19] The seventy elders of Israel who participate in the meal represent the people.[20] God's presence is also with them in a startling way. They saw the God of Israel without being destroyed. No doubt they did not see the fullness of His glory but only saw 'under his feet' a pavement of sapphire and stone (similar to Isaiah 6:1-8 and Ezekiel 1:22). The point of this remarkable manifestation of the presence of God is to show that He is a willing party to the covenant and desires to be in a relationship with Israel.[21]

---

15. Currid, *Exodus Chapters 19–40*, p. 136 and Oswalt, 'Exodus,' p. 484.

16. Oswalt, 'Exodus,' p. 483. He comments that normally gods serve as witnesses but in place of gods the pillars are a historical witness to the covenant ceremony.

17. Currid, *Exodus Chapters 19–40*, p. 135. Exodus 24:4 notes that Moses wrote down all the words of Yahweh which included the Ten Commandments and the Book of the Covenant.

18. Currid, *Exodus Chapters 19–40*, p. 137.

19. Stuart, *Exodus*, p. 552.

20. Currid, *Exodus Chapters 19–40*, p. 134. Seventy is symbolic of the totality of Israel.

21. Stuart, Exodus, p. 557 and Oswalt, 'Exodus,' p. 484.

Deuteronomy: Covenant Renewal

While Moses was receiving the Law of God on Mt. Sinai, the people rebelled against God in the golden calf incident. Although idolatry almost led God to destroy the people and to start over with Moses (Exod. 32:7-10), his intercession caused God to relent from this course of action (Exod. 32:11-14). Eventually the covenant was renewed, and God promised that His presence will continue with the people (Exodus 33–34). The rebellion of the people showed itself again in the wilderness where they did not believe in the promise of God to give them the land and so they rejected their mission (Numbers 13–14). The rebellious wilderness generation must die in the wilderness (Num. 14:20-35), but God will raise up the next generation to fulfill His covenant promises. The census of the next generation is for the purpose of preparing them to take the land of Canaan. The emphasis is on those who are twenty years old and upward and able to go to war (Num. 26:2). Deuteronomy is the renewal of the Mosaic Covenant with that generation so they will fulfill God's covenant purposes.

There are several things that demonstrate that Deuteronomy is a covenant renewal document. First, there is continuity between Deuteronomy and the covenant at Mt. Sinai. The same Ten Commandments are given as the foundation of the covenant (Exod. 20:1-17; Deut. 5:1-21), followed by case laws that apply those commandments to Israel's situation (Exod. 20:22–23:19; Deut. 12–26).[22] Deuteronomy expands on the case laws because guidance is needed for the people as they cross the Jordan river to take the land.[23] Second, Deuteronomy is preached law. Moses reviews the past history of the people in order to exhort them to be faithful to God (1:5–4:43).[24]

---

22. Several commentaries view the case law of Deuteronomy 12–26 to be elaborations or applications of the Ten Commandments (Eugene H. Merrill, *Deuteronomy* [(NAC; Nashville: B&H Publishers, 1994], p. 31; John D. Currid, *A Study Commentary on Deuteronomy* [Darlington: Evangelical Press, 2006], pp. 21-23; and Christopher J. H. Wright, *Deuteronomy* [NIBC; Peabody, MS: Hendrickson Publishers, 1996], p. 5. Wright calls it broadly convincing.

23. Merrill comments that the change in language in Deuteronomy as compared with Exodus is due to the changed historical and theological circumstances (*Deuteronomy*, p. 52).

24. Richard L. Pratt, Jr., *He Gave Us Stories* (Phillipsburg, NJ: P&R Publishing, 1990), p. 286. He shows that Deuteronomy can be understood as three addresses (1:5–4:43; 4:44–28:68; 29:1–30:20).

Third, Moses asserts the continuity of the new generation who are receiving the Law of God with the generation who received the law at Mt. Sinai. He speaks to them as if they were present, 'The LORD spoke with you face to face at the mountain' (v. 4). He also states, 'The LORD our God made a covenant with us at Horeb. Not with our fathers did the LORD make this covenant, but with us, who are all of us here alive today' (Deut. 5:2-3). This is an interesting statement because it confirms that the covenant at Mt. Horeb/Sinai was made with the new generation even if they were not alive at the time. There is debate concerning how to understand Moses' statement that the covenant was not made with our fathers but with us who are alive here today. One solution is to say that Moses wanted to make the covenant-making event of the past vivid for his contemporaries who were not present at Mt. Sinai.[25] Thus, Moses drove home forcefully the direct identification of the new generation with the previous generation who entered into the covenant at Mt. Sinai. The essence of the covenant was its present reality[26] and Deuteronomy 5:2-3 emphasizes the immediate responsibility of the present generation.[27] This view argues that even though there seems to be a contrast with the generation at Sinai ('not with our fathers') Moses' words are merely rhetorical to focus on the responsibility of the new generation.

Another solution is to understand 'not with our fathers did the LORD make this covenant' as referring to the patriarchs, which means that 'this covenant' does refer to the covenant at Sinai.[28] Whenever the phrase 'your fathers' is used in Deuteronomy it always refers to the patriarchs Abraham, Isaac, and Jacob (1:8; 6:23). The focus is on covenant renewal as each generation, including the generation Moses is addressing, must make a commitment to the covenant.[29] This seems to be the best solution. A clear principle related to covenants is expressed in these

---

25. Gerhard von Rad, *Deuteronomy* (OTL; Philadelphia: The Westminster Press, 1966), p. 55.

26. Peter Craigie, *Deuteronomy* (NICOT; Grand Rapids: Eerdmans, 1976), p. 148.

27. McConville, *Deuteronomy* (AOTC; Downers Grove, IL: InterVarsity Press, 2002), p. 124. Wright (*Deuteronomy*, p. 62) argues that the phrase 'not with our fathers ... but with us' is an example of relative negation where the meaning is 'not only but also'.

28. Merrill, *Deuteronomy*, p. 141.

29. Currid, *Deuteronomy*, pp. 126-27.

verses. Whenever a covenant is made, future descendants are included in the covenant. This is why Moses is able to say that the covenant at Sinai was made with the generation about to take the land even though most of them were not alive when that covenant was made.[30]

Fourth, the treaty form of Deuteronomy emphasizes the need for covenant renewal. There is a consensus that Deuteronomy fits a suzerain-vassal form of treaty that was common in the ancient Near East.[31] The basic elements of the treaty and their relationship to Deuteronomy are listed in the following chart:

Preamble	Covenant Mediator	1:1-4
Historical Prologue	Covenant History	1:5–3:29
Stipulations	Covenant Life	4:1–26:19
Sanctions	Covenant Ratification	27:1–30:20
Dynastic Disposition	Covenant Continuity	31:1–34:12[32]

A treaty between a great king and a vassal people would need to be renewed with each successive generation or if the stipulations of the treaty were broken. The passing away of Moses and the transition to new leadership made it essential that the covenant be put into writing with a full and final statement of the terms of the covenant.[33] The form of a treaty with the emphasis on law (stipulations) and blessings for

---

30. McConville comments that 'Here is the clearest expression in Deuteronomy of the principle that Israel in all its generations stands in principle once again at Horeb, confronted with the covenant commands as if about to be given for the first time' (*Deuteronomy*, p. 124). Wright states that 'Moses' point is that the present generation and thereby by implication all future generations was just as much a partner in the covenant concluded at Sinai as those who actually stood at the foot of the mountain' (*Deuteronomy*, p. 62). The same principle is found in Deuteronomy 29:14-15 where the renewal of the covenant is also being made with future generations yet to be born.

31. Merrill comments that after forty years of scholarship a near consensus has been reached (*Deuteronomy*, p. 29).

32. Kline, *Treaty of the Great King*, pp. 49-50. For a similar presentation of the elements of the treaty and Deuteronomy, see Merrill, *Deuteronomy*, pp. 30-32 and Currid, *Deuteronomy*, pp. 14-18. For a list of the elements of a treaty in the context of the ANE in the second millennium, see Delbert R. Hillers, *Covenant: The History of Biblical Idea* (Baltimore: John Hopkins, 1969). One should not expect there to be exact correspondence between Exodus or Deuteronomy and the treaty form (see Appendix 1 for a discussion of covenants in the ANE).

33. Merrill, *Deuteronomy*, p. 27.

obedience and curses for disobedience (sanctions) impacts the character of this covenant (see below).

The Mosaic Covenant and the Abrahamic Covenant

The Mosaic Covenant is a result of God's faithfulness to His covenant promises to Abraham. When the people cried out to God from their bondage in Egypt, God heard their cries and remembered His covenant with Abraham, Isaac, and Jacob (Exod. 3:6, 8). In order to fulfill the promises God had made to Abraham He delivered His people from Egypt, brought them to Mt. Sinai, and entered into a covenant with them. Although the Mosaic Covenant has its distinctive elements, it also includes God's promises to Abraham and helps to fulfill those promises. The promise which takes center stage in the Mosaic Covenant is the promise of land. The reason that God acted to deliver Israel was to bring them to the land of Canaan (Exod. 3:8; 23:20-33). The Mosaic Covenant is to prepare the people to take the land by making them into a nation so that they can fulfill God's purposes for them (Exod. 19:5-6). God had promised to make Abram into a great nation so that the families of the earth would be blessed (Gen. 12:2). If Israel takes the land and lives in obedience to God, they will become a blessing to the nations.

There is unity to the Covenant of Grace that includes the Mosaic Covenant. This unity is based on several factors. There is continuity between the Mosaic Covenant and the promises of the Abrahamic Covenant. In fact, the Mosaic Covenant was necessary for the Abrahamic promises to be fulfilled. Israel had to be organized as a nation in order to take the land that God had promised to Abraham's descendants.[34] Once the land was taken the other promises could be fulfilled, at least in a provisional way. During the kingdom of Solomon, Israel's name became great as the descendants of Abraham became as many as the sand by the sea (1 Kings 4:20). They also became a blessing to the nations as kings and rulers came to see the wonders of the kingdom of Solomon (1 Kings 4:21; 10:1-13). Of course, this was not the final

---

34. Dumbrell states that '… Israel is the agent used by God to achieve the wider purposes which the Abrahamic covenant entails, purposes which involve the redemption of the whole world' (*Covenant and Creation*, p. 89).

fulfillment of God's promises to Abraham because Solomon's heart turned away from Yahweh and the division of the kingdom followed. The use of 'my covenant' in Genesis 6:18 (Noah), 17:2 (Abraham), and Exodus 19:5 (Moses) shows the unity of the Covenant of Grace with the Mosaic Covenant being part of the development of that covenant. WCF 7.5 associates the Covenant of Grace with the administration of the law when it states that 'This covenant [the Covenant of Grace] was differently administered in the time of the law, and in the time of the gospel.' The Mosaic Covenant did not supplant the Abrahamic Covenant because it remained in force,[35] nor did it annul it, but it stands in unity with it. Thus, the primary way the Mosaic Covenant should be understood is part-and-parcel of the Covenant of Grace.

The Distinctive Nature of the Mosaic Covenant

The nature and role of the Mosaic Covenant in the history of redemption is greatly debated. The emphasis on the law, Israel's keeping of the law to keep the land, and Paul's use of Leviticus 18:5 in Romans 10:5 has led to a variety of views of the relationship between the Covenant of Works and the Mosaic Covenant. Many describe the Mosaic Covenant as 'in some sense' having a principle of works embedded in it. But the meaning of 'in some sense' is the major question.[36] The best view of this matter is that the Mosaic Covenant is not a republication of the Covenant of Works, but that the requirement to keep the law in the Covenant of Works continues and everyone who does not keep the law perfectly stands condemned by it. This view does not argue that the Jews misrepresented the requirements of the law because those requirements have not been revoked for humanity. The requirement to keep the law

---

35. Berkhof, *Systematic Theology*, p. 297.

36. The phrase 'in some sense' is used to acknowledge that the Covenant of Works was a unique, unrepeatable administration of a covenant. It is used by some who argue for republication: the Covenant of Works was 'in some sense' echoed in the Mosaic Covenant ('The Report of the Committee to Study Republication: Presented to the Eighty-third (2016) General Assembly of the Orthodox Presbyterian Church' [hereinafter 'The OPC Report'] accessed through the OPC website [opc.org/GA/republication.html], p. 2). It is used by others to refer to the ongoing obligation to keep the moral law perfectly, as in the second use of the law (Robert J. Cara, *Cracking the Foundation of the New Perspective on Paul* [Ross-shire: Christian Focus, 2017], p. 46, n. 24).

through personal and perfect obedience still stands and everyone who is born into this world stands condemned by the law because no one is able to keep it perfectly.[37] The problem with many of the Jews, including the Pharisees, was that they misappropriated the law by making it the basis of salvation. The law is unable to save anyone because of human sinfulness, but the righteous requirement of the law still needs to be met. It is important to keep this distinction because there is a tendency to omit or overlook the fact that the obligation of perfect obedience to the law continues even as the basis of the law as a way of salvation is denied.[38] This obligation to keep the law is the 'righteousness that is based on the law' that Paul writes about in Romans 10:5 over against the 'righteousness based on faith'.

This principle of a 'righteousness based on the law' is particularly relevant to unbelievers because they stand condemned by their inability to keep the law. Believers, on the other hand, have come to realize that they are condemned because they are not able to keep the law and have put their faith in the One who has kept the law for them ('the righteousness based on faith'). Israel at first rejected her mission to take the land because of unbelief (Num. 14:11) and then later lost the land because of unbelief and idolatry (Jer. 25:1-14). Israel did not trust in God, broke the Law of God, and so experienced the curse of the law in the judgment of exile. This scenario is unique to Israel only in the sense that she had a mission to fulfill and failed to fulfill it through disobedience. The role of the law in condemning those who do not believe in God's promises is not unique to Israel in the Mosaic Covenant.[39] Even if someone argues that there is a parallel between Adam and Israel because both lose their land (the garden of Eden and the land of Canaan) through disobedience, the differences between Adam and Israel show that the Mosaic Covenant is not a republication of the Covenant of Works. Adam was sinless and had the ability to perfectly keep the law, but Israel was fallen and did not have the ability to keep the law perfectly. Thus, when Israel sinned,

---

37. Vos, *Reformed Dogmatics*, p. 2:45.

38. The blanket statement is usually made that the law was never meant to bring salvation without any recognition that one of the original purposes of the law in the Covenant of Works was for Adam to earn a more blessed life by perfectly keeping the law.

39. 'The OPC Report', p. 23.

she was not immediately cast out of her land. Israel was not under a probationary test in the same way as Adam. Only Christ is the proper parallel to Adam's situation (Rom. 5:12-21). The requirement for Israel to keep the law perfectly remains. The question is whether Israel will have faith in God or not.

In Deuteronomy 29 Moses calls the people together to renew the covenant. He summarizes God's past dealings with Israel, restates the present situation of the offer to accept the covenant, and addresses the options of covenant disobedience and obedience.[40] He highlights the problem of unbelief by stating that Yahweh has not given the people a heart to understand or eyes to see (29:4),[41] which will eventually lead to the curse of exile from their land (29:25-27). In Deuteronomy 30 the people will return to God, obey His voice (30:1-3), and God will bring them back to the land and circumcise their hearts and the hearts of their offspring (30:5-6). Apart from God's regeneration the people have no hope to keep the covenant. The history of Israel's disobedience to God demonstrates this truth. Israel loses the land because she breaks the covenant and lives in disobedience to God (second use).

The law also functions as a guide and blessing for the people (third use).[42] God hears the cry of His people and delivers them from Egypt in order to fulfill the promise of land that He had made to Abraham. The law is given in Exodus 20 in the context of redemption. In the historical prologue to the law God identifies Himself as Yahweh 'who brought you out of the land of Egypt, out of the house of slavery' (20:2). God gives the law to help the people understand how to live in a way that pleases God and brings blessings into their lives. Israel has the opportunity to fulfill God's mission and be a blessing to the nations.

Both second and third uses of the law are embedded in the law and sometimes it is difficult to tell which is in view. Sometimes the emphasis is on obedience, as in Exodus 19:5, 'Now therefore, if you

---

40. Merrill, *Deuteronomy*, p. 375.

41. Paul quotes Deuteronomy 29:4 in Romans 11:8 in regard to the hard heart of the Jews to the truth of the gospel message (Currid, *Deuteronomy*, p. 455).

42. The second and third use of the law as used here is based on the Formula of Concord 6. Calvin has the same three uses but reverses the first two (*Institutes of the Christian Religion* 2.7.6–13)

will indeed obey my voice and keep my covenant, you shall be my treasured possession ...' Sometimes the emphasis is on God's elective love (Deut. 7:6-8). Sometimes God's law is presented as the life of the people (Deut. 4:5-8) and sometimes as the instrument of judgment (Deut. 29:24-28). Whether a law is second or third use depends on the condition of the people before God. In fact, any moral law can be either second or third use. Paul uses the seventh commandment as second use (Rom. 7:7) and third use (Rom. 13:8-10). If an Israelite is not a believer in Yahweh and is not keeping the covenant, then the second use of the law is in view. If an Israelite is a believer and is seeking to live a life that is pleasing to God by keeping the covenant, the third use is in view.[43]

These principles also apply to the nation of Israel and the king who is a representative of the people. The king took on a more elevated, representative role in the Davidic Covenant, which is also reflected in Psalm 2. Israel is God's firstborn son (Exod. 4:22) and the king is adopted as son: 'You are my son, today I have begotten you' (Ps. 2:7). For much of their history the nation of Israel and the kings were disobedient to God. The prophets were sent by God as covenant prosecutors calling His disobedient people back to Him. They held out blessings to the people if they returned to the Lord by preaching oracles of salvation based on the blessings of the covenant (Lev. 26:1-13; Deut. 28:1-14). They held out covenant judgment to the people if they did not return to the Lord by preaching oracles of judgment based on the curses of the covenant (Lev. 26:14-46; Deut. 28:15-68). Both kings (Jer. 22:1-30) and people (Jer. 4:1-18) were held responsible for the judgment of exile that came on Israel because of their disobedience. In response to the growing apostasy of king and people, God preserved a remnant who were faithful to him. Although this remnant was important as a witness to the truth and a testimony against the nation, they were not able to stop the covenant curse of exile that resulted when people and king broke the covenant.

The second use of the law that brought judgment against disobedience in the Mosaic Covenant presupposes that the requirements of the Covenant of Works are still operative even if the Covenant of Works

---

43. Cara, *Cracking the Foundation*, p. 50. Paul also uses the seventh commandment for the first use of the law in 1 Timothy 1:10.

itself is no longer in force. The penalty for breaking the law shows that the requirement of the law is perfect obedience in order for someone to inherit eternal life. Of course, no one can keep the law perfectly so that everyone stands condemned under the just requirements of the law. Also, everyone needs a mediator who can keep the law perfectly and pay the penalty for breaking the law. Paul himself understands the law in this way (Rom. 10:5; Gal. 3:12). In Romans 10:5 he argues that there is a righteousness based on the law that is contrasted with a righteousness based on faith. Paul highlights a specific aspect of the Mosaic Law as the standard of righteousness required by the Covenant of Works. He is not arguing that God placed Israel under a Covenant of Works at Mt. Sinai. The Mosaic Covenant should not be identified with the Covenant of Works as a covenantal administration, but the requirement of perfect obedience set forth in the Covenant of Works is an abiding requirement.[44] Paul references Leviticus 18:5 in Romans 10:5, as he does in Galatians 3:12, for the principle that there is a righteousness based on the law in contrast to the righteousness based on faith. There are two ways to earn righteousness before God, the way of law/works and the way of faith, and both are proved from Old Testament texts.[45] The Westminster Standards agree with this view of the Mosaic law as demonstrated in the proof-texts. The WCF 7.2 uses the principle 'do this and live' to confirm the Covenant of Works with Adam.[46] After speaking of the law as a Covenant of Works in WCF 19.1, WCF 19.2 goes on to state that 'This law, after his fall, continued to be a perfect rule of righteousness; and, as such, was delivered by God upon Mt Sinai.'[47] Waters points out that Romans 10:5 is not cited as proof of the Covenant of Works itself, but as proof for the moral law at the heart of the Covenant of Works.[48] This demonstrates that there is a works principle still operative in the Covenant of Grace in a secondary sense

---

44. Waters, 'Romans 10:5 and the Covenant of Works,' pp. 211-12.

45. Cara, *Cracking the Foundation*, p. 47. Paul refers to Deuteronomy 30:11-14 to argue for the righteousness based on faith in Romans 10:6-13.

46. WCF 7.2 references Galatians 3:12 and Romans 10:5 which both refer to the principle 'do this and live' in Leviticus 18:5.

47. The phrase 'as such' shows that the law continued its role as a perfect rule of righteousness.

48. Waters, 'Romans 10:5 and the Covenant of Works,' p. 212.

related to the second use of the law which is particularly evident in the Mosaic Covenant. Of course, an emphasis on the second use of the law does not negate the third use of the law. The former refers to justification and the latter to sanctification.[49]

In summary, the Mosaic Covenant is primarily a development of the Covenant of Grace. It shows great continuity with the promises of the Abrahamic Covenant and is necessary for those promises to be fulfilled.[50] Although there is significant overlap between the Abrahamic Covenant and the Mosaic Covenant, they are not the same because of the emphasis in the Mosaic Covenant on the law and how the law functions. There is continuity with the Covenant of Works in the second use of the law showing that the requirements of the law still need to be met for there to be salvation. But the Mosaic Covenant is not the Covenant of Works because there was no provision in the Covenant of Works for salvation if the law was broken. God had to initiate the Covenant of Grace to secure salvation. The elements of salvation for sinners who have broken the covenant, such as substitutionary atonement in the sacrificial system, are part of the Mosaic Covenant because it is part of the Covenant of Grace. The 'righteousness based on the law' associated with Leviticus 18:5 in the Mosaic Covenant highlights the continuing obligation to keep the law perfectly (second use). This principle ultimately serves the Covenant of Grace pointing people to their need of salvation through an obedient mediator. Thus, the design of the types and symbols of the Mosaic Covenant are meant to teach the gospel (WCF 7.5).[51]

The Blessings and Curses of the Mosaic Covenant

The Mosaic Covenant is part of the Covenant of Grace, so it is concerned about Israel's spiritual relationship with God. The types and shadows of the Mosaic Covenant that deal with the priesthood and the sacrifices

---

49. The distinction between second use (justification) and third use (sanctification) of the law helps to explain how Paul can speak both positively and negatively about the law.

50. Robertson calls the Mosaic law an advancement beyond all that precedes it by presenting an externalized summation of the will of God and the revelation of God's purposes in redemption (*The Christ of the Covenants*, pp. 172-86).

51. Charles Hodge, *Systematic Theology: Volume 2* (Grand Rapids: Eerdmans, 1952), p. 275.

are geared toward establishing and furthering the people's spiritual life and to enable a holy God to continue to dwell in their midst. And, yet, the sanctions of the Mosaic Covenant focus on temporal and material blessings and curses. The blessings of the covenant (Lev. 26:1-13; Deut. 28:1-14) can be divided into blessings in nature and blessings in warfare.[52] The former includes agricultural plenty, livestock fertility, health and prosperity, and population increase. The latter includes defeat of enemies, end of warfare, relief from destruction, and return of captives. The curses of the covenant can also be divided into judgment in nature and judgment in warfare. The former includes drought, pestilence, famine, disease, wild animals, and population loss. The latter includes defeat, siege, occupation, death, destruction, and exile. These blessings and curses are material in nature and focus on Israel's temporal life in the land of Canaan.

How are we to understand the emphasis in the Mosaic Covenant on physical and temporal blessings and curses? This is part of the types and symbols of the Mosaic Covenant that point to other realities that are both spiritual and material. The land of Canaan is a type of the new heavens and earth so that the physical blessings of the Mosaic Covenant will be experienced by God's people in a form that is appropriate to their glorified existence. The physical curse of judgment will fall on unbelievers who will experience the curse in both spiritual and physical ways appropriate to their eternal existence. But the blessings and curses of the Mosaic Covenant are not limited to the new heavens and new earth, because they also have relevance for God's people today. The WCF 19.6 discusses this. It recognizes that true believers are not under the law as a Covenant of Works to be justified or condemned, but that the law can be of great use to them to inform them of the will of God and their duty to God (third use) and to show them the pollutions of their heart and their need of Christ (second use). This section of the confession goes on to mention the threatenings of the law (the curse) and the promises

---

52. These divisions come from Richard L. Pratt, Jr., *He Gave Us Prophets* videos, Lesson 4: 'Dynamics of the Covenant' (available on thirdmill.org); for a longer list of the blessings and curses of the covenant along with passages from Leviticus and Deuteronomy listed, see Douglas Stuart, *Hosea-Jonah* (WBC; Dallas: Word Books, 1987), pp. xxxii-xliii.

of blessings. For the regenerate, the threatenings show what their sins deserve and what afflictions in this life they may expect even though they are freed from the curse threatened in the law. Although the curse of the law reminds believers what their sins deserve, they are freed from it because Christ has taken the curse for them (Gal. 3:14). Even though believers have no fear of eternal judgment for sin, there can be temporal judgments related to the consequences of sin (1 Cor. 11:32; WCF 17.3). There is no longer a one-to-one relationship between bad things that happen and covenant judgment. The focus of the nation on obedience to the law in the land is shattered by the work of Christ and the mission He has given to His people. The rain falls on the just and the unjust (Matt. 5:45). Persecution for the sake of Christ is a reality for the church (John 15:18-21). Famines, hurricanes, and earthquakes are reminders of God's coming judgment (Matt. 24:3-14). The WCF 19.6 also states that the promises of the covenant show to believers God's approval of obedience and what blessings they may expect when they obey,[53] even though these blessings are not due to them by law as a Covenant of Works. The Old Testament emphasizes material blessings without ignoring spiritual blessings. The New Testament emphasizes spiritual blessings without ignoring physical blessings. The new heavens and new earth will have an abundance of both. Thus, believers in the New Covenant can benefit from the teaching of the blessings and curses of the Mosaic Covenant.

---

53. The Scriptural proof in the WCF for this statement is the blessings of the covenant stated in Leviticus 26:1-14.

CHAPTER 7

The Davidic Covenant

GOD'S covenant with David represents the culmination of all the promises of the previous covenants. It not only consolidates those promises but also sets the stage for the further outworking of them in Old Testament history and for their fulfillment in Jesus Christ. The Davidic Covenant is a high point of Old Testament theology because it advances to a new stage prior Old Testament concepts apart from which the hope of a coming king cannot be fully understood.[1] God's purposes to redeem a people reach their climactic stage as far as the Old Testament is concerned. The kingdom of God arrives in a formal manner with indications of how God will rule among His people. God situates His throne in a single locality and the Davidic line is established as the line through which God will exercise His rule on the earth. This chapter will examine the key texts that explain the Davidic Covenant in order to understand the promises God makes to David, how those

---

1. Robert D. Bergen calls the Davidic Covenant the flowering of a Torah prophecy, the climax of David's life, and the foundation for a major theme in the writings of the Latter Prophets (*1, 2 Samuel*, NAC (Nashville: Broadman & Holman Publishers, 2002], p. 336). Walter Brueggemann calls it the 'dramatic and theological center of the entire Samuel corpus', and 'the most crucial theological statement of the OT' (*First and Second Samuel* [Louisville: John Knox Press, 1990], pp. 253, 259).

promises are fulfilled in Old Testament history, and also how those promises find their fulfillment in Jesus Christ.

God's Promises to David (2 Samuel 7)

Background and Setting

David's life as king reaches a turning point in 2 Samuel 7. The chapter begins with David secure in his kingdom, living in his house, and enjoying rest which the LORD had given him from his enemies. David has time to reflect on the accomplishments of his kingdom and what this period of rest means for the future. He wants to honor God and proposes that a house of cedar be built for Him wherein the ark of God will dwell. This suggestion makes sense in the Old Testament context where it is the duty of the king to build a temple for the gods who have given him victory. Anything less would be considered ingratitude to God.[2] Other events in 2 Samuel have made this request by David possible. In chapter 5 David was made king over all Israel and moved his capital to Jerusalem after conquering the Jebusites. This location was more centrally located in Israel than Hebron, the previous capital.[3] In chapter 6 David brought the ark of God to Jerusalem, a relocation that left no doubt as to the divine designation of the city. The ark was the visible symbol of God's presence and came to be identified with His rule over Israel. God is enthroned and seated as king upon the cherubim above the ark. It is the footstool of the divine throne.[4] With the ark of God in Jerusalem and with David experiencing rest from his enemies, the time is ripe to contemplate building a more permanent temple for God.

The setting to 2 Samuel 7 is given in verses 1-3. God gave David victory over his enemies that led to a period of rest. This rest did not mean the end of warfare for David, because God also promised him future rest from his enemies in verse 11. David enjoyed a period of peace that allowed him to reflect on God's blessings and to contemplate that he dwelt in a house of cedar whereas God dwelt in a tent. When David first suggested that he

---

2. Joyce G. Baldwin, *1 & 2 Samuel* (TOTC; Downers Grove: InterVarsity Press, 1988), pp. 213-14.

3. Robertson, *Christ of the Covenants*, p. 230.

4. Dumbrell, *Covenant and Creation*, pp. 142-43.

wanted to build a house for God, Nathan gave his blessing to the idea. And yet, the request to build a temple is rejected by God, but not because He was angry with David. There were reasons that he was not the man to build the temple; plus, God had something greater planned for him. Instead of David building a house/temple (*bayit*) for God, God will build a house/dynasty (*bayit*) for David. This promise is the main focus in 2 Samuel 7 around which the basic elements of God's other promises to David are given. Although 2 Samuel 7 does not use the term covenant (*bᵉrît*) to describe the relationship established there, other passages identify it as a covenant (2 Sam. 23:5; Pss. 89:3, 28, 34; 132:12). These passages confirm that God gave to David an enduring, unconditional promise, sworn on divine oath.[5]

The Dynastic Oracle

Very quickly the word of the LORD came to Nathan to communicate to David an oracle concerning the building of the temple and God's plans for his future (2 Samuel 4–17).[6] This oracle first contains a reversal of Nathan's positive response to David's desire to build a temple (7:5-7). God asks David why he wants to build a house for God to dwell in. God has never dwelt in a house from the days He brought Israel out of Egypt, nor has He ever requested that a temple should be built for Him. In fact, the tent structure of the tabernacle allowed God's presence to travel with His people, a tremendous benefit throughout Israel's history. The section ends with the same question, but this time set in the period of the judges (7:7). The fact that this question frames this section (7:4-7) shows how important the question is. The point seems to be that the building of a temple should be at God's initiative.[7] The question of verse

---

5. Baldwin, *1 & 2 Samuel*, p. 213. For further evidence that the covenant is part of the intention of the author of 2 Samuel 7, see David G. Firth, 'Speech Acts and Covenant in 2 Samuel 7:1-17,' in *The God of the Covenant: Biblical, Theological, and Contemporary Perspectives*, eds. Jamie A. Grant and Alistair I. Wilson (Downers Grove: Inter-Varsity Press, 2005), pp. 79-99.

6. Bill T. Arnold notes that up to this point speeches were used sparingly but the content of 2 Samuel 7 is composed almost entirely of speeches. The narrator takes a long pause to consider the magnitude of these developments (*1 & 2 Samuel* [NIVAC; Grand Rapids: Zondervan, 2003], p. 471).

7. Dumbrell, *Covenant and Creation*, p. 148. The fact that Yahweh must initiate the move should have been discernible from David's experience of having to wait for the

5 puts the pronoun 'you' in an emphatic position indicating a rejection of the person (David) rather than a rejection of the action itself (the building of the temple).[8]

Nathan's oracle also reviews David's rise to power (2 Sam. 7:8-9b).[9] God Himself took David from being a shepherd and made him a prince over His people Israel. God had been with him wherever he had gone and given him victory over all his enemies. God's presence has been the source of his success. Even though David has been elevated to a high position as king, there is an emphasis on his subservient role to God. God calls him 'my servant', a title of honor but also a reminder that David himself is a servant of God. The use of the word 'prince' (*nāḡîḏ*) reminds him that he is subservient to the real king of Israel, God Himself.[10] But God also reminds David that He will bless him with future blessings (7:9c-11). There is debate concerning whether the verbs in these verses should be translated as past or future. The form of the verbs would normally be translated as future.[11] However, some argue against a future translation on grammatical grounds, but also because the blessings mentioned in these verses have already been provided for David at the beginning of the chapter (a great name, a place for Israel to dwell securely, and rest).[12] Hertzberg thinks the statements refer to

divine pleasure before moving the ark to Jerusalem, as well as the fact that Jerusalem had been put into David's hands by Yahweh. The marking off of the site and the movement of the ark were divine decisions. The timing of building the temple and the person who would build it must also be divine decisions.

8. A. A. Anderson, *2 Samuel* (WBC; Dallas: Word Books, Publisher, 1989), p. 118.

9. The verb forms are imperfect *waw* consecutives recounting what God has done for David in the past.

10. Baldwin, *1 & 2 Samuel*, p. 215.

11. The verbs in vv. 9b-11 change to perfect *waw* consecutives.

12. O. Loretz, 'The *Perfectum Copulativum* in 2 Sam. 7, 9-11', *CBQ* 23 (1961): pp. 294-95 and H. W. Hertzberg, *I & II Samuel: A Commentary* (OTL; Philadelphia: Westminster Press, 1964), p. 286. The grammatical argument against translating the perfect *waw* consecutives as future is that there is no imperative or imperfect preceding them. In support of translating the perfect *waw* consecutives as future is that in verse 10 there are two imperfect verbs with the negative that have to be translated as future (P. Kyle McCarter, Jr., *II Samuel: A New Translation with Introduction, Notes, and Commentary* [ABT; Garden City: Doubleday, 1984], p. 202). These are followed by two more perfect *waw* consecutive verbs after a parenthetical remark about the past days of the judges that uses a perfect verb.

the past but translates them as present because of the possibility that they have been left intentionally ambivalent. What the Lord has done in the past continues to have relevance.[13] And yet, just because God has granted to David a great name, rest, and a secure dwelling place does not mean that these blessings are permanent. In fact, verses 9c-11 provide the one blessing that God is going to grant to David that will be the lynchpin of these other blessings and that will ensure their continuing relevance. The last blessing mentioned in these verses is the key blessing. God will build David a house, a dynasty that will endure forever.[14] Part of the history of Israel shows that without a stable kingship, the other blessings are in jeopardy (Judg. 17:6; 21:25).

David had wanted to build God a house (temple) but God promises that He will build David a house (dynasty). This promise is mentioned at the end of verse 11 and then is further explained in verses 12-17. This promise will be fulfilled in the future after David has died. The focus is on the one who will immediately follow David and will begin the fulfillment of the promise of an enduring dynasty and will build a house for God. This son will be a descendant of David 'from your own body' (CSB, NIV) whose kingdom will be established (7:12).[15] The relationship between the kingdom, the temple, and this son born to David is important. David, the man of war, was not allowed to build the temple which was reserved for his son, Solomon, the man of peace.[16] The early reign of Solomon reflected this peace (rest from enemies) which was the proper setting for the building of the temple because the temple, as the symbolical representation of the kingdom, was to correspond to the nature of that kingdom.[17] God grants this by His grace

---

13. Hertzberg, *I & II Samuel*, p. 286.

14. The promise of an enduring dynasty is introduced with the solemn declaration 'The LORD declares to you' (McCarter, *II Samuel*, p. 205).

15. Baldwin comments that the use of the word 'seed' implies not only one generation, but many, although the immediate reference is to David's heir and successor (*1 & 2 Samuel*, p. 215). The general reference to the Davidic dynasty is made clear by verse 16.

16. Anderson points out that the emphatic 'he' in 7:13 is the positive counterpart to the negative emphatic 'you' of 7:5 where God rejects David's plan to build God a temple (*2 Samuel*, p. 118).

17. C. F. Keil and F. Delitzsch, 'Joshua, Judges, Ruth, I & II Samuel,' in *Commentary on the Old Testament in Ten Volumes* (Grand Rapids: Eerdmans, 1978), p. 2:345.

in first establishing David's dynasty and then allowing that dynasty to establish the Lord's temple. This binds David's rule to God's rule and vice-versa.[18] God will maintain His permanent dwelling place as king in Israel through the kingship of the Davidic line.[19]

Other promises that God makes to David are important for understanding the Davidic Covenant and its role in the history of Israel (2 Sam. 7:14-16). The Davidic Covenant establishes a father-son relationship between God and the kings of the Davidic line (7:14). This represents a significant development in redemptive history (see below). The king's relationship to God as son, along with his responsibilities to keep the covenant, raises the issue of the discipline of the king and what happens to God's promise of a continuing dynasty if the king breaks the covenant. God specifically states that when the son commits iniquity, God will discipline him with the rod of men, but His steadfast love (*ḥeseḏ*) will not be taken from him as it was taken away from Saul (7:14-15). The covenant has a conditional aspect that relates to each individual king. Each king must keep the covenant, and if a king does not keep it, God may use other nations to bring judgment against him and the people. The covenant also has an unconditional element to it so that the promises of an enduring dynasty and kingdom are not ultimately dependent on the obedience of individual kings. God will not remove His covenant loyalty from the line of David and choose another dynasty in place of it, as He did with Saul.[20] David's dynasty, kingdom, and throne will be established forever (7:14-16). The ultimate realization of the promises made to David are assured because the Davidic Covenant fits into God's purpose to redeem a people for

---

18. Roland de Vaux comments that because Yahweh was considered to be the true king of Israel, the royal throne was called the throne of Yahweh (1 Chron. 29:23), and more explicitly, the throne of the kingship of Yahweh (1 Chron. 28:5) over Israel (*Ancient Israel: Its Life and Institutions* [Grand Rapids: Eerdmans, 1997], p. 106).

19. Robertson, *The Christ of the Covenants*, p. 233.

20. The verb used in 7:15 in a negative way to describe that God's steadfast love will not depart from David's descendant (*sûr*) is also key to understanding the turning points in Saul's story (Sara Japhet, *I & II Chronicles: A Commentary* [Louisville: Westminster/ John Knox Press, 1993], p. 334). The Spirit of the Lord departed from Saul (1 Sam. 16:14), the Lord was with David, but he had departed from Saul (1 Sam. 18:12), and Saul even acknowledges that God has turned away from him (1 Sam. 28:15-16).

Himself. God's plan to establish a kingdom among redeemed sinners will come to pass.[21]

The Implications of the Davidic Covenant

The remainder of 2 Samuel 7 consists of David's prayerful, grateful response to the promise of God to build him a dynasty. David appears before the LORD and expresses humility and surprise at the great promises that God has given to him (7:18-21).[22] God's blessing is greater than what David deserves because of the implications for the future of his house and for the rest of mankind (for a discussion of the phrase 'this is instruction for mankind', see below). God's blessings to David are no different from the way He has blessed His people in the past (7:22-24). He is great and unique among the gods which makes His people Israel unique as demonstrated by their redemption out of Egypt through the power of God as He makes a name for Himself and establishes His people. Then David asks God to confirm the promises he Has made to him so that his house will be established and continue forever (7:25-29).[23] Several times throughout this section David uses Adonai Yahweh (Lord GOD) for the name of God. This name does not appear anywhere else in Samuel or in the parallel passage in Chronicles. It is used in Genesis 15:2 and 8 by Abraham when God spoke to him about the promise of a seed. This seems to be a conscious, deliberate response by David indicating that he is aware that the blessing of Abraham is continued in the blessing that God has promised to him.[24]

The implications of the Davidic Covenant for the rest of humanity is expressed in the phrase 'this is instruction for mankind' (2 Sam. 7:19). Questions related to this phrase include whether it is a question or

---

21. Robertson, *The Christ of the Covenants*, p. 246.

22. The division of these verses comes from Walter C. Kaiser, Jr., 'The Blessing of David: The Charter for Humanity,' in *The Law and the Prophets*, ed. John H. Skilton (Nutley, NJ: Presbyterian and Reformed, 1974), p. 310.

23. This section begins with 'And now' which indicates a transition from praising God for his past actions on behalf of God's people to praying for the future fulfillment of God's promises (Baldwin, *1 & 2 Samuel*, pp. 218-19). This phrase also occurs in verses 28 and 29, highlighting the truth of God's word (v. 28) and supplicating God to bring it to pass (v. 29).

24. Kaiser, 'The Blessing of David,' p. 310.

a statement and what is the meaning of the word *tôrāh* (it normally means 'law' or 'instruction'). One view is that this is the typical way that God deals with humanity. God makes great plans and graciously makes them known.[25] This view is reflected in the NIV (1984) translation, 'Is this your usual way of dealing with man, O Sovereign LORD?'[26] There are no contextual or grammatical grounds to translate this as a question and 'instruction' or 'law' is a better meaning for *tôrāh* in this context.[27] Another view is that 'the law of man' is the law that regulates the conduct of man as exemplified in the love shown to David by God. This law states that you should love your neighbor as you love yourself.[28] In other words, the way God treats David is the way human beings should treat each other. But the usual meaning for *tôrāh* is not 'manner' or 'custom' (meanings usually associated with the Hebrew words *ḥôq* and *mišpāṭ*).[29] Perhaps the best view of this phrase is that it refers to the Davidic Covenant as God's plan for the establishment of His kingdom that will bless all humanity. The word 'this' (*zō'ṯ*) refers to the content of God's gracious revelation to David concerning the promises of the covenant. The meaning of *tôrāh* is 'law' or 'teaching' and it regularly refers to divine instruction. It refers here to a divinely constituted ordinance which takes its place among the laws which govern human affairs. The word *hā'āḏām* refers to humanity in general because the promises to David will be the channel of blessing for all the nations, the principle by which all humanity will be blessed. Kaiser calls the phrase in 7:19 the Charter of Humanity and translates the phrase, 'this is the Charter for mankind, O Lord God.'[30]

---

25.   Baldwin, *1 & 2 Samuel*, p. 217.

26.   The NIV (2011) translates this phrase as 'and this decree, Sovereign Lord, is for a mere human', with a note that says, 'for the human race'. This translation seems to support Kaiser's view.

27.   Peter J. Gentry and Stephen J. Wellum, *Kingdom through Covenant: A Biblical-Theological Understanding of the Covenants* (Wheaton: Crossway, 2018), pp. 456-57.

28.   Keil and Delitzsch, 'Joshua, Judges, Ruth, I & II Samuel', p. 2:350.

29.   Kaiser, 'The Blessing of David', p. 314.

30.   Kaiser, 'The Blessing of David', p. 314. He argues against the view that *hā'āḏām* refers to 'the Man', namely, the man of Psalms 8:5-6 and 80:17 (as in A. W. Pink, *The Life of David: Two Volumes in One* [Swengel, PA: Reiner Publications, 1977], p. 1:337). Although these promises will be fulfilled in the Messiah, the proper name Adam or a reference to a covenant made with him is not emphasized here.

The parallel phrase to 2 Samuel 7:19 in 1 Chronicles 17:17 seems very different. The context is that David expresses amazement to God that 'You have also spoken of your servant's house for a great while to come' (NKJV), and the next phrase, 'and have shown me future generations,' is the parallel phrase. This is a general statement that God has shown David important things in the future concerning God's promises to David and to God's people.[31] There seems to be very little connection with the statement in 2 Samuel 7:19. Kaiser argues that 1 Chronicles 17:17 supports his understanding of 2 Samuel 7:19. He translates the verse as 'and thou are regarding me according to the upbringing *torah* of mankind'. It is not clear that the word $k^e\underline{t}ôr$ should be translated 'torah' or that the word 'upbringing' should go with 'torah'. Kaiser discusses the possibility that $k^e\underline{t}ôr$ is a shortened form of 'torah', but he acknowledges it is difficult to cite linguistic parallels that would support this view. He sees it as a by-form of $k^e\underline{t}ō'ar$, meaning 'according to the outline' of mankind, and understands the phrase to be synonymous with the idea expressed in 2 Samuel 7:19 ('the charter of mankind'). Yet, the word 'upbringing' (*ma'ălāh*) stands closer to 'mankind' (*hā'ǎḏām*) and many translate these two words together instead of taking 'upbringing' with $k^e\underline{t}ôr$ (understood as 'torah'). The third option is to translate 1 Chronicles 17:17 as 'and [you] have regarded me according to the rank of a man of high degree' (NKJV; see also NIV and NAS). This seems to be an interpretation of 2 Samuel 7:19 that emphasizes that the Davidic king has the highest rank among human beings because he represents the supreme and universal God. This is equivalent to what David says in 2 Samuel 23:1-7 where he refers to Nathan's oracle as a covenant and calls himself 'the man raised on high, the one anointed by the God of Jacob' (v. 1 CSB).[32]

---

31. There are difficulties with the ESV translation. The phrase 'you have shown me' should be translated 'you regard me' or 'you see me' (reflecting a Qal verb instead of a Hifil verb). Also, the phrase 'future generations' is very general for the Hebrew phrase $k^e\underline{t}ôr$ *hā'ǎḏām ma'ălāh*. Thus, the ESV offers the marginal reading 'and you look upon me as a man of high rank'.

32. Gentry and Wellum, *Kingdom through Covenant* (hereinafter *KTC*), 458. They translate 1 Chronicles 17:17 as 'you see me according to the rank of the man placed high.' 2 Samuel 23:1-7 is David's prophetic oracle that presents the reign of a righteous king guided by the fear of the Lord (Bergen, *1, 2 Samuel*, pp. 464-67). David was a man 'who was raised on high' and his 'house' should rule in righteousness and the fear of God so

Differences between 2 Samuel 7 and 1 Chronicles 17

There are other differences between 2 Samuel 7 and 1 Chronicles 17 that are a result of the different focus of the author of Chronicles. The books of 1 and 2 Samuel focus on the need for godly leadership in the transition from the period of the judges to the monarchy and show why David is the king chosen by God instead of Saul to lead God's people. The books of 1 and 2 Chronicles were written to the post-exilic community to answer the question, 'Are God's promises to Israel, David, and Jerusalem still valid for us?' The post-exilic community had experienced limited success as many were still in exile, Israel was under the control of powerful nations, and the promises of the covenant were not evident. The author wrote a history of God's people going all the way back to Adam to demonstrate that God will fulfill His promises. However, it is a selective history that presents the ideal reigns of David and Solomon as models for the post-exilic community.[33]

The different purpose of Chronicles explains some of the different emphases in 1 Chronicles 17 in comparison with 2 Samuel 7.[34] The main differences will be commented on here.[35] First, 1 Chronicles 17:1 does not mention that God had given rest to David from all his enemies, as in 2 Samuel 7:1, and that God will give rest from enemies in 2 Samuel 7:11 is changed to 'I will subdue all your enemies' (NKJV) in 1 Chronicles 17:10. Both 2 Samuel 8 and 1 Chronicles 18 recount David's victories over his enemies after the account of the Davidic Covenant so that the main reason for the omission of 'rest' in 1 Chronicles is to avoid confusion

---

that God's blessings would be poured out on God's people. The blessings that accompany a king who rules in righteousness are also expressed in Psalm 72, which could be a psalm written by David 'for Solomon' (for a discussion of this possibility, see Belcher, *Messiah and the Psalms*, p. 268, n. 81).

33. Pratt, *He Gave Us Stories*, pp. 297-98. Japhet writes, 'The period of David and Solomon is a unified whole' and 'is the zenith of Israel's virtues and achievements' (*I & II Chronicles*, p. 48).

34. This is true even though there is almost universal consent that 1 Chronicles 17 is dependent on 2 Samuel 7 (Roddy Braun, *1 Chronicles*, [WBC; Waco, TX: Word Books, 1986], p. 198). Many of the differences are minor due to stylistic variations or problems in transmission, but some variations reveal intentional changes (Richard L. Pratt, Jr., *1 and 2 Chronicles* [Ross-shire: Christian Focus, 1998], p. 148).

35. See Pratt for a chart that compares 2 Samuel 7 and 1 Chronicles 17 (*1 and 2 Chronicles*, p. 147).

concerning the future victories of David. The focus in 1 Chronicles is on Solomon as the man of rest who will build the temple of God. David only had a partial rest, but Solomon will be 'a man of rest' who will be given rest from all his enemies (1 Chron. 22:9-10). Solomon is the culmination of the rest that began with David, and when God gives peace and quiet to Israel in the days of Solomon, he will build a house for God.[36]

Second, the statement that when the son commits iniquity he will be disciplined in 2 Samuel 7:14b is omitted in 1 Chronicles 17:13. This omission causes some to think that the unconditional nature of God's promise is not retained in 1 Chronicles 17.[37] The issue is not whether one text is unconditional and the other text is conditional because both elements are present in the overall presentation of both books. Human failure in the Davidic line is well known from 1–2 Kings and royal obedience is still important for Israel to receive God's blessings.[38] The Chronicler focuses on the role of Solomon in building the temple, emphasizing the positive aspects of the reign of Solomon so that the house of David still provided permanent hope for God's people even after the exile.[39] The reigns of both David and Solomon are presented as in agreement concerning the goal of building a temple for God's people.[40]

Third, there is an explicit connection made in 1 Chronicles 17:14 between the human throne of Israel and God's throne. The emphasis in 2 Samuel 7 is on God's promises to David that 'your house and your kingdom will be made sure forever before me' (7:16 NIV). God's promise in 1 Chronicles 17:14 is that 'I will confirm him in my house

---

36. Martin J. Selman, *1 Chronicles: An Introduction and Commentary* (TOTC; Downers Grove: InterVarsity Press, 1994), p. 177. He calls Solomon the man of peace and rest *par excellence.*

37. Japhet, *I & II Chronicles*, p. 334. She writes, 'The Chronicler deviates from the central premise of II Sam. 7 and approaches more closely the Deuteronomistic redaction of 1 Kings, which does see God's promise as conditional.' Others, interestingly, think that the 2 Chronicles text is more unconditionally stated (Arnold, *1 & 2 Samuel*, p. 488, n. 59).

38. Selman, *1 Chronicles*, p. 180.

39. Pratt, *1 and 2 Chronicles*, p. 154.

40. H. G. M. Williamson, *1 and 2 Chronicles* (NCB; Grand Rapids: Eerdmans, 1982), p. 133.

and in my kingdom forever'.[41] The kingdom is God's kingdom with His rule manifested through the reign of the son of David who sits on the throne. The kingdom of God on earth is established through the Davidic Covenant.[42]

Finally, the focus on Solomon and the close association of the Davidic kingdom with God's kingdom in the post-exilic context of Chronicles, gave hope to God's people that David's throne would be established as necessary for the restoration of God's rule on the earth. Such restoration would not be complete until the throne of David was occupied. One of the major things lacking in the post-exilic period was the establishment of a king which caused this hope to shift to the future.[43] These ideas provide essential background for the teaching of the New Testament that the kingdom of God is established in Jesus, son of David (Matt. 12:28; Luke 17:20-21), who sits on David's throne (Acts 2:22-36).[44]

The Culmination of God's Covenant Promises

The Development of the Idea of Kingship

The promises of the Davidic Covenant are the culmination of previous promises that are found in covenants God made with His people. In this way the Davidic Covenant sets the stage for the future of God's people and the ultimate fulfillment of His promises. The idea of kingship did not just appear in Israel's history at the time of the institution

---

41. The focus on Solomon in Chronicles is further supported by looking at the clause that follows God's promise to David concerning house and kingdom. In 2 Samuel 7:16 the next sentence is 'Your throne will be established forever', but in 1 Chronicles 17:14 the next sentence is 'his throne shall be established forever'.

42. Pratt, *1 and 2 Chronicles*, pp. 25, 154. Selman calls this a significant contribution to the development of the idea of the kingdom of God (*1 Chronicles*, p. 180).

43. Pratt, *1 and 2 Chronicles*, p. 25. He comments that the lack of attention to royal matters in the ministries of Ezra and Nehemiah shows that the hopes for the immanent restoration of the line of David had faded, causing messianic hopes to be cast into the indefinite future.

44. Pratt, *1 and 2 Chronicles*, p. 154 and Selman, *1 Chronicles*, pp. 180-81. A focus on Solomon in Chronicles does not preclude a messianic emphasis because Chronicles clearly points to both the special significance of Solomon and another son of David who would establish God's house and kingdom *forever* (Selman, *1 Chronicles*, pp. 176, emphasis original).

of kingship with Saul. The concept of rule goes back to Genesis 1–2, particularly Genesis 1:26-28, where every human being is to rule over creation for the glory of God. God's rule on the earth was accomplished through the agency of human dominion. The Fall made dominion more difficult because the earth was cursed. For restoration to take place, an individual will arise who will conquer the serpent so that dominion can be established again. The promise in Genesis 3:15 uses the language of warfare to describe the conflict between the seed of the serpent and the seed of the woman. The covenant with Abraham includes the promise of kings (Gen. 15:12-16; 17:6) and the prospect of Abraham's descendants establishing dominion over the land of Canaan (Gen. 17:8). One will come with royal power from the tribe of Judah whose dominion is demonstrated in the unleashing of abundant blessings in creation (Gen. 49:8-12).

Deuteronomy 17 sets forth how this king shall rule 'when you come to the land' and desire a king 'like all the nations'. God will grant them their desire for a king, but he must be a king 'whom the LORD your God shall choose'. Deuteronomy sets out the parameters of kingship in a theocracy where Yahweh is the true king by keeping the king aware of his relationship to Yahweh and to his fellow Israelites. Limits on the rule of the king in Deuteronomy is antithetical to the usual assumptions of royal power. Deuteronomy 16:18–18:22 places all authority in the nation under the authority of Yahweh and within the covenant character of the law for the nation.[45] The law is a higher power than the word of the king (17:18-20), keeping the king from the temptations of royal power and the abuses of it. The law will be the standard by which the nation and the king will be judged, so that obedience will bring covenant blessings and disobedience will bring covenant curses (Deut. 27–28). A balance of power among the leaders limits the power of all the offices, particularly the king, so that the laws work together as a constitution for the nation. The typical marks of success among kings are limited by Yahweh. The limit on horses (17:16) signifies a limit on a professional standing army and has implications concerning Yahweh's leadership in

---

45. Patricia Dutcher-Walls, 'The Circumscription of the King: Deuteronomy 17:16-17 in its Ancient Social Context', *JBL* 121.4 (2002): pp. 603-04.

'holy war'. They are to trust in Yahweh for victory, not military strength. The limit on wives (17:17) limits foreign entanglements and temptations to apostasy. Wives would come as a part of treaties and would bring foreign influence and the temptation to worship false gods. The limit on wealth signifies a limit on commerce with foreign nations and a limit on the king's accumulation of power and status above other Israelites.[46]

As the ministry of Samuel ended, the elders of Israel requested 'a king to judge us like the nations' (1 Sam. 8:5 NKJV). When Samuel warned the people of the dangers of kingship, the people responded with 'But there shall be a king over us, that we also may be like all the nations, and that our king may judge us and go out before us and fight our battles' (8:19-20 CSB, NKJV). God told Samuel to give them a king because they had rejected God as their king (8:7, 22). Although Deuteronomy 17 had mentioned the future appointment of a king, the people's request for a king had the wrong motivations. Israel wanted to be like the nations and a king would give her power and political influence with the nations. Deuteronomy 17 did not mention that the king would be responsible for fighting the battles of Israel, probably because it was clear that Yahweh was the one who fought for His people and won their battles (see the descriptions of the battles in Joshua and in the victory over the Philistines in 1 Samuel 7:5-11). The request for a king to lead them in battle was a lack of trust in Yahweh to defend Israel. Samuel made it clear in his farewell address that both the people and the king were subject to the Word of God and that if either one did not obey the Law of God, then the hand of God would be against both of them (1 Sam. 12:13-16). The prophets would be raised up by God to speak the Word of God to the king. Throughout the history of Israel the kings rejected the word from God. Saul is such an example. Israel requested a king like the nations, and God granted them a king like they requested. Saul looked like a good choice,[47] but he was rejected by God because he rejected the Word of God (1 Samuel 15). David was God's choice[48] and through the promises

---

46. Ibid.

47. Bergen, *1, 2 Samuel*, pp. 118-19. He has an excellent discussion of the character of Saul.

48. The statement that Yahweh 'has sought out a man after his own heart' (1 Sam. 13:14) has been understood to refer to David as God's choice (Jason Derouchie, 'The Heart of

of the Davidic Covenant the kingdom of God reached its zenith in the early reign of Solomon.

Fulfillment of Earlier Covenant Promises

The culmination of the promises of God in the Davidic Covenant is evident in how the Davidic Covenant and the early reign of Solomon fulfills prior covenant promises. The Davidic Covenant stands in an organic relationship with the other covenants so that the Davidic Covenant builds on and assumes the promises of the other covenants but does not replace them.[49] God promised Abraham many descendants who would one day inherit the land that Abraham experienced only as a sojourner. God promised to make Abraham's name great (Gen. 12:2) and to give him many descendants, as numerous as the stars of heaven (Gen. 15:5) and the dust of the earth (Gen. 13:16). These promises are restated to David (2 Sam. 7:9-10) and fulfilled in the early reign of Solomon. The people are as numerous as the sand by the sea (1 Kings 4:20) and the kingdom experienced peace and safety throughout the whole region (1 Kings 4:24-25). Also, the promise that all families of the earth will be blessed (Gen. 12:3) is fulfilled as 'people of all nations came to hear the wisdom of Solomon, and from all the kings of the earth, who had heard of his wisdom' (1 Kings 4:34).[50] Several promises in the Mosaic Covenant are also fulfilled in the Davidic Covenant, including the rest God granted David, the experience of covenant blessings by God's people in the land (Deut. 28:1-14; 1 Kings 4:25), and the nations witnessing God's blessings on Israel (Deut. 28:10; 1 Kings 4:30). The promise that God will be with the people, expressed in some form of the phrase 'I will take you to be my people, and I will be your God' (Exod. 6:6-7), is fulfilled in David (2 Sam. 7:9) and God's people (Ezek. 34:24).[51] This

---

YHWH and His Chosen One in 1 Samuel 13:14,' *BBR* 24.4 (2014): pp. 467-89) or to refer to David as a man who will be like-minded with the Lord and surrender to His word (Bergen argues that both views are possible meanings of 1 Samuel 13:14 [*1 Samuel*, p. 151]).

49. Robertson, *The Christ of the Covenants*, pp. 27-52.

50. The early reign of Solomon is a partial fulfillment of the mission of Israel to the nations (Belcher, *Prophet, Priest, and King*, pp. 13-16).

51. Robertson, *Christ of the Covenants*, pp. 46-48. He summarizes this phrase as 'I shall be their God and they shall be my people' and discusses it as the thematic unity of the covenants.

principle is also fulfilled when God dwells among His people through the temple that Solomon built (1 Kings 8:54-61). The Davidic dynasty is fully integrated into the religious and social dimensions of the Mosaic Covenant so that the covenant is administered by the Davidic king who takes on a prominent role in the leadership of the nation.[52]

The King as Mediator of God's People

The Davidic Covenant is not only the culmination of the covenant promises of God, but the king's position is also advanced as the nation stands on the threshold of a new political era.[53] Up to this point, Israel was God's firstborn son (Exod. 4:23), but now the king of Israel is the son with God as his Father.[54] This special relationship of sonship means that he serves as a covenant mediator. As son he shares the throne with God his Father and has access to the Father. He represents God to the people, but he also represents the people to God.[55] The special status of the king as son of God has implications for his role within the nation of Israel.

First, the king was empowered to perform certain religious functions in relationship to worship. David set up the first altar for Yahweh in Jerusalem (2 Sam 24:25), conceived the idea of building the temple, and then made plans for it. The kings were able to perform certain priestly acts. Solomon offered sacrifices at the dedication of the temple (1 Kings 8) and then at the three great feasts of the year (1 Kings 9:25). Both David and Solomon blessed the people in the sanctuary (2 Sam. 6:18; 1 Kings 8:14) and David wore the loincloth which was the vestment of officiating priests (2 Sam. 6:14).[56] However, this special role of the king did not mean that he was a priest or could perform all the priestly functions (2 Chron. 26:16-21).[57] The king's role

---

52. Bergen, *1, 2 Samuel*, p. 334, n. 52.

53. Dumbrell, *Covenant and Creation*, p. 136.

54. Adoption does not mean deification of the king. The character of Yahweh as transcendent and unique made deification of the king impossible. Plus, the prophets do not condemn the kings for claiming deity (de Vaux, *Ancient Israel*, pp. 112-13).

55. Robertson, *Christ of the Covenants*, pp. 235-36.

56. de Vaux, *Ancient Israel*, pp. 113-14.

57. For a discussion of the view that a royal priesthood was established in Israel in relationship to David and his descendants, see Belcher, *Prophet, Priest, and King*, pp. 131-38.

in worship occurred in special or exceptional circumstances, such as the transference of the ark to Jerusalem, the dedication of an altar, or the great annual festivals. Ordinarily the conduct of worship was left to the priests (2 Kings 16:15). The king was the religious head of the people, but he was not a priest in the strict sense.[58]

Secondly, the special status of the king as son has implications for the role of the king in keeping the covenant. The king represented the people so that his actions of obedience or disobedience become part of the basis for whether God's people experience His judgment or His blessings. The people were still indicted for their sin and they were held responsible for the judgment of exile (Jeremiah 2–6), but special responsibility fell on the king to follow God and obey the law; otherwise, he was held responsible for God's judgment (Jeremiah 22; Ezekiel 34).

There were also implications for Jerusalem as the center of God's plan for the nations. The throne of God was identified with the throne of the Davidic king so that Jerusalem became the center from which God would exercise His sovereignty over the nations through the king.[59] When Solomon built the temple, Jerusalem became the place of God's presence and the focal point of the religious life of God's people in worship and in looking to Jerusalem for God's help in times of need (1 Kings 8). It also became the geographical location for the fulfillment of Israel's mission to the nations to become a kingdom of priests and a holy nation. As king and people lived in obedience to God, the nations would see the abundant blessings that God would pour out on His people and they would come to learn about the great God who Israel worshiped and the wonderful law that He had given to His people (Deut. 4:5-8). The early reign of Solomon was a partial fulfillment of this mission (1 Kings 4:29-34; 10:1-13). The promises of the Davidic Covenant were

---

58. de Vaux, *Ancient Israel*, p. 114.

59. The correlation of God's rule in Jerusalem through the Davidic king with the temple as His dwelling place factors into the development of 'Zion theology'. Mount Zion, a high mountain, is the place of God's rule with a river flowing out of Zion to bring fertility to the land. The Lord as the divine king rules over heaven and earth, providing security for Jerusalem as the place where the nations will come to acknowledge God's sovereignty (John T. Strong, 'Zion: Theology of', in *NIDOTTE*, pp. 4:1314-21).

fulfilled in David's son Solomon, and the early reign of Solomon brought Israel as a nation to the height of her power and influence.[60]

The Davidic Covenant established God's rule in Israel through the line of David. The king of Israel was established as the son of God who was to lead God's people in faithfulness to God. Israel had the opportunity to fulfill her mission as a light to the nations. The disobedience of Solomon and the kings following him led to the judgment of exile and the loss of kingship. But the promises of the Davidic Covenant kept the hope alive that one from the throne of David would come to rule over God's people. Christ established a kingdom that will never end and even today He rules over this world at the right hand of the Father for the sake of His people (Eph. 1:22-23). The promises of the Davidic Covenant should bring great comfort to God's people for we live in a world that does not recognize the rule of our King. We can be assured that one day He will return as the King of kings to defeat all His enemies. God made a promise to David that He has already begun to fulfill and there is no doubt He will bring it to completion for our good and His glory.

---

60. Even after the division of the kingdom the mission of Israel is kept alive in various prophetic passages, such as Isaiah 2:2-5; Zechariah 8:20-23; and 14:16-21.

CHAPTER 8

The New Covenant

Israel's History of Disobedience

THIS history of God's people in the Old Testament was primarily a history of disobedience. The blessings of Solomon's reign did not last because he turned away from the Lord (1 Kings 11:1-8). God raised up adversaries against Solomon and took ten tribes away from David's line with the division of the kingdom under Rehoboam. But God kept His promise to David by not taking the whole kingdom away from his descendants (1 Kings 11:34-36), represented in the dynasty that continued in the southern kingdom of Judah. God even told Jeroboam that he was leaving one tribe to Solomon's son 'that David my servant may always have a lamp before me in Jerusalem, the city where I have chosen to put my name' (1 Kings 11:36). The division of the kingdom did not terminate the covenant commitment on behalf of David and Jerusalem.

God's faithfulness to His covenant promise to David is expressed in the phrase 'for the sake of my servant David' (1 Kings 11:32, 34 CSB, NIV, NKJV). This phrase, or the shortened 'for David's sake', occurs at several points of the history of the southern kingdom.[1] Two times it is

---

1. Robertson, *The Christ of the Covenants*, pp. 236-43. Robertson gives a brief review of the history of Israel from the perspective of God's faithfulness to David.

used in a positive sense as a promise to Hezekiah that God will defend the city of Jerusalem from Sennacherib (2 Kings 19:34; 20:6). The other uses are in response to the disobedience of the kings of the southern kingdom. It is used with Abijam, the first king to rule after Rehoboam. Abijam walked in the sins of his father before him and his heart was not wholly true to the Lord (1 Kings 15:4). The phrase is used when the northern kingdom influenced the southern kingdom to do evil during the reign of Jehoram, son of Jehoshaphat, 'yet the LORD was not willing to destroy Judah, for the sake of David his servant' (2 Kings 8:19).

The apostasy of the kings of Judah culminated in the reign of Manasseh (see 2 Kings 21 for a list of his idolatrous practices, even setting up idols in the temple of Jerusalem). His evil is characterized as more despicable than the practices of the nations who inhabited the land before Israel (2 Kings 21:2, 11). Such idolatry, including child sacrifice (2 Kings 21:6), led to a pronouncement of God's judgment against the city of Jerusalem. The same disaster that had overtaken Samaria of the northern kingdom will also overtake Jerusalem (2 Kings 21:13-16).[2]

The destruction of the temple and the city of Jerusalem leading to exile is a momentous event. All the covenant promises of God seem to be in jeopardy. The promises of the Abrahamic Covenant of a great name, descendants as numerous as the stars of heaven, and possession of the land are dashed in the loss of land and the scattering of God's people to Babylon. Israel has failed in her mission to be a holy nation and a kingdom of priests to the nations by adopting the ways of the nations rather than by following God. Thus, she experienced the covenant curse of exile. The promise of an enduring kingdom and a descendant of David to occupy the throne is in jeopardy because the kings have disobeyed God and Babylon has removed the king from Jerusalem. Such events were hardly believable to the people (see the sentiment in Jeremiah 7:4) even though Jeremiah and Ezekiel had prophesied these very events. There was perhaps no lower point of Israel's history than the devastating events of 587 B.C.

---

2. August H. Konkel, *1 & 2 Kings* (NIVAC; Grand Rapids: Zondervan, 2006), pp. 622-23.

Will the Davidic Promises Be Fulfilled?

Several passages of Scripture wrestle with the implications of the apparent failure of the covenant promises. Of course, the failure is not found in the promises themselves, or in the God who made them, but in the sin of the king and people. And yet, God had committed Himself to fulfill the covenant promises, so there are questions whether God will be faithful to the promises He had made to Abraham, Moses, and particularly to David. Did the removal of the Davidic king from Jerusalem and the lack of a king to rule over God's people in the post-exilic period mean that God's promises to David had come to an end?

Where is God's Covenant Faithfulness (Psalm 89)?

Psalm 89 wrestles with these questions. It has three sections: a hymn to Yahweh for His faithfulness (89:1-18), a review of the promises of the Davidic Covenant (89:19-37), and a lament over the apparent failure of the promises to David in light of the condition of the monarchy (89:38-51).[3] The psalm closes with a doxology (89:52) that marks the end of Book 3 of the Psalter (Psalms 73–89).

The key words of the psalm are 'steadfast love' (*ḥeseḏ*) and 'faithfulness' (*'ĕmûnāh*). The hymn praises God's faithfulness by showing how the heavens and the heavenly hosts praise the power of God, whose rule exemplifies God's steadfast love and faithfulness (89:5, 14). The promises of God to David display the same enduring stability as the creation because the God who rules creation made an oath to His servant David (89:3) to establish his throne (89:29). The close relationship between Yahweh and the Davidic king that was expressed in Psalm 2:7 is also expressed in the cry of David 'You are my Father' (89:26) and in the close relationship between Yahweh and David.[4] Just as Yahweh is head of the heavenly assembly (89:6-8) so He will make David the firstborn, the highest of the kings of the earth (89:27).[5] Just as Yahweh rules the

---

3. For a discussion of the setting and date of the psalm, see Belcher, *Messiah and the Psalms*, p. 270, n. 101.

4. Marvin E. Tate, *Psalms 51–100* (WBC; Dallas: Word Books, 1990), pp. 423.

5. The firstborn as the highest of the kings of the earth does not refer to the one born first but to the one who has the privileges and blessings that come with having the highest place (Belcher, *Messiah and the Psalms*, p. 140).

raging sea and scatters His enemies by the strength of His hand (89:9-10, 13), so Yahweh will place David's hand on the sea and His right hand on the rivers (89:25). David, as Yahweh's representative, rules the sea. The heavenly rule of Yahweh is manifested on earth through the reign of David. The blessings to David (89:20-28) are also extended to his descendants (89:29-37), in line with the promise of 2 Samuel 7:36 that David's throne will last as long as the sun.

The strong statements of God's 'steadfast love' and 'faithfulness' to establish David's throne and His affirmations that He will not lie to David or violate the covenant make the lament that questions God's faithfulness all the more jarring to the reader (89:38-45). Instead of being the highest of the kings of the earth, the throne and the crown are cast down to the dust (89:39, 44). Instead of David's right hand ruling the sea, the right hand of the enemy is exalted (89:42) and the kingdom has experienced the humility of defeat (89:43-44).

The current humiliation of the king has an explanation that goes back to the Davidic Covenant itself (2 Sam. 7:14-15). The Davidic kings have not obeyed God and His wrath has been poured out against His anointed (89:31-33, 38). The problem is not the faithfulness of God but the unfaithfulness of the king. The questions in verses 46-51 are a cry for God to fulfill His covenant promises to David by moving beyond discipline and wrath to show His faithfulness again to the Davidic line. Even though the disobedience of the king has led to the destruction of the kingship and temple, the issue of God's steadfast love is raised in the question in Psalm 89:49, 'Lord, where is your steadfast love of old, which by your faithfulness you swore to David?' God has been faithful to the covenant to bring the discipline of judgment; will He also be faithful to show His steadfast love as promised?

The Restoration of the Davidic King (Psalm 132)

The conditional nature of the Davidic Covenant is demonstrated in the removal of the king in Judah, but the unconditional nature of the covenant is seen in the continued hope that God would establish the Davidic line again at some point in the future. The loss of kingship in the Babylonian exile puts a strain on the promises of God to David that one of his descendants would sit on the throne forever. The hope that the

Davidic dynasty would rise again was kept alive during the post-exilic period in the royal psalms. Two groups of Davidic psalms in Book 5 of the Psalter (Psalms 108–110; 138–145) remind God's people of the need for a Davidic king to complete the restoration.[6] Psalm 132 is a royal psalm that focuses on God's promise to David that one of his descendants will sit on the throne 'forever' (132:12). Jerusalem as God's dwelling place is also emphasized in the psalm. The basic structure of the psalm highlights the parallels between David's concern to establish a dwelling place for Yahweh (132:1-10) and Yahweh's covenant promises concerning David's descendants (132:11-18), with reference to the 'anointed one' (*māšîaḥ*) in verses 10 and 17. The first section asks God to remember all the hardships that David endured in finding a proper place for the ark, Yahweh's dwelling place, to rest (2 Samuel 6). The significance of the ark cannot be overlooked as it represents the rule of God on the earth.[7] God is to remember the efforts of David for the ark so that He will act on behalf of the Davidic king to establish his throne (132:11-12). God promises that the strength ('horn') of David would be restored and his dynasty would not be extinguished, but rather would shine like a lamp.[8]

Psalm 132 is part of the Songs of Ascent and it gives a rationale for making the pilgrimage to Jerusalem: Zion is God's dwelling place and the site of the Davidic throne.[9] It is also a call for the restoration of the Davidic dynasty in the post-exilic period.[10] It demonstrates that the rejection of the king in Psalm 89 is not final. Psalm 89:39 laments the defilement of the crown of the 'anointed one', but 132:18 affirms

---

6. For how kingship and the Davidic Covenant relate to the theme and structure of the Psalter, see Belcher, *Messiah and the Psalms*, pp. 17-18.

7. Belcher, *Messiah and the Psalms*, p. 150.

8. Both horn and lamp may refer to the permanence of the Davidic dynasty (Willem A. VanGemeren, 'Psalms', in *The Expositor's Bible Commentary*, rev. ed., eds. Tremper Longman III and David E. Garland [Grand Rapids: Zondervan, 2008], p. 5:930).

9. For an analysis of the Songs of Ascent that treats them as a unity with the theme of Yahweh's restoration of Zion, see Philip E. Satterthwaite, 'Zion in the Songs of Ascents', in *Zion, City of our God*, eds. Richard S. Hess and Gordon J. Wenham (Grand Rapids: Eerdmans, 1999), pp. 105-128. -

10. For a discussion of the possible setting of Psalm 132, see Belcher, *Messiah and the Psalms*, p. 274, n. 168.

that the crown of the 'anointed one' will shine.[11] In Psalm 89:42 the enemies have triumphed over the king, but in 132:18 the enemies are defeated and humiliated. Psalm 132 gives hope that the promises of the Davidic Covenant will be fulfilled. A king will come, a horn will sprout for David.

The Promise of a New Covenant

Hope is also expressed in the promise of a New Covenant, particularly in Jeremiah 31:31-34. Although in the call of Jeremiah, God gave him the message of overthrowing and planting (1:10), the book of Jeremiah focuses on God's judgment that is coming to Jerusalem and Judah with only a few chapters given to prophecies of restoration (chapters 30–33). Part of the problem is the character of the people who have broken the covenant by living lives of disobedience (chapters 1–6). They have put their faith in the temple of God without understanding the need to obey God (chapter 7). If they do not turn to God, an army from the north will destroy them (6:22-28). Part of the problem is the character of the kings of Judah who have rejected the Lord by rejecting His word (chapter 36) and by not enforcing justice in the land (chapter 22). Prophets (5:31; 23:9-22; 28:1-17) and priests (1:26; 5:31) are also condemned by Jeremiah, showing that the whole country is corrupt. The people deported to Babylon in 597 are identified as the good figs, leaving the bad figs in Jerusalem who will experience the judgment of God (chapter 24). God's purposes will be fulfilled in the good figs in Babylon, who will eventually be brought back to the land (29:10-14). The prophecies of restoration are found in Jeremiah 30–33. The key text is 31:31-34 which deals primarily with Israel's relationship with God, but the broader prophecies of restoration (Jeremiah 30–33) mention many of the other covenant promises of God.

Although Jeremiah 31:31 is the only place in the Old Testament where the term 'new covenant' is used, the concept is expressed in other passages of Scripture, particularly Ezekiel 36, along with other

---

11. For connections between the sprouting of the horn in Psalm 132 and the passages in the prophets that speak of the branch (Isa. 4:2; Jer. 23:5; Zech. 3:8 and 6:12), see F. Delitzsch, 'Psalms', in *Commentary on the Old Testament in Ten Volumes*, C. F. Keil and F. Delitzsch (Grand Rapids: Eerdmans), p. 5:316.

prophecies of restoration (Ezekiel 33–39) that also mention covenant promises of God. Ezekiel begins with the problem of bad leadership and puts much of the blame on the shepherds (kings) of Israel who have not been good shepherds. But God promises to be their shepherd and to raise up a shepherd, 'my servant David', who will feed the flock (34:23-24). God also promises peace, prosperity, and security (33:25-31), including judgment against the enemies of God's people, represented by Edom (35:1–36:7), and return to their own land (36:8-21). The heart of the restoration is to establish the relationship between God and His people, summarized in the phrase that God is their God and Israel is His people (34:30; 36:28). When God brings them back to their land, He will cleanse them, give them a new heart, and put His Spirit within them (36:24-38). Israel is so dead that she is like a valley of dry bones that needs to be transformed through the power of the Word of God (37:1-10), so dramatic will this be that it is like a resurrection (37:11-14). When God brings them back to their land, they will experience unity (37:15-23), a king called 'my servant David' will rule them (37:24-25), and God will dwell with His people (37:27). God will bring about this restoration by making a 'covenant of peace' with His people that shall be an everlasting covenant (37:26).

Jeremiah 30–33 can be divided into two sections. The first section, chapters 30–31, contains six poems, each beginning with 'Thus says the LORD' (30:4-11; 30:12-17; 30:18-31:1; 31:2-6; 31:7-14; 31:15-22).[12] The conclusion of chapters 30–31 contain five short salvation oracles that form a chiasm centered on 31:31-34. The first (31:23-26) and the fifth (31:38-40) are about Jerusalem. The second (31:27-30) and the fourth (31:35-37) emphasize the importance of personal human responsibility and God's enduring faithfulness to His corporate people. These oracles are more future oriented and draw out the implications of what precedes them.[13] Chapters 32–33 are mostly prose and each begins with the formula 'The word that came to Jeremiah from the LORD' (CSB, NKJV) with 33:1 adding 'a second time'. These two chapters come from the

---

12. Barbara Bozak, *Life 'Anew': A Literary Theological Study of Jeremiah 30–31* (Rome: Pontifical Biblical Institute, 1991), pp. 18-25.

13. Gerald L. Keown, Pamela J. Scalise, and Thomas G. Smothers, *Jeremiah 26–52* (WBC; Dallas, TX: Word Books, Publisher, 1995), pp. 126-27.

period when Jeremiah was imprisoned in the court of the guard that was in the palace of the king (32:2; 33:1). Chapter 32 revolves around Jeremiah's purchase of a field in his hometown of Anathoth while the city of Jerusalem is under siege. Chapter 33 further develops material from chapter 32 so that these two chapters should be taken together.[14]

The prophecies of restoration in Jeremiah 30–33 are introduced by 30:1-3.[15] There is a double statement that these words come from God and Jeremiah is told to 'Write in a book all the words I have spoken to you' (v. 2 NIV). In other places Jeremiah has been told to write 'all the words that I have spoken to you against Israel and Judah and all the nations' (36:2), but here the focus is on the restoration of Israel and Judah (30:3). This refers to a reversal of divine judgment and a reinstatement of covenantal favor (29:14), including release from captivity and a return to the land that God had given to their fathers.[16] The land is a key promise made to Abraham and for restoration to take place the people must be brought back to their land. In the prophecies of 30:4–31:22, restoration to the land is also mentioned in the first oracle (30:4-11). The people will be released from the bondage of strangers and be brought back to the land to experience security (30:8-11). The remaining oracles highlight what restoration in the land means for God's people, including repentance and forgiveness (30:12-17), the repopulation of the land, a reversal of the judgment suffered by God's people (31:2-6), a rejoicing over the goodness of God and renewed blessings (31:7-14), and a call for God's people to respond appropriately to His mercy (31:18-22). The covenant relationship with God is emphasized twice: 'And you shall be my people, and I will be your God' (30:22; 31:1). In the five oracles that conclude chapter 31, the first (31:23-26) and fifth (31:38-40) emphasize the restoration and rebuilding of Jerusalem.

The land promise is also at the heart of chapters 32–33. Jeremiah is imprisoned in Jerusalem for prophesying that Babylon would capture

---

14. Keown, Scalise, and Smothers, *Jeremiah 26–52*, pp. 145, 167.

15. J. A. Thompson, *The Book of Jeremiah* (NICOT; Grand Rapids: Eerdmans, 1980), 553. He calls these verses the editorial preface to the whole collection. This makes verse 4 the beginning of the prophecy.

16. John L. Mackay, *Jeremiah: An Introduction and Commentary. Volume 2: Chapters 21–52* (Mentor; Ross-shire: Christian Focus, 2004), p. 185.

Jerusalem. The city is under siege by Babylon for months before the downfall of the city. The end is near, but God tells Jeremiah to redeem a field from his hometown of Anathoth (32:6-8). He redeems the field and seals the deed of purchase in an earthenware vessel as a witness that houses and lands will again be bought in the land (32:9-15). Even though the situation is hopeless, God gives the people hope for the future. The destruction of temple and city does not mean the end of God's people because He will one day bring life back to the land. After his redemption of the field, Jeremiah prays to the Lord (32:16-25), highlighting God's power and mercy in redeeming His people from Egypt and bringing them to this land, even though now their disobedience has brought them to the brink of destruction. God responds to Jeremiah's prayer by explaining the reason for His judgment, but He promises future restoration (32:26-44). Fields will be bought again in the land, but the emphasis is on the restoration of God's relationship with His people. They will dwell in safety and become the people of God again (vv. 37-38) by an everlasting covenant that will give them one heart and one way so that they will fear God again.[17] The first part of Jeremiah 33 highlights again the immediate future of devastation for the city (vv. 2-5) and the restoration that God will bring, including healing and forgiveness (vv. 6-9), abundant joy (vv. 10-11), and prosperity (vv. 12-13).

The rest of Jeremiah 33 focuses on the promise of a king in the Davidic Covenant and the implications for God's people (vv. 14-26). Without a king there can be no kingdom and no full restoration of the people. It is not a surprise that the prophesies of restoration end with an emphasis on the Davidic Covenant as a capstone to it. In 33:14-16 God declares that at some point in the future He will fulfill the promise of someone from the Davidic line to be raised up to execute righteousness in the land and to save His people. This one is identified as 'a righteous Branch to spring up for David' (v. 15) and the name of Jerusalem will be 'The LORD is our righteousness' (v. 16). This passage seems to allude to Jeremiah 23:5-6 where the word 'branch' (ṣemaḥ) is also used and the

---

17. The phrases 'one heart' and 'one way' refers to integrity of life, the agreement between will and way of life, as well as unity and solidarity among God's people (Keown, Scalise, Smothers, *Jeremiah 26–52*, p. 160).

king is named 'The LORD is our righteousness'. The image of a new shoot sprouting from the stump of a tree fits the condition of the diminished Davidic dynasty.[18] The name given to the king in Jeremiah 23:5-6 is given to the city of Jerusalem in 33:16 as an embodiment of the character of the king who establishes the city once again as the capital of the kingdom.[19]

The next two verses are introduced with 'Thus says the LORD' and offer strong statements of assurance that God's covenant promises to David and the Levitical priests will be fulfilled (33:17-18). David shall never lack a man to sit on the throne and the Levitical priests shall never lack a man to offer sacrifices in God's presence. It is clear that these two promises come from covenants that God has made with David and with the Levitical priests (33:21). The Davidic Covenant is clearly laid out in 2 Samuel 7. Some argue that the covenant with the Levitical priests goes back to the covenant with Levi in Numbers 25:10-13. The promise given to Phinehas that he and his descendants should have the priesthood as their rightful possession is termed 'my covenant of peace' and a covenant forever.[20] Others argue that the covenant of Levi arose in association with the events of Exodus 32 where Moses ordained the Levites for the service of the Lord (v. 29). The book of Numbers also mentions the covenant of salt in connection with the offerings for priests and Levites (ch. 18) and the covenant of peace established with Phinehas, son of Aaron (Num. 25:1-13). These two passages in Numbers assume the covenant of Levi and specify the role of priests and Levites.[21]

There must have been doubt concerning the fulfillment of these promises because some are reported as saying, 'The LORD has rejected the two clans that he chose' (Jer. 33:24). This statement is made by

---

18. Keown, Scalise, and Smothers, *Jeremiah 26–52*, pp. 145, 173. The term 'branch' (*ṣemaḥ*) is also used in Zechariah 3:8 and 6:12 with messianic significance (Tremper Longman III, *Jeremiah, Lamentations* [NIBC; Peabody, MA: Hendricksen Publishers, 2008), p. 222.

19. Mackay, *Jeremiah*, p. 278. Just as the term 'branch' is also used of the remnant in Isaiah 4:2 and 6:13, so 'The LORD our righteousness' is applied to the city of Jerusalem.

20. Mackay, *Jeremiah*, p. 282; Longman, *Jeremiah*, p. 222.

21. Pieter A. Verhoef, *The Books of Haggai and Malachi* (NICOT; Grand Rapids: Eerdmans, 1987), p. 245 and Timothy R. Ashley, *The Book of Numbers* (NICOT; Grand Rapids: Eerdmans, 1993), p. 523.

'these people' with the comment that 'Thus they have despised my
people so that they are no longer a nation in their sight'. This statement
does not reflect the self-perception of God's people but the attitude
of the surrounding nations who are the enemies of 'my people'.[22] The
focus of their contempt is that the LORD has rejected the two clans
that He chose. The word for 'clan' (*mišpāḥāh*) means 'family' and
it could refer to the two kingdoms of Israel and Judah, but in light
of the context of Jeremiah 33 it probably refers to the descendants of
Levi and David who no longer function as priests and kings as they
were set apart to function in their respective covenants. This fact could
be seen as a colossal failure of God's covenant promises. Jeremiah
addresses this concern by using terminology that reminds the people
of the Abrahamic Covenant, but he centers on the Noahic Covenant to
make the case that God has not rejected His people and His covenant
promises will not fail. The descendants of David and the Levites will
be as countless as the stars of the sky and as measureless as the sand on
the seashore (33:22). The patriarchal promise to Abraham (Gen. 15:5;
22:17) is still relevant and will be fulfilled through the descendants of
David and Levi. Yahweh also refers to 'my covenant with the day and
my covenant with the night' (33:20 CSB, NIV, NKJV) and 'the fixed order
of heaven and earth' (33:25) as a way to show that there is no possibility
that His covenant with David and the Levitical priests will be broken
(33:20) or that He would ever reject the descendants of Jacob and David
(33:26). In other words, if anyone can break the terms of the Noahic
Covenant so that day and night do not come at their appointed time,
then the covenant with David and the Levites can be broken (33:20-21).
The divine commitment to the regular succession of day and night and
the fixed order whereby God has structured the creation is evidence
that God will not reject the offspring of Jacob and that a son of David
will rule over God's people.[23] These are impossible scenarios meant to
demonstrate that even though it appears God's covenant promises are
in jeopardy, God will fulfill them.[24]

---

22. Mackay, *Jeremiah*, p. 283; Longman, *Jeremiah*, p. 223.

23. Mackay, *Jeremiah*, pp. 282, 284.

24. The fact that the Levitical priesthood becomes obsolete in the new covenant
would seem to go against what this passage promises. Christ, however, fulfills the

The promise of a New Covenant (31:31-34) is given in the context of the assurance of the fulfillment of other covenant promises, including return to the land, the rebuilding of Jerusalem, and promises made to Abraham, Levi, and David. There are also promises of healing, forgiveness, joy, and prosperity. The promise of a New Covenant seems to be the central promise of Jeremiah 30–33 so that the fulfillment of the other covenant promises will be dependent on the fulfillment of the promises of a New Covenant. In the five oracles that conclude chapter 31, the first (31:23-26) and fifth (31:38-40) emphasize the restoration and rebuilding of Jerusalem. The third oracle is the prophecy of the New Covenant (31:31-34).

The second (31:27-30) and fourth (31:35-37) form a contrasting pair concerning the responsibility of each person for his or her sin set in tension with God's commitment for the survival of the nation. The second oracle highlights the positive side of the message God had given to Jeremiah (1:10) to sow the house of Israel and the house of Judah with the seed of man and beast. God will build and plant them once again. When that happens, the people will no longer utter the proverb, 'The fathers have eaten sour grapes, and the children's teeth are set on edge.' This represents a common view of the exilic period that the people were suffering unjustly for what their forefathers had done (Ezek. 18:2). It was an excuse to avoid their own sinfulness spoken in a spirit of self-righteousness that is blind to their own culpability.[25] The proper view is that everyone will die for his own sin (v. 30). Individuals should take responsibility for their own iniquity. This is not a new doctrine because individual responsibility has always been emphasized alongside corporate responsibility (Deut. 24:16). There are situations where someone might suffer because of the actions of a representative (Adam and Achan), but there are also situations where the individual person

---

Old Testament offices and transforms them so that they continue in greater ways. For example, He now sits on the throne of David, which is not an earthly throne but the heavenly throne at the right hand of God the Father. Christ transforms the temple and the priesthood so that the ministry of the church, the new temple of God, is carried out by the sacrifices of His people. This fulfills Isaiah 66:21 in that Gentiles can serve as priests and Levites.

25. Mackay, *Jeremiah*, p. 232.

suffers for what he or she has done. Jeremiah emphasizes individual responsibility because the corporate side has been used as an excuse.[26] The fourth oracle (31:35-37) affirms the corporate side by emphasizing the continuing existence of Israel as a nation.

The first saying (31:35-36) stresses the power of Yahweh as the one who set up the sun, moon and stars to function as light bearers in the order of creation and established the waves of the sea. Only if this fixed order departs from God's control could the offspring of Israel ever cease from being a nation. The second saying (31:37) presents the impossible 'if' statement that only if someone can measure the heavens or explore the foundations of the earth, then God would reject the offspring of Israel for all they have done.[27] These are impossible situations to show God's commitment to His corporate people and their continuing existence. The establishment of the New Covenant cannot be stopped, and it will be the instrument to bring about all the other promises of God.

The Fulfillment of the Covenant Promises

Each of the covenants have their distinctive promises that are developed in redemptive history and are fulfilled in Jesus Christ. In the initiation of the Covenant of Grace in Genesis 3:15, God promised that the seed of the woman would crush the head of the serpent. The godly line develops through the line of Seth, but wickedness increases on the earth until God decides to destroy the world by a flood. Noah, who finds favor with God, and his family are preserved by God in the ark. After the Flood, God enters into a covenant with Noah and all creation, promising to preserve the created order so redemptive history can move forward. Noah is a second Adam who continues the mandate given to Adam in the midst of a fallen world. Sin is still a problem as seen in the drunkenness of Noah and the Tower of Babel. In response to the increase of sin, God decided to work out His purposes for the salvation of the world through one man and his family. He called Abram to go to a land that He would show him, promising to give to him and his

---

26. If this is a brand-new way for God to interact with his people, then it is strange that Jeremiah (31:35-36) and Isaiah (45:25; 61:8-9) continue to mention that God will continue to bless the offspring of Israel according to his covenant promises.

27. Bozak, *Life 'Anew'*, p. 125.

descendants (seed) the land of Canaan, to make his name great, and to make him a blessing to the nations. God committed Himself to fulfill these promises in the covenant of Genesis 15, including the promise to make Abraham's descendants as numerous as the stars of heaven (15:5). God's commitment to Abraham's descendants (seed) is further confirmed in the sign of circumcision (17:9-14) with the promise 'to be God to you and your offspring after you' (17:7). God changes Abram's name to Abraham to show that he will be a father of many nations with kings coming from him (17:6).

The full promise of kingship related to a descendant of Abraham awaits further developments, but God promised that the scepter will be associated with the tribe of Judah (49:8-12) and that a ruler will arise to crush the enemies of God's people (Num. 24:17-18). Regulations related to the king are given in Deuteronomy 17:14-20 'when you come into the land' (NKJV). These regulations are part of the Mosaic Covenant where Israel is made into a nation, given a law, and a mission focused on the land of Canaan. The Mosaic Covenant is foundational for the development of kingship and for understanding the history of Israel and her loss of the land in exile, which is related to the blessings and curses of the covenant (Deuteronomy 27–28). God's covenant commitment to the dynasty of David is expressed in 2 Samuel 7; but His promises appear to be in jeopardy in the destruction of Jerusalem, including the temple and the monarchy, in 587 B.C. (Ps. 89:38-51). The particular promises of each covenant revolve around Israel existing as a nation in the land God had given to her. The loss of king, nation, and land makes it difficult to see how those promises can ever be fulfilled.

God told Israel through Isaiah the prophet that He was able to fulfill His promises by bringing the people back to their land. He will raise up Cyrus, king of Persia, who defeated Babylon in 539 B.C. and issued a decree in 538 that Israel could return. The Israelites returned to their land and began the slow process of trying to reconstitute themselves as a nation under the control of Persia. Conditions were difficult when they returned: they cleared rubble from the temple site and built an altar, but they got caught up in trying to establish their own lives and built their own houses (Hag. 1:2-6). God raised up two prophets, Haggai and Zechariah, to get the people to rebuild the temple and it was dedicated in 516 B.C. Ezra the scribe returned to Judah to help in the restoration by focusing on the Mosaic Covenant with an emphasis on law, purity, and separation. Nehemiah became governor of Judah and rebuilt the wall of Jerusalem. By 400 B.C. many Israelites had returned to their land, the temple was operating, the walls of Jerusalem had been built, and attempts had been made to live by the Mosaic Covenant. Israel was trying to become a nation, with a law, living in the land given to them by God. It was important that Israel sought to live according to the Mosaic Covenant, but there were major problems in the post-exilic community. The book of Malachi shows that the people were not faithful in their relationships with each other and the priests were allowing the people to bring blemished animals for sacrifice which was against the regulations of the Mosaic Covenant. Israel was in the land and had the law, but they were not fulfilling their mission to the nations, and were lacking a king to sit on the throne according to the promise of the Davidic Covenant. The scene was set for a king to come to fulfill God's covenant promises.

It is significant that Jesus came proclaiming, 'The time is fulfilled, and the kingdom of God is at hand; repent and believe in the gospel' (Mark 1:15; see also Matthew 4:17). The King has come to establish His kingdom. The nature of this kingdom is very important for understanding the fulfillment of God's covenant promises. The people of Jesus' day were expecting a king like David to destroy their enemies and establish Israel as a great nation. They were expecting a powerful king who would establish a political kingdom, a territory or realm over which the king would rule. This expectation is encouraged by the fact that Jesus is of the line of David. He is called the son of David (Matt. 1:1; 12:23), the king of the Jews (Matt. 2:2), the Messiah (Christ) who fulfills Old Testament prophecies (Matt. 2:4-6), and the beloved Son in whom God is well pleased (Matt. 3:16). Mary is told by the angel that the son she will bear will be 'called the Son of the Most High' and 'the Lord God will give him the throne of his father David, and he will reign over the house of Jacob forever, and of his kingdom there will be no end' (Luke 1:31-33 NKJV). But Jesus did not meet their expectations of a king who would lead Israel in a revolt against the Roman government, which meant they also did not understand His kingdom. The evidence of Jesus' kingship is seen in His power to rule creation (Matt. 8:23-27; Mark 4:35-41; Luke 8:24), His healing illness and disease (Matt. 4:25; Mark 1:29-33), and His power over the spiritual forces of wickedness in casting out demons (Mark 1:21-28; Luke 4:31-37). He also demonstrated power over life and death by raising people from the dead (Matt. 9:22-26; Mark 5:35-43; Luke 8:49-58).

Jesus came to establish a spiritual kingdom that could be entered immediately by submitting to the rule of Jesus through faith in Him. The word 'kingdom' can refer to the authority of a king to exercise rule and all those who believe in Jesus submit their lives to His rule. The nature of the kingdom that Jesus came to establish is also a spiritual kingdom as He heals a paralytic to show His power to forgive sins (Mark 2:1-12). He overcomes Satan's temptations (Matt. 4:1-11) and does battle with the demons (Matt. 12:22-32). Jesus defines His kingdom as operating differently than the kingdoms of the world by bearing witness to the truth (John 18:36-37). The present, spiritual reality of the kingdom means, according to the parables, that the kingdom begins small, is hidden in the way it works, and can be rejected by people. Yet Christ reigns now as King as He sits at the right hand of the Father after His resurrection and ascension, governing the world for the sake of His people (Eph. 1:22). The promises of the Davidic Covenant are fulfilled in Christ who is the descendant of David, the Son who occupies the throne of David.[28] He is the horn who sprouted for David (see also Ezek. 29:21, Luke 1:69) and the highest of the kings of the earth as the firstborn of creation (Ps. 89:27; Col. 1:15), both Son of David and Son of God (Rom. 1:3-4). Jesus fulfilled the conditions of the covenant by keeping the law perfectly and bearing in Himself the chastening judgments deserved by David's seed through their covenant violations (Ps. 89:38-45).[29] God was faithful to His covenant promises to

---

28. Robertson, *Christ of the Covenants*, pp. 251-252. He argues that even in the Old Testament there is a convergence of the throne of David as the throne of God (1 Chron. 29:22), which intensifies in some of the prophecies related to the coming Davidic king (Isa. 9:6), and is confirmed in the New Testament (Acts 2:30-36). Peter connects the oath made to David that God would seat one of his descendants on his throne with the resurrection and exaltation of Christ to the right hand of the Father.

29. Belcher, *Messiah and the Psalms*, pp. 142-43. Robertson comments that the role of Jesus as the seed of David speaks to the question of the conditionality of the covenant (*Christ of the Covenants*, p. 248).

David and those who believe in Jesus Christ are the beneficiaries of the rest, salvation, and security that results from His person and work.

The fullness of Christ's kingdom, however, has not yet come. The manifestation of Christ as king to the world awaits His future coming when He will appear in glory at the end of the age, the enemies of God will be defeated, and God's people will receive the fullness of their inheritance. Christ will reign not only in the hearts of His people, but also over the whole world (Rev. 11:15). This kingdom comes by the power of God, not by wisdom or human effort. The present, spiritual reality of Christ's kingdom that will not come in its fullness until Christ comes again is important for understanding the fulfillment of the Old Testament. The promises of the Old Testament are fulfilled now for God's people in a provisional way and will be fulfilled in a complete way in the future when Jesus comes to establish the fullness of His reign. Then they will experience the fullness of salvation in the new heavens and earth.

The land promise is central to the covenant promises of the Old Testament. God called Abram to leave his father's house and go to the land He would show him with the promise that He would give it to his descendants. The land is the place where the other covenant promises of God will be fulfilled and where Israel will fulfill her mission to the nations as a kingdom of priests and a holy nation. The nations would come to Israel to learn about the beneficence of God and the great law that He had given to His people. Although this mission was partially fulfilled under Solomon's reign, he turned away from the Lord and the kingdom divided. The Servant Songs of Isaiah (49:1-5; 52:13–53:12) show that, even though Israel failed in her mission, God will raise up another Servant who would succeed in bringing Israel back to God and in ministering to the nations. Jesus is that Servant who shows that where one worships is no longer important in light of His ministry. Rather, the Father seeks those who will worship in spirit and in truth (John 4:23-24). Focus on land as a specific geographic location is expanded in light of the mission the resurrected Christ gives to His people to go into all the world.[30] The good news of the message of the

---

30. With the fulfillment of the Old Testament covenant promises in Jesus Christ certain changes take place related to the existence of God's people and their mission. No

gospel is to be taken to every nation. Abraham in the Old Testament was heir of the land, but in the New Covenant he is the heir of the world (Rom. 4:13). The inheritance of the followers of Christ is the world, but they have not yet fully received that inheritance. Christ now rules the world, including all the nations, and the mission of His people is to the world/nations, and the reality of that will not be clear until Christ comes again (Rev. 19:1-21).

The promise of a New Covenant focuses on the spiritual relationship between God and His people. It begins with the phrase 'Behold the days are coming' (NKJV) which introduces several oracles in this section (Jer. 31:27, 31, 38). This is an 'eschatological formula'[31] that refers to a future time period when Yahweh will act to restore the fortunes of His people.[32] The covenant is made with the house of Israel and the house of Judah, a designation that emphasizes the reunification of the divided people of God. The New Covenant is contrasted with the Mosaic Covenant that was made when God delivered them from Egypt. Although the people made a commitment to keep the terms of this covenant (Exod. 24:7), they broke the covenant through their disobedience. God then declares the character of the New Covenant by laying out what it will accomplish in the lives of the people:

(1) 'I will put my law within them, and I will write it on their hearts'

(2) 'I will be their God and they shall be my people'

(3) 'they shall all know me, from the least of them to the greatest'

(4) 'I will forgive their iniquity, and I will remember their sin no more'

longer is there a commitment to one geographical location but the mission encompasses the whole world. No longer are God's people constituted a nation with a civil government but now God's people are a spiritual people scattered among many nations. The church is not dependent on physical warfare to accomplish its purposes but advances its cause through spiritual warfare focused on proclaiming the good news of the gospel. These changes hinge on the nature of the kingdom that Christ came to accomplish.

31. Keown, Scalise, and Smothers, *Jeremiah 26–52*, p. 127.

32. Mackay, *Jeremiah*, p. 233. The post-exilic period sees the beginning of the fulfillment of the covenant promises with the people returning to the land and trying to reconstitute the community based on the Mosaic Covenant (Haggai, Ezra, Nehemiah). Even though there are major struggles in the post-exilic period it prepares the way for the coming of Christ to fulfill God's covenant promises.

The four promises of the New Covenant were also part of the purposes of the Mosaic Covenant to establish a relationship with God. The people were to love Yahweh with all their heart (Deut. 6:5) and the law itself was to be on their heart (Deut. 6:6; 11:18; 30:14). God's purpose in delivering them from Egypt was to solidify His relationship to them: 'I will take you to be my people, and I will be your God, and you shall know that I am the LORD your God' (Exod. 6:7). The result was to be that the people would know the LORD (Deut. 4:35), a relationship built on God's mercy and forgiveness (Exod. 34:6-7; Num. 4:18-19) through the sacrificial system (Lev. 1:4; 4:27-31). The Mosaic Covenant failed to bring about these purposes on a broad scale among the people because of their continuing disobedience to God, leading to His judgment by exile. The Mosaic Covenant clearly showed people their sin (second use) but it had no power to transform their lives apart from God's sovereign intervention (Deut. 29:4; 30:1-6).[33]

There are a number of reasons why the Mosaic Covenant failed to transform the people.[34] As great a leader as Moses was, he was only a servant in God's house to testify of things that were to be spoken later related to Christ, the Son, who would build God's house, the church (Heb. 3:5-6). Moses had no power as mediator of the covenant to bring about the things he was proclaiming, but Christ as the mediator of the New Covenant would have the power to establish it. The covenant under Moses partook of the provisional, shadowy nature of types and ordinances (sacrifices, circumcision, the paschal lamb) that all foreshadowed the Christ to come. These were sufficient and efficacious by the operation of the Spirit to instruct and build up the elect in the promised Messiah by whom there is full remission of sins and eternal salvation (WCF 7.5). The earthly tabernacle was a copy of the heavenly tabernacle so that the earthly priests served only a copy and shadow

33. Deuteronomy 29–30 demonstrates that after the judgment of exile God will fulfill His covenant promises for them by bringing them back into the land and circumcising their hearts so that they will love the Lord with all their hearts and obey Him. Jeremiah declares that these promises will come about through the New Covenant.

34. One should not conclude that there were not any true believers in the Mosaic Covenant. Justification and sanctification language are used of David in Psalms 32 and 51, and God told Elijah that there were 7,000 in Israel who had not bowed the kneel to Baal (1 Kings 19:18), even though Elijah thought he was the only one left (1 Kings 19:14).

of the heavenly things (Heb. 8:5). This impacted the ministry of the priests who dealt with washings and regulations of the body (Heb. 9:6) and offered sacrifices that could not perfect those who drew near (Heb. 10:1-2) because the blood of bulls and goats cannot take away sins (Heb. 10:4, 11). On the other hand, Christ ministers in the heavenly tabernacle, and having offered His own blood once for all, He secured eternal redemption (Heb. 9:11-13). The fact that Jesus has a superior priesthood (according to the order of Melchizedek), serves in the true sanctuary, and is also the King who sits at God's right hand, ensures that the covenant He mediates will effectively accomplish the purposes of the covenant (Heb. 8:1-6). He is the mediator of the New Covenant enacted on better promises than the Old Covenant.[35] The author of Hebrews quotes the full passage from Jeremiah 31:31-34 in Hebrews 8:8-12. A New Covenant was needed because the first covenant failed to bring to fruition its promises in the lives of the people (8:7-8a).[36] The establishment of the New Covenant makes the first covenant obsolete and ready to vanish away (8:13).[37]

The promises of the New Covenant take on the provisional nature of the kingdom that Christ established in line with Paul's statement that we have only received a down payment of our full inheritance (Eph. 1:13-14). The internal transformation that comes about in the New Covenant is presented in the first promise that God makes in that He will write His law in the hearts of His people. The power to obey will come from an inner renewal of the heart. This promise has already begun in the lives of believers, but it has not yet been completed because

---

35. The word 'enacted' (*nomotheteō*) means 'to enact on the basis of legal sanction, ordain, found by law' (BDAG, p. 676). This word is also used in Hebrews 7:11 where it refers to the law received by the people through the Levitical priesthood. This shows that the New Covenant not only focuses on a spiritual relationship with God, but it is also a legal agreement with a legal basis (Peter T. O'Brien, *The Letter to the Hebrews* [Grand Rapids: Eerdmans, 2010], p. 292, n. 36).

36. There are several reasons given in the book of Hebrews to explain the inadequacy of the first covenant, including the inadequacy of animal sacrifices (10:1-4), the Levitical priesthood (7:11-25), and the earthly tabernacle (8:1-6).

37. O'Brien points out that the noun translated 'vanish away' (*aphanismos*) does not simply signify a vanishing, but signifies a deliberate destruction, usually due to God's judgment. Thus, the Old Covenant is destined for imminent destruction (O'Brien, *Hebrews*, p. 303).

obedience is not yet perfected in God's people. There is still the need to watch for corruption in their thinking (Eph. 4:17-32; 2 Pet. 3:17-18)[38] because battling the old nature is still a part of the believers' experience (Gal. 5:16-26). The essence of the covenant relationship (Exod. 6:7; Jer. 7:23; 11:4) will also become a reality: 'I will be their God and they shall be my people' (CSB, NIV, NKJV).[39] Although this covenant relationship cannot be broken for those who are true believers, they still need to be disciplined by God to keep them from straying away from Him in their pursuit of holiness (Heb. 12:3-17).

The third promise of the New Covenant, fully stated, is, 'And no longer will each one teach his neighbor and each his brother, saying, "Know the LORD," for they shall all know me, from the least of them to the greatest, declares the LORD' (Jer. 31:34). This promise is greatly debated and is a water-shed issue between Baptists and Presbyterians. Many Baptists argue that, since the New Covenant cannot be broken (Jer. 31:31), there cannot be anyone who is part of the New Covenant who falls away or breaks the covenant. Everyone who is part of the New Covenant is a true believer. Sometimes the same language is used of those who compose the New Covenant and the church, the New Covenant community: both are made up of only those who truly believe.[40] It is true that there are believers who will never break the New Covenant because they belong to the elect. They have an immediate relationship with God through Christ that is not dependent on an external mediator or approaching God through an earthly tabernacle. The New Testament mentions this relationship as an anointing from God that brings the knowledge of God with it so that such persons do not need anyone to teach them (1 John 2:20, 27). This comment does not mean that teachers are not needed in the New Covenant—there is room to grow in the knowledge of God (Col. 1:10). The focus is on what happens in regeneration where

---

38. Richard L. Pratt, Jr., 'Infant Baptism in the New Covenant,' in *The Case for Covenantal Baptism*, ed. Gregg Strawbridge (Phillipsburg, NJ: P&R Publishing, 2003), p. 171.

39. Mackay, *Jeremiah*, p. 237.

40. Gentry and Wellum, *KTC*, p. 555. The following statements are made: 'There will be no such thing as an unregenerate member of the new covenant community' and 'There are no covenant members who are not believers' (see Chapter 13 for further discussion of this issue).

the knowledge of God is communicated directly to persons in their conversion.[41] This anointing is an anointing with the Holy Spirit.

It is an impossible ideal to equate the elect of the New Covenant with the members of the church, the New Covenant community, because of the 'now, but not yet' character of the church before the second coming of Christ. Presbyterians recognize an administration of the New Covenant where someone can be part of the New Covenant in a legal sense but not necessarily have a relationship with God. In Romans 11:16-24 Paul affirms the unity between Israel and the church by means of an olive tree. The branches of the olive tree are holy by virtue of being connected to the root of the tree which is holy. But some of the branches were broken off because of their unbelief (v. 20).[42] Paul then warns the Gentiles who have been grafted into the olive tree that the same thing could happen to them (vv. 21-22). They too are considered part of the olive tree, and are thus holy, but they can also be cut off from the tree. In other words, it is possible for a branch to be considered holy because it is connected to the olive tree even though that branch is removed because of unbelief. If someone falls away through unbelief it shows that they did not have a vital relationship with God. The visible church displays the character of a mixed community as distinguished from the invisible church that is composed of the elect, who will not break the covenant. It is clear in 1 John that some who had been part of the church had left the church (1 John 5:19). Not everyone who is part of the New Covenant community is a true believer. Not every confession of faith is a true confession. The book of Hebrews issues warnings to its members not to drift away (2:1-4) and not to fall away with an unbelieving heart (3:12), lest there be grave consequences (6:1-7). Every church is a mixed

---

41. Robertson argues that the point of the covenant is to establish a oneness between God and His people so that no human mediator (like Moses, the Levites, or the prophets) is needed for this relationship. The knowledge of God will be the immediate possession of everyone who is truly part of the New Covenant. Galatians 3:20 supports this idea: 'Now an intermediary implies more than one, but God is one.' As long as intermediaries will function in the covenant relationship the intention of oneness cannot be achieved (*Christ of the Covenants*, pp. 295-97). Oneness can be achieved through Christ because Christ is God.

42. Paul does not have spiritual Israel in view because the branches that manifest unbelief were part of the covenant.

community because people give false professions of faith. At some point most churches have to exercise church discipline, as is clear in the churches even in the period of the apostles (1 Cor. 5:1).[43] Only in the new heavens and earth will God's people experience perfected natures that no longer need to be exhorted to holiness because they will no longer struggle with sin. This fits with the final promise that emphasizes the forgiveness of sins and that God will remember their sin no more (31:34). Unlike the blood of bulls and goats in the Old Testament, the blood of Christ has the power to remove sin and to procure an eternal redemption (Heb. 9:12). The sins of believers in this world are truly forgiven and removed, but they still continue to sin and thus need to ask for forgiveness. This situation will continue until God's people are completely transformed and freed from sin when Christ comes again.[44]

---

43. Jonty Rhodes makes the point that there are plenty of examples in the New Testament of people who seemed to have accepted the gospel, were welcomed into the church, but who later revealed themselves to have never sincerely believed (*Covenants Made Simple: Understanding God's Unfolding Promises to His People* [Phillipsburg, NJ: P&R Publishing, 2013], pp. 153-54).

44. J. Andrew Dearman comments that the complete transformation of God's people is still in the future beyond the 'already' that the church has tasted as it waits for the 'not yet' of the future (*Jeremiah/Lamentations* [NIVAC; Grand Rapids: Zondervan, 2002], p. 289). MacKay states that 'the ultimate realization of this [Jeremiah's] prophecy is found not in the earthly reality of the New Testament church but in its glorified heavenly consummation' (*Jeremiah*, p. 238).

CHAPTER 9

Major and Minor Variations to Covenant Theology

THE purpose of this chapter is to analyze different approaches to covenant theology that have made an impact in the reformed community in some way, or that serve as an example of how covenant theology can impact other doctrines. This chapter will first analyze two important reformed scholars, O. Palmer Robertson and John Murray, who do not always line up with the confessional language of the Westminster Standards, but are solid on justification by faith. Then a few other approaches will be examined to show how covenant theology, or aspects of it, impacts justification by faith.

Minor Variations to Covenant Theology

O. Palmer Robertson: The Christ of the Covenants

This book has become a classic and is very helpful in laying out the covenant framework of Scripture, in discussing the relationships of the covenants to each other, and in highlighting the particulars of each of the Old Testament covenants. The main thing that students struggle with is that he uses different terms than the Westminster Standards in discussing covenant theology.

Robertson introduces the divine covenants by discussing the nature, extent, unity, and diversity of the covenants. He then presents substantive, beneficial chapters on each of the covenants in the Old Testament, along with a chapter that addresses how Christ brings about the consummation of the covenants. He begins by defining a covenant as a 'bond in blood sovereignly administered'.[1] This definition highlights that God takes the initiative in the covenant relationship and that there are promises made through the taking of oaths that are confirmed by the shedding of blood. This definition works with most covenants, especially those covenants between God and His people, but it has limitations. Robertson denies that there is a covenant relationship between the members of the Trinity (usually called the Covenant of Redemption). He affirms that God intended from eternity to redeem a people but that is not the same thing as proposing the existence of a pre-creation covenant between the Father and the Son. Such a 'covenant' seems artificial, goes beyond the Scriptural evidence, and does not fit the definition of a covenant as a sovereignly administered bond.[2]

Robertson acknowledges the difference between a pre-fall and a post-fall covenant and even commends the Covenant of Works and Covenant of Grace terminology. This distinction recognizes the necessity of a pre-fall probation period that required perfect obedience as the meritorious ground of blessing and provided an overarching structure to unite the totality of God in relation to man in his fallen state.[3] Thus, Robertson affirms a bi-covenantal structure to Scripture. He believes, however, that these terms do not express the whole picture. The term 'works' suggests that grace was not operative in the pre-fall covenant, that works have no place in the Covenant of Grace, and that the 'work' required of Adam is confined to the one command of not eating from the tree of knowledge of good and evil.[4] Robertson opts to call the pre-fall covenant the Covenant of Creation and to refer

---

1. O. Palmer Robertson, *The Christ of the Covenants* (Phillipsburg, NJ: P&R, 1980), p. 4.
2. Ibid., p. 54.
3. Ibid., p. 55.
4. Ibid., p. 56.

to the unfolding covenants in redemptive history as the Covenant of Redemption. Although he clearly defines these terms and the reasons for using them, students become confused when these terms are compared with the WCF.[5] These minor criticisms, however, should not take away from the value of Robertson's work.

John Murray: 'The Adamic Administration'

Murray calls for a 'recasting' of covenant theology to make it more biblically articulated.[6] He does not want to limit covenant theology to the developments that occurred in the seventeenth century. He uses the Noahic Covenant as the model to discover the essence of a covenant. On the basis of this analysis he defines a covenant as a sovereign administration of grace and promise. The following covenants fit this definition: Noahic, Abrahamic, Mosaic, Davidic, and the New Covenant.[7] Each covenant emphasizes grace and the proper response to the covenant. The conditional fulfillment of obedience is the same in the Abrahamic and the Mosaic Covenants, two covenants that are usually contrasted with each other. The conditional element relates to the enjoyment of the blessings of the covenant. The Mosaic Covenant is also an administration of grace.[8] The essence of all the covenants is the assurance that 'I will be your God and ye shall be my people'.[9]

Murray does not consider the pre-fall relationship between God and Adam as a covenant because the term 'covenant' is not used in Genesis 1–3 and, Murray believes, it is always used in Scripture in a situation that needs redemption. Also, the phrase 'Covenant of Works' does not allow for elements of grace that are present in the pre-fall relationship between God and Adam. Murray calls this relationship 'the Adamic Administration' whereby God, by a special act of providence, established for Adam the provision that would enable him to pass from

---

5. This is especially true if a student adopts Robertson's terminology and then is examined by a church body that adheres to the WCF.

6. John Murray, *The Covenant of Grace* (Phillipsburg, NJ: P&R, 1983), p. 5.

7. Ibid., pp. 12-16.

8. Ibid., p. 22.

9. Ibid., p. 32.

the state of contingency (able not to sin) to the state of holiness (not able to sin) by means of a probationary test.[10]

Although Murray does not call the relationship between God and Adam before the Fall a covenant, many of the elements that make up the Covenant of Works are part of his Adamic Administration.[11] It was a sovereign administration whereby Adam acted as a representative for his descendants. The condition of this arrangement was obedience, focused on the command not to eat of the tree of knowledge of good and evil (Gen. 2:16). The promise held out to Adam, if he obeyed God's command, was everlasting life, symbolized in the tree of life (Gen. 3:22). Murray did not want to associate this promise with the principle of 'do this and live' (Lev. 18:5; Rom. 10:5; Gal. 3:12) or with any notion of meritorious reward. If Adam passed the test of obedience, he could only claim the fulfillment of the promise on the basis of God's faithfulness, not on the basis of justice. If Adam failed the test of probation, he and his descendants would experience the full impact of sin and death, which is defined as spiritual (moral and religious), judicial, and psycho-physical.[12]

Murray's definition of the covenant as a sovereign administration of grace and promise, based on his analysis of the covenant with Noah, forced all the covenants into a single type of covenant which flattened the different nuances found in them. His emphasis on grace and the continuity of the covenants is good, but the way he develops the covenant leads to an emphasis on the third use of the law. Concerning the Mosaic Covenant, he writes,

> In reality there is nothing that is principally different in the necessity of keeping the covenant and of obedience to God's voice, which proceeds from the Mosaic covenant, from that which is involved in the keeping required

---

10. John Murray, 'The Adamic Administration,' in the *Collected Writings of John Murray: Volume Two, Select Lectures in Systematic Theology* (Carlisle, PA: The Banner of Truth Trust, 1977), p. 49.

11. Venema states, 'Murray's treatment of the WCF's doctrine of the covenant of works, then, is not so much a repudiation of any of its essential teaching as a revision and refinement of some aspects of the WCF's formulation that he finds objectionable or misleading' (*Christ and Covenant Theology*, p. 22).

12. Murray, 'The Adamic Administration', pp. 49-56.

in the Abrahamic. In both cases the keynotes are obeying God's voice and keeping the covenant.[13]

The Abrahamic and the Mosaic Covenants are not different from each other and the requirements of fulfilling the covenant are the same in each.[14] His view of the Mosaic Covenant stems from the fact that there is not a Covenant of Works with continuing obligations that people are required to keep and are condemned for not keeping. This view is especially evident in his exegesis of New Testament texts, particularly Romans 10:5. Paul expresses the fact that there is a righteousness that is based on the law, expressed in Leviticus 18:5, that the person who does the commandments shall live by them. Murray argues that Leviticus 18:5, in its original setting, does not refer to legal righteousness as opposed to grace, but occurs in a redemptive context where the emphasis is on the blessings that come to God's people because of obedience. In other words, the context of Leviticus 18:5 is sanctification, not justification. The formal statement of Leviticus 18:5 can express the principle of law-righteousness, but the concept that 'the man who does shall live' is inoperative in the realm of sin so that 'do this and thou shalt live' has no validity as the way of justification and acceptance with God. Murray affirms that this principle is operative in the state of integrity but is not relevant after the entrance of sin.[15]

Murray has a point if he is arguing against the false idea that in the Old Covenant the basis of salvation was works, but now it is faith,[16] but he is short-sighted not to see that the obligation to keep the demands of the law still remain for fallen humanity and that the 'do this and live' in Leviticus 18:5 expresses this principle. In other words, it is appropriate to use any law in the Old Testament, including Leviticus 18:5, to express the condemnation that comes to those who break the law (second use). The WCF 7.2 uses the principle 'do this and live' expressed in Leviticus 18:5 to refer to the condition of personal and perfect obedience that was required of Adam to obtain life in the

---

13. Murray, *The Covenant of Grace*, p. 22.

14. Ibid., p. 20.

15. John Murray, *The Epistle to the Romans* (Grand Rapids: Eerdmans, 1968), pp. 2:51, 249-51.

16. Ibid., p. 2:50.

Covenant of Works.[17] Calvin comments concerning Romans 10:5 that the righteousness of the law is not taught by the whole law, but is taught in a restricted sense in the law. Paul understands Leviticus 18:5 as offering the promise of eternal life to those who would keep the law, but the purpose of this is to show that no one can attain righteousness in this way.[18] Hodge writes, 'There are but two possible ways in which this righteousness can be obtained – by works or by faith.'[19] The righteous requirement of the law is either met by us, through personal and perfect obedience, or it is met by another, in whom we trust, so that we receive a righteousness that is not our own.

Although Murray denied a Covenant of Works, he included in his discussion of 'The Adamic Administration' the elements of this covenant. Thus, he can affirm the necessity of the obedience of Christ as our federal head who kept the law where Adam failed.[20] He understands Adam's representative role so that his sin explains why every descendant of Adam is born a sinner. Adam's sin was imputed to them.[21] Although Adam failed to keep God's law, Christ obeyed the law and became the vicarious sin-bearer in His death on the cross so that the righteousness of Christ can be imputed to those who have faith in Him.[22] Murray states, 'By Adam sin-condemnation-death, by Christ righteousness-justification-life.'[23] He confirms the importance of the basic elements of the probationary test for Adam, the impact of his disobedience, and that these elements are foundational for the work of Christ. Thus, Murray affirms the traditional view of justification by faith.[24]

---

17. WCF 7.2 references Galatians 3:12 and Romans 10:5 which both refer to the principle 'do this and live' in Leviticus 18:5.

18. John Calvin, *The Epistles of Paul the Apostle to the Romans and to the Thessalonians* (Grand Rapids: Eerdmans, 1960), p. 223.

19. Charles Hodge, *A Commentary on Romans* (London: The Banner of Truth Trust, 1972), p. 337.

20. Murray, 'The Adamic Administration,' p. 58.

21. Murray, *Redemption Accomplished and Applied* (Grand Rapids: Eerdmans, 1955), p. 25.

22. Murray, *Redemption*, pp. 123-28. Murray uses the term merit to refer to the work of Christ (*Collected Writings*, pp. 2:286-87).

23. Murray, 'The Adamic Administration,' p. 59.

24. For a comparison of Murray and Kline's views of the covenants, see the end of Chapter 11.

Major Variations to Covenant Theology

Although Murray denied the Covenant of Works, he ended up with a confessional (traditional), biblical view of justification by faith because he affirmed other key doctrines in Scripture that are foundational for such a view. A denial of the Covenant of Works does not always mean that someone will have a wrong view of justification, but such a denial can lead to faulty views of this doctrine.[25] The first two authors reviewed in this section (Dumbrell and Williamson) are not directly connected to John Murray's legacy of calling for a recasting of covenant theology. The first is an example of someone who denies the Covenant of Works and is weak on justification by faith, and the second is an example of someone who denies a Covenant of Works but is good on the traditional view of justification. Some proponents of Federal Vision (FV), the final position reviewed, express indebtedness to Murray and see themselves as following in his footsteps.[26] Many in this movement deny a Covenant of Works and are weak on the traditional view of justification by faith.

W. J. Dumbrell, *Covenant and Creation*

This book is a substantial work on the covenants and has many beneficial discussions of the various covenants in the Old Testament. Dumbrell denies the existence of a Covenant of Works because it is argued from biblical inference rather than from biblical content.[27]

---

25. It is impossible to be comprehensive in this section, but N. T. Wright is an example. His views on justification can be found in *The Letter to the Romans* in *The Interpreter's Bible*, 12 vols. [Nashville: Abingdon Press, 2002], p. 10:440. For evaluation of his views from a traditional standpoint of justification, see Stephen Westerholm, *Perspective Old and New on Paul: The 'Lutheran' Paul and His Critics* (Grand Rapids: Eerdmans, 2004); Guy Waters, *New Perspective on Paul: Review and Response* (Phillipsburg, NJ: P&R Publishing, 2004); Thomas Schreiner, *Faith Alone: The Doctrine of Justification* (Grand Rapids: Zondervan, 2015); and Robert Cara, *Cracking the Foundation of the New Perspective on Paul: Covenantal Nomism and Reformed Covenant Theology* (Ross-shire: Christian Focus, 2017).

26. James B. Jordan, 'Merit Versus Maturity: What Did Jesus Do For Us?' in *The Federal Vision*, eds. Steve Wilkins and Duane Garner (Monroe, LA: Athanasius Press, 2004), p. 155.

27. W. J. Dumbrell, *Covenant and Creation: A Theology of the Old Testament Covenants* (Grand Rapids: Baker, 1984), p. 46. This book was first published in 1984 by Thomas Nelson Publishers and then was republished in 1993 by Baker.

The first time that covenant occurs in Scripture is in the context of Noah and the Flood. Noah is referred to as a righteous man, blameless, and one who walked with God. The word 'righteous' (*ṣādîq*) refers to conduct arising from a prior relationship that exhibits an attitude of trust and fidelity toward God.[28] Noah's behavior is contrasted with the wickedness of his generation. God instructs Noah to build the ark in preparation for the Flood that God will send to judge the earth because of the wickedness of humanity (Gen. 6:5). God tells Noah, 'I will establish my covenant with you, and you shall come into the ark, you, your sons, your wife, and your sons' wives with you' (Gen. 6:18). The normal verb for the inauguration of a covenant is 'to cut' (*kārat*) a covenant. The word 'establish' (*qûm*) is used in Genesis 6:18, which indicates that God is not beginning a covenant relationship with Noah but is continuing a covenant that is already in place. Genesis 9:1-17 presents Noah as a second Adam, armed with the same mandate God gave to Adam, within the context of a fallen world.[29] Genesis 6:18 refers to a divine relationship established by creation itself. Therefore, there can only be one divine covenant. The Covenant of Works is rejected because the biblical evidence for it is lacking.[30]

Dumbrell discusses Genesis 1–3 to show its relationship to Genesis 9. He recognizes that there was a condition established by God in His relationship with Adam that focused on the prohibition concerning the tree of knowledge of good and evil (Gen. 2:16). This condition regulated fellowship in the garden and Adam failed to meet the condition. Adam's failure impacted all of his descendants because all were somehow involved (Rom. 5:19).[31] The difference between the pre-fall and post-fall condition of Adam is that before the Fall Adam was able to determine the course of action to be adopted, but after the Fall he is in the grip of the consequences of the course of action which he had chosen. By eating the forbidden fruit Adam intruded into an area reserved for God alone and asserted equality with God. Adam's moral defiance of God meant

---

28. Dumbrell, *Covenant and Creation*, pp. 13-14.
29. Ibid., pp. 26-28. He understands the Noahic Covenant as a redemptive covenant (p. 39), including the redemption of creation (p. 43).
30. Ibid., pp. 32, 44-46.
31. Ibid., pp. 36-37.

that his life would be full of tension and absolute moral uncertainty.[32] Dumbrell does not discuss further the implications of Adam's failure for his descendants (imputation) or for the obedience of Christ in fulfilling the law (justification).

The situation in Genesis 1–3 is complex because of how sin impacts the original mandate that God gave to Adam and Eve. In standard Reformed theology, there is a distinction between the relationship of God with Adam before the Fall and after the Fall. Before the Fall there is no sin to impede their relationship, but after the Fall sin radically impacts all the relationships of Adam, including his relationship with God. It is impossible for Adam to have fellowship with God without God covering his shame and taking care of his guilt. God promises to send someone to do battle with the serpent in order to redeem humanity and restore God's creation (Gen. 3:15). Contrary to Dumbrell, the pre-fall and post-fall relationship between God and humanity cannot be conflated or subsumed under one covenant relationship. They are two different ways of how Adam related to God. There was an initial covenant relationship between God and Adam, but that relationship was broken. A different relationship needed to be established so that sinners could have fellowship with God. These two different situations would need to have two different covenants. God's word of judgment to Adam includes the mandate that God had originally given to him concerning marriage and dominion (Gen. 3:16-19). When Genesis 6:18 refers to a previous covenant, it is referring to the original mandate that God had given to Adam but not apart from the changes that came with the Fall. The instructions related to marriage, dominion, and the image of God continue to be relevant for humanity after sin entered the world. The obligations of the Covenant of Works continue for humanity because everyone is required to keep the Law of God, but now it is impossible to do so.

One of Dumbrell's emphasis is that righteousness in the Old Testament indicates behavior consistent with the nature of a relationship already established. He uses this definition with Noah in Genesis 6 and with Abraham in Genesis 15.[33] This view of righteousness impacts

---

32. Ibid., pp. 37-39.
33. Ibid., p. 13 (Noah) and p. 54 (Abraham).

his understanding of Genesis 15:6. Abraham is already in a covenant relationship with God and his response is an example of covenant fidelity, a response of further trust in God that is appropriate at this point in light of the promises of Genesis 12:1-3 and Abraham's prior response to them. He argues that Paul in Romans 4 moves this verse into the area of justification. He does not dispute this move, because it is appropriate for the New Testament writers to use Abraham as a paradigm of the appropriate response to God's promises, but originally this verse has more to do with Abraham's righteous response of covenant fidelity.[34] This view muddies the waters concerning the role of faith as the instrument of someone being declared righteous by God not on the basis of what they have done. This leaves open the question of whether Genesis 15:6 originally has justification by faith in view.

Dumbrell views the Sinai Covenant as particularizing the promises of the Abrahamic Covenant through the nation of Israel so that God's purposes of redemption for the world can be carried out by Israel as a kingdom of priests and a holy nation (Exod. 19:5-6). Israel is to be the vehicle through which the divine will is displayed. The law is the distinctive element in the Sinai Covenant, and it is given in a context of grace. The law is significant only within the framework of a relationship already established by covenant. The Ten Commandments make clear how Israel is to express covenant loyalty to God and how to translate faith into action. Israel will be blessed by God according to the measure by which she is faithful to the divine will. Dumbrell emphasizes the relational aspect of the law so that obedience to the law is not the fulfillment of a legal demand but is the expression of a relationship that leads to God's blessing.[35] Yet there is a relationship between Israel's occupancy of the land and her loyalty to the covenant. The future of Israel is guaranteed but it was not certain that the land would be kept by Israel. The blessings of nationhood and land depended entirely on how Israel responded to God.[36] There are appropriate parallels between Adam and Israel. Both were put into sacred space to exercise kingly/

---

34. Ibid., pp. 53-54.
35. Ibid., pp. 87-92.
36. Ibid., p. 99.

priestly roles, both were given laws to maintain the divine space, and both broke the law and were expelled from the divine space. Their continued existence in the divine space was dependent upon their obedience to the divine mandate.[37] The Old Testament becomes a history of Israel's national failure.[38] Although both Adam and Israel are driven from their land because of disobedience, there is very little emphasis on covenant curse (second use) but a lot of emphasis on the blessing of the covenant relationship (third use). This approach fits with Dumbrell's view that both righteousness and the law should be understood as primarily relational, not legal.

Dumbrell also published a commentary on Romans where he explored further the topics of righteousness and justification. He defines justification primarily in relational, not forensic terms. Justification expresses covenant membership or covenant identification. He also rejects the traditional view of imputation.[39] Without a Covenant of Works there is little room in Dumbrell's view of the covenant for the legal aspect of fulfilling the law in order to obtain righteousness. God and Noah were already in a covenant relationship where righteousness was defined solely in relational terms. This move impacts his view of Abraham's response of faith in Genesis 15:6, the role of the law in the Sinaitic covenant, and Paul's discussion of justification in the book of Romans. Apart from the legal aspect of the law that condemns sinners who do not keep it perfectly, there is no need for the active obedience of Christ or the imputation of His righteousness.

Paul R. Williamson: Sealed with an Oath

Williamson provides a biblical theological look at the covenants that emphasizes that the primary function of covenant is to advance God's creative purpose of universal blessing.[40] He is an example of someone who denies the Covenant of Works but affirms a traditional view of

---

37. Ibid., pp. 119-20.

38. Ibid., p. 99.

39. Dumbrell, *Romans: A New Commentary* (Eugene, OR: Wipf & Stock, 2005), pp. 40-41, 67-68, 102.

40. Paul R. Williamson, *Sealed with an Oath: Covenant in God's Unfolding Purpose* (NSBT; Downers Grove, IL: InterVarsity Press, 2007), p. 11.

justification by faith. The distinctives of his approach will be highlighted with attention to his basis for arguing for justification.

A covenant ratifies an already existing relationship by means of a verbal and/or enacted oath. Promises are made and obligations are required, including some form of divine sanction implied for covenant-breakers. The promises and obligations are sealed with the oath.[41] The first time the word 'covenant' ($b^e r\hat{\imath}t$) is used is Genesis 6:18, which is not looking back to a prior covenant but is looking forward to its ratification after the Flood in Genesis 8:20–9:17.[42] There is no evidence of a covenant between God and Adam in the garden. Although there may be parallels between Adam and Israel (both receive a prohibition with the possibility of punishment and both share a role as royal priests), the absence of a divine promise and an oath calls into question the existence of a covenant with Adam. There is also no external textual support in the rest of Scripture to confirm a covenant between God and Adam. Hosea 6:7 has too many questions related to its interpretation to rely on it to establish a pre-fall covenant. The disobedience of Adam and Eve leads to exile from the garden, but this does not undo the purpose of creation, demonstrated in the birth of their children (Genesis 4) and the promise of a seed who would defeat the serpent (Gen. 3:15).[43]

Williamson also rejects the idea of one Covenant of Grace that encompasses all the Old Testament covenants because it imposes on Scripture a hypothetical covenantal framework.[44] Although all the divine covenants ultimately serve the same overarching divine purpose, it is preferable to explore the unity and continuity of the various divine-human covenants apart from one unifying Covenant of Grace. The promise in Genesis 3:15 is not the intiation of the Covenant of Grace because there is no oath expressed and the promise was made to the serpent rather than directly to Adam and Eve. There are seven

---

41. Ibid., pp. 39, 43.

42. Ibid., p. 59. He comments that Genesis 6:18 is proleptical, anticipating the covenant ratified in Genesis 9.

43. Ibid., pp. 51, 56.

44. He also rejects the Covenant of Redemption, a covenant between the Father and the Son before the world was created; see 'The *Pactum Salutis*: A Scriptural Concept or Scholastic Mythology,' *TynBul* 69.2 (2018): pp. 259-82.

covenants in Scripture: the universal covenant with Noah, his family, and all creation, the patriarchal covenants with Abraham and his seed, the national covenants with Israel and its priestly representatives, the royal covenant with David and his seed, and the New Covenant with a spiritually renewed and reconstituted Israel.[45]

The purpose of the covenant with Noah is to reaffirm God's original creation intent that the Flood had placed in abeyance. The primary obligation imposed on humanity is to fulfill the original role appointed by God from the beginning (Gen. 1:28), but now in a fallen world.[46] Williamson argues against a covenant with creation to which the Flood account refers because creation takes priority over covenant. This means that the focus of the covenant of Noah is not just with the divine-human relationship but with the renewal of creation itself, an eschatological objective that each of the divine-human covenants advance.[47]

Williamson argues that there are two covenants with Abraham that go back to two distinct promises that God makes to Abraham in Genesis 12:1-3, setting forth a twofold agenda. These two promises are distinct from each other and must be clearly defined. The first promise relates to making Abraham's descendants into a nation that will inherit a land through which his name will become great. The second promise focuses on the international community through whom Abraham will mediate blessing. There is a shift from nation to 'all the families of the earth'. Although these two promissory blessings are distinct, the second promised blessing is in some way dependent on the first promise given to Abraham. This is the basis for the argument that God establishes two covenants with Abraham. The covenant in Genesis 15 deals with posterity and land (nationhood). There is no mention of international dimensions or royal descendants. The covenant is established by a sacrificial ritual but there is no sign to this covenant, nor are there any human obligations given to Abraham (it is unilateral). Nothing is revealed concerning events subsequent to nationhood and the covenant is not called 'everlasting'. The covenant in Genesis 17 is different. It is

45. Williamson, *Sealed with an Oath*, pp. 31, 58.
46. Ibid., pp. 61, 63.
47. Ibid., pp. 72-76.

called 'everlasting' and there is a sign of the covenant (circumcision) which is part of the human obligations attached to it.[48] The international dimension is seen in the promise that Abraham will be the father of many nations and there will be royal descendants in his line.[49] Genesis 17 also anticipates a further ratification which takes place in Genesis 22 with the extraordinary test of Abraham's faith. Abraham typified the kind of righteous behavior expected of his covenant heirs (Gen. 18:18-19) and demanded of his national descendants (Gen. 26:5; Neh. 9:13).[50]

Williamson's view of the 'national covenant' with Israel is fairly straightforward. The giving of the law was not meant to set aside the promise to Abraham but was a means by which the goal of the promise could be advanced through Abraham's national decendants. The purpose of this covenant was to show how the promised divine-human relationship between Yahweh and the people could be expressed and maintained. Thus, Israel must fulfill the obligations given to her in the law in order to maintain the covenant relationship.[51] The goal of the covenant was to help Israel fulfill her mission by establishing her as a special nation for the purpose that Yahweh could make Himself known to the families of the earth.[52] The Sinai Covenant is bilateral (Exodus 24), which is related to the obligation to keep the sabbath, the sign of the covenant.[53] It is interesting that there is very little discussion by Williamson of the role of the law. The blessings and curses of the covenant are mentioned, but only in passing. The sacrifices restore favor with God by averting the wrath of God because of sin (the term propitiation is used), but the need for this is assumed. There is no explicit discussion of the role of the law as showing Israel her need for substitionary sacrifice or as a guide to help her live.

---

48. Ibid., pp. 82-83, 86-87.

49. Williamson understands the multinational fatherhood of Abraham in a non-physical way. In other words, the focus is not on biological ancestry but on mediating divine blessing to the nations. This is based on the grammatical construction of the inseparable preposition (l^e) joined to the noun 'father' ($'\bar{a}\underline{b}$) used in a resultative sense (Ibid., p. 88).

50. Ibid., pp. 87, 90-91.

51. Ibid., pp. 94-96.

52. Ibid., p. 114.

53. Ibid., p. 100.

There is nothing unusually distinctive in his discussion of the Davidic Covenant. Williamson understands it as a land grant that is primarily associated with the Abrahamic Covenant. He argues for the continuity between these two covenants, but there is little discussion of how the Davidic Covenant relates to the Mosaic Covenant.[54] The chapter on the New Covenant looks at Old Testament texts that speak of the New Covenant, including Jeremiah 31:31-34. There is both continuity and discontinuity between the New Covenant and the Sinai Covenant. Continuity includes the same people, the same obligation of the law, and the same objective of a divine human relationship. Discontinuity includes the law written on the heart, an intimate relationship with God, and a covenant that cannot be broken. What is particularly new about the New Covenant is not the covenant partner, but the quality of the community created by God.[55]

The chapter on the covenant in the New Testament covers the Gospels and Acts, the letters of Paul, Hebrews, and Revelation. Justification by faith is addressed in the discussion of the New Covenant in Paul. Recent views on Paul serve as background to highlight Paul's views. Williamson rejects Sander's covenantal nomism because it does not fully understand Jewish literature of the second temple period.[56] It also reinterprets the doctrine of justification by faith to fit the underlying premise that good works are instrumental in salvation. The concept of 'righteousness' is understood in divine terms as God's covenant faithfulness and in human terms as being in the covenant. This is a reductionist view of righteousness that limits it to the realm of relationships whereas Paul

---

54. Ibid., pp. 120-21.

55. Ibid., p. 156.

56. Covenantal nomism is the term used by E. P. Sanders to describe Second Temple Judaism as a religion of grace and not works-righteousness (*Paul and Palestinian Judaism: A Comparison of Patterns of Religion* [Minneapolis, MN: Fortress, 1977]). It is the foundation of the NPP. For analysis and critique, see D. A. Carson, Peter T. O'Brien, Mark A. Seifrid, eds., *The Complexities of Second Temple Judaism*, vol. 1 of *Justification and Variegated Nomism* (Grand Rapids: Baker, 2001); Simon J. Gathercole, *Where is Boasting? Early Jewish Soteriology and Paul's Response in Romans 1–5* (Grand Rapids: Eerdmans, 2002); and Robert J. Cara, *Cracking the Foundation of the New Perspective on Paul: Covenantal Nomism Versus Reformed Covenantal* Theology (Ross-shire: Christian Focus Publications, 2017).

uses righteousness to mean 'accordance with a norm'. These views also lead many to deny the imputation of Christ's righteousness to His people. Williamson highlights aspects of justification by faith in discussing Paul's view of the law. In 2 Corinthians 3:7-18, the condemnation of the law, as opposed to justification through faith in Christ (mentioned in a footnote), and the emphasis by Paul's Judaizing opponents on keeping the law in accordance with the Old Covenant, are highlighted. In Galatians, Paul establishes the significance of the Abrahamic Covenant over against the Mosaic Covenant with the argument that those like Abraham are justified before God by faith rather than by the law (Gal. 3:6, 11). Jesus' death is the remedy for the curse of the law (Gal. 3:13) so that covenant blessings are inherited by faith and not through the works of the law (Gal. 3:15-18).[57] The summary of Paul's view of the New Covenant is that it has been inaugurated by Christ and ratified by His death on the cross. The true heirs of God's promises are not primarily the biological descendants of Abraham but those who are the true seed through faith.[58]

Evaluation of Williamson's Views

In a day and age when justification by faith has been redefined, it is encouraging to read someone who upholds the traditional view. It is more important that people understand justification by faith correctly than that they agree with all the facets of covenant theology. Williamson is good on justification by faith because he understands the condemnation of the curse of the law that can only be remedied through faith in the death of Christ. He also defines righteousness in a legal sense instead of a relational sense. There are shortcomings, however, in Williamson's examination of covenant. There is no discussion of the relationship between Adam and Christ in Romans 5:12-21 or of Paul's discussion of the righteousness that is based on the law (quoting Leviticus 18:5) versus the righteousness based on faith in Romans 10:5-13. Perhaps, the representative principle is not related to the covenant when there is no covenant between God and Adam in the pre-fall state. Disobedience to the law brings condemnation, based on Galatians 3, but there is very

---

57. Williamson, *Sealed with an Oath*, pp. 188, 192-95.
58. Ibid., p. 200.

little discussion of this role of the law in the Sinai Covenant. Thus, the concepts highlighted in Paul's view of the New Covenant do not seem to have a firm basis in the Old Testament.

Williamson denies that there is a Covenant of Works in Genesis 1–2 because of the absence of a divine promise and an oath. But do all the elements of the covenant have to be present for someone to recognize the existence of a covenant? In discussing Deuteronomy, Williamson acknowledges that the ratification of the covenant is missing. He explains this by arguing that the record of Deuteronomy is selective and that an actual ceremony took place at the conclusion of Moses' speech. Concerning the Davidic Covenant, there is also no covenant ceremony or sacrificial right described and no sworn oath, which he calls the key defining characteristic of any biblical covenant.[59] The lack of the former is explained on the premise that the Davidic Covenant is an extension of the Abrahamic Covenant and the omission of the latter by the fact that it is clear in other passages of Scripture that this is a covenant. The same arguments can be used for affirming a Covenant of Works in Genesis 1–2. One of the elements of a covenant is some form of divine sanction against covenant breakers.[60] In Genesis 2:17, God gives a negative command with the penalty of death if the command is broken. Nothing specific is said concerning what happens if Adam and Eve obey this command, but it is surely implied that this test of obedience would lead to further blessing. This is the pattern throughout Scripture. Israel's obedience will ensure that she keeps her land inheritance, and Christ's obedience has implications for His work and those whom He represents. Obedience leads to greater blessings. One might also argue that there is an implied oath in the emphatic statement of the penalty: 'you shall surely die' (Gen. 2:17). There are as many elements of a covenant in Genesis 1–2 as there are in 2 Samuel 7. The Covenant of Works lays the foundation for the work of Christ by establishing that disobedience to the law brings a curse. If someone sees elements of a covenant in Genesis 2, then it makes sense to understand Hosea 6:7 to be referring to that covenant.

---

59. Ibid., pp. 113-14, 120.
60. Ibid., p. 39.

Williamson also denies an all-encompassing Covenant of Grace that includes the individual covenants of the Old Testament because it imposes on Scripture a hypothetical covenantal framework. When he talks about covenant as a unifying theme, however, his arguments are very similiar to the arguments for an all-encompassing Covenant of Grace. For example, he affirms that the concept of the covenant is more pervasive in both Testaments than the mere frequency of the use of covenant terminology, so that even when not explicitly mentioned in the text, it is seldom far from the surface. The idea of covenant is essential for unlocking numerous biblical texts. All the covenants serve the same overarching divine purpose of restoring God's universal blessing for all of creation.[61] Such statements sound very much like those who argue for one Covenant of Grace that is worked out in redemptive history through the individual covenants to fulfill God's purposes of salvation (WCF 7.5–6).[62] Although one can be thankful that Williamson affirms justification by faith, his discussion of certain New Testament texts concerning justification could be strengthened considerably with a more robust understanding of the relationship between covenant and the role of the law, including the requirement of perfect obedience to the law, and the need for a representative to fulfill that law for us.

Federal Vision

Federal Vision (FV) represents a movement rather than a particular person.[63] Not everyone associated with the movement will agree on

---

61. Ibid., pp. 31, 33.

62. Geerhardus Vos defines Biblical Theology as the division of the course of revelation into different periods that center on the various covenants which he subsumes under the term Covenant of Grace (*Biblical Theology* [Grand Rapids: Eerdmans, 1948], pp. 25, 32).

63. The proponents of Federal Vision set forth their views in *The Federal Vision*, eds. Steve Wilkins and Duane Garner (Monroe, LA: Athanasius Press, 2004). Contributors to this volume include Steve Wilkins, John Barach, Rich Lusk, Mark Horne, James B. Jordan, Peter J. Leithart, Steve Schlissel, and Douglas Wilson. The movement has also been called Auburn Avenue Theology after Auburn Avenue Presbyterian Church where conferences were held to promote the movement's ideas. Federal Vision is the preferred name because it addresses the root concern of the system, which is the covenant (Guy P. Waters, *The Federal Vision and Covenant Theology: A Comparison Analysis* [Phillipsburg, NJ: P&R Publishing, 2006], p. 3).

every point, but their system develops from covenant theology and they offer a comprehensive and sweeping vision articulating an epistemology, a Trinitarian theology, a doctrine of redemption and its application, and a conception of the church, culture, and Christian living in the world.[64] Some see themselves following in the footsteps of John Murray, who called for a recasting of covenant theology,[65] by seeking a better systematic construction of God's relationship with Adam and how Jesus fulfilled it for us.[66] Some Federal Vision proponents have expressed their appreciation of Norman Shepherd's teachings on justification, election, and covenant.[67] Several evaluations of their views have been written.[68] The purpose of this section is to provide orientation to those who are not familiar with their basic views. The focus will be on the way they understand the covenants in Scripture in order to see how it impacts their view of justification by faith.

In order to understand FV, it is imperative to understand their view of the covenant. There is a broad-based consensus that a covenant is primarily a relationship with the living Triune God that is loving, personal, ordered, and formally binding. There is resistance to defining the covenant in legal or administrative terms whereby a person can be in the covenant but not in a personal relationship with God. Instead, they affirm that everyone in the covenant is in a relationship with God

---

64. Waters, *The Federal Vision,* p. 2.

65. Murray, *The Covenant of Grace,* 5; see the discussion in this chapter of Murray's view.

66. Jordan, 'Merit Versus Maturity: What Did Jesus Do For Us?' p. 155.

67. Particularly, Peter Leithart, *The Kingdom and the Power* (Phillipsburg, NJ: P&R Publishing, 1993), p. 237 n. 2 and Mark Horne, 'Book Review: *The Call of Grace: How the Covenant Illuminates Salvation and Evangelism,* 2002. Norman Shepherd was professor of systematic theology at WTS from 1961 to 1982. For a critical analysis of Shepherd's view, see Waters, *The Federal Vision,* pp. 97-107, and Jeong Koo Jeon, *Covenant Theology and Justification by Faith: The Shepherd Controversy and Its Impacts* (Eugene, OR: Wipf & Stock, 2006). Jeon shows how a loss of the distinction between law and gospel impacts justification by faith.

68. Waters, *The Federal Vision* (part of the bibliography has a section on 'Critical Responses to the FV'), Brian M. Schwertley, *Auburn Avenue Theology: A Biblical Critique* (Kearney, NE: Morris Publishing, 2005), and *The Auburn Avenue Theology, Pros & Cons: Debating the Federal Vision,* ed. E. Calvin Beisner (Fort Lauderdale, FL: Knox Theological Seminary, 2004).

and experiencing real communion with the Triune God through union with Christ. This means that everyone in the covenant experiences the blessings of union with Christ. This view is supported by the biblical metaphor of marriage that is used to describe the covenant relationship. The members of the Trinity are a paradigm for our covenant relationship with God as the three persons of God are in a vital personal relationship with each other.[69]

The definition of a covenant as a relationship with God through union with Christ leads to 'covenant objectivity'. How should someone who is in the covenant view their standing before God? A distinction is made between the objective relationship of being in the covenant and the subjective understanding a member of the covenant might have of the strength or the nature of that relationship. A person is in a covenant relationship with God even if he or she does not feel it or believe it (much like a person is still married even if he stops believing it). Every baptized person is in covenant with God and in union with Christ. There is no distinction between being internally in the covenant versus being in the covenant externally. In other words, it is not possible to be in the covenant legally and not have a relationship with God. Everyone who is baptized, including children, are in a relationship with God through union with Christ. Baptism joins us to Christ so that those who are baptized are the elect.[70] Membership in the covenant is not to be defined by drawing distinctions along the lines of regeneration and conversion.[71]

This view of the covenant impacts other doctrines, but the focus here will be on a few issues directly related to the definition of the covenant as a relationship. Problems result if the covenant is understood only as a relationship without affirming the legal aspect of the covenant. Even marriage has a legal side that lays out the rights and responsibilities

---

69. Steve Wilkins, 'Covenant, Baptism, and Salvation' in *Debating the Federal Vision*, p. 262, writes that 'covenant is a real relationship, consisting of real communion with the triune God through union with Christ .... Thus, being in covenant gives all the blessings of being united to Christ.' See also Waters, *The Federal Vision*, pp. 10-14.

70. John Barach, 'Covenant and History,' 2002 AAPCPC lecture (accessed at enigstetross.org/pdf/Barach-Covenant). Waters in *The Federal Vision* gives annotated bibliography on the unpublished papers and lectures of FV proponents.

71. Waters, *Federal Vision and Covenant Theology*, pp. 17-19.

of the parties and cannot be collapsed into the marriage relationship. This does not reduce marriage to a contract because the legal side gives security to the relationship by highlighting the commitment of each to the covenant.[72] A covenant cannot be revoked without grave consequences. The legal aspect of the covenant allows for the proper administration of the covenant in relationship to children and in relationship to those who disobey God's commands. The apostles draw distinctions between those who are true members (1 Pet. 5:12) and those who are not true members of the covenant (1 John 2:19-20).[73]

Proponents of FV conceive of the order and progress of the covenants in biblical history differently, including whether the relationship between God and Adam is a covenant. Many of them, however, reject a Covenant of Works and the concept of merit, while arguing for a gracious relationship between God and Adam. The condition of this relationship is faith-filled obedience. These ideas are emphasized by Jordan in the book written by the proponents of FV and is used here as an example.[74]

Jordan sees problems with the traditional Reformed understanding of the Covenant of Works, particularly, the idea of earning eternal life through meritorious works.[75] He calls this arrangement Pelagian in character. The reward earned seems out of proportion to the merits required. Another problem is that the reward earned should not be eternal life but glorification; in other words, the reward should not just be the perpetuation of original life but a new glorified life. He believes the statement in WCF 19.1 that

---

72. The marriage metaphor, like all metaphors, has its limitations. Although marriage has both legal and relational aspects, without the consummation of the relationship a marriage can be annulled. But someone can be in the covenant in a legal sense through baptism and/or a false profession of faith without having a personal relationship with God. If it becomes evident that such a person does not have a relationship with God through unbelief or consistent disobedience to God, then church discipline seeks to restore the offender, but the outcome could be excommunication if the person does not repent.

73. Schwertley discusses the denial of the visible/invisible church distinction by FV and its importance (*Auburn Avenue Theology*, pp. 113-28).

74. Jordan, 'Merit versus Maturity,' pp. 151-202. In reading FV proponents, it is clear that many of them are either influenced by Jordan or follow his views.

75. Other proponents of FV who reject merit include Ralph Smith, *Eternal Covenant: How the Trinity Reshapes Covenant Theology* (Moscow, ID: Canon, 2003), pp. 62-65 and Rich Lusk, 'A Response to "The Biblical Plan of Salvation",' pp. 118-22.

'God gave to Adam a law ... by which he bound him and all his posterity, to personal, entire, exact, and perpetual obedience' with the promise of life for fulfilling it, and the threat of death for breach of it, is confusing and misleading. He asks, 'Where is faith in all of this?'[76]

A better way to understand God's relationship with Adam is to see a two-stage process, consisting of a stage of human life and then a glorified stage which Adam failed to attain. These two stages are found in Paul's discussion of Romans 5 and 1 Corinthians 15. Specifically, the two stages are a stage of childhood and a stage of maturity. A person does not become a mature adult by earning it through good works. Good behavior prepares a person for mature responsibilities and bad behavior disqualifies a person from mature responsibilities. Good behavior does not earn points. If Adam had remained faithful to God, he would have matured to the point of being aware that he needed a fuller kind of life from God, which God would have freely given him at the proper time. There is nothing here of merit, but the choice is whether to exercise faith or not. Adam rejected the God-given process of maturation because Adam prematurely seized the privilege that God held out at the end of the process. Thus, the garden was a kindergarten, a place where Adam could grow from childhood to kingly maturity, a place of easy life with free food, a place to learn how to cultivate and guard.[77]

This view of Adam in the garden impacts Jordan's view of the work of Christ. He does not want to use the term 'merit' to speak of Christ's accomplishments because it is a hangover of medieval theology and creates the idea that Jesus earned by works His translation into glory.[78] Although he does not disagree with the idea of double imputation (our sins were imputed to Jesus and His glory to us), he rejects the active and passive obedience of Christ. Instead, Jesus became the first mature man, perfect in faith toward the Father and perfect in obedience. He

---

76. Jordan, 'Merit Versus Maturity,' pp. 153-55. An answer to this question is that this describes the righteousness based on the law that Adam was capable of obeying.

77. Jordan, 'Merit Versus Maturity,' pp. 153, 157-60. Lusk also uses maturity to explain the relationship between the Old and New Covenants ('A Response to "The Biblical Plan of Salvation",' pp. 130-32).

78. For the appropriate use of merit, see the discussion in Chapter 2, 'The Covenant of Works.'

thus became eligible for transformation into glory through death, not because He had earned the right to it but because He had matured to the point of being fit for it. We do not receive Jesus' merits but His maturity, His glorification. The reigning paradigm for Adam, for Christ, and for us is growth into maturity instead of breaking or keeping the law.[79]

In this view Adam's relationship with God centers on faith, not on works or merit. This impacts Jordan's understanding of the work of Christ who does not fulfill the law on our behalf but becomes the first perfect, mature man through faith, which makes Him eligible for transformation into glory. This approach flattens the confessional understanding of the relationship between the covenants by denying the distinction between the law and the gospel.[80] The role of the law as a legal basis for our relationship with God that brings conviction of sin is downplayed in favor of formulations that stress biblical obligations as 'gospel'.[81] Imputation is not defined according to the historic definition because it is the glory of Jesus that is imputed to us instead of His righteousness.[82] This impacts the understanding of Christ's work as a basis for our justification because it is His righteousness, derived from the perfect obedience and full satisfaction of His work, imputed to us, whereby God pardons our sins (as in WLC 70-71).[83] A reworking of the Covenant of Works impacts how one understands the work of Christ and the basis of justification by faith.[84]

In order to summarize and highlight some of the problems with FV in relationship to justification by faith, a short review of things they

---

79. Jordan, 'Merit Versus Maturity,' pp. 193-95.

80. Others who reject the law/gospel distinction among FV proponents are Doug Wilson, *'Reformed' is not Enough: Recovering the Objectivity of the Covenant* (Moscow, ID: Canon Press, 2010), pp. 65-66 (he argues that the law/gospel distinction is grounded in the subjective state of the sinner, not within the biblical covenants); Rich Lusk, 'A Response to "The Biblical Plan of Salvation",' p. 128 (he argues that the law does not require perfection); and Steve Schlissel, 'Covenant Reading', 2002 AAPCPC lecture, quoted by Waters, *Federal Vision and Covenant Theology*, p. 51.

81. Waters, *Federal Vision and Covenant Theology*, p. 33. Waters' remarks are made in reference to another Federal Vision proponent, but they apply well to Jordan's views.

82. This view of imputation is also argued by Smith, *Eternal Covenant*, p. 83.

83. Waters, *Federal Vision and Covenant Theology*, p. 40.

84. For further analysis of different views of God's relationship with Adam among proponents of Federal Vision, see Waters, *Federal Vision and Covenant Theology*, pp. 30-44.

affirm will be given here. Typically, FV proponents deny imputation and/or define it differently. Lusk denies that the active obedience of Christ is imputed to the believer, focusing rather on union with Christ so that my in-Christness makes imputation redundant. He writes, 'I do not need the moral content of his life of righteousness transferred to me; what I need is a share in the forensic verdict passed over him at the resurrection.'[85] Lusk emphasizes the resurrection as Christ's vindication and the righteousness of God whereby we are vindicated because of our union with Christ. This changes the focus of justification away from the perfect obedience and full satisfaction of Christ imputed to the believer in his justification (as in WCF 11.1, 3), and raises the question of whether the believer's covenantal faithfulness becomes the ground of his acceptance on the day of judgment.[86]

The way some FV proponents define righteousness is a problem. Leithart argues that the Reformers were too narrow in their view of justification and so, to some extent, distorted the doctrine. By defining righteousness in relational terms as loyalty within a covenant relationship, 'righteousness' and 'justification' can have a wider scope than just strictly judicial. God's righteousness in justification is defined as God's keeping His covenant promises with those counted righteous. Justification is not the mere declaration of a verdict but includes counting someone as a loyal friend or servant, and the execution of the verdict of righteousness is demonstrated in deliverance from enemies. Paul in Romans 3 understood justification as a favorable judgment of God rendered through deliverance from enemies.[87] By defining righteousness in relational terms, justification is then understood in non-forensic, transformational categories.[88]

---

85. Lusk, 'A Response to "The Biblical Plan of Salvation",' p. 142.

86. Waters, *Federal Vision and Covenant Theology*, pp. 79-80. He clarifies that WLC 52 affirms that Christ was raised for our justification, but that Lusk argues that the resurrection *is* our justification (emphasis original), not just that it was necessary for our justification.

87. Peter J. Leithart, '"Judge Me, O God": Biblical Perspectives on Justification,' in *The Federal Vision*, pp. 209-11, 222.

88. Waters, *Federal Vision and Covenant Theology*, p. 85. He correctly points out that it is inappropriate to argue the biblical doctrine of justification from the sum total of the biblical uses of the term 'justify'.

There is also confusion concerning the role of faith, faithfulness and final justification. Lusk argues that justification partakes of the already/not yet dynamic of salvation. This impacts the role of works in our justification. He defines works as faith-filled obedience that, in a secondary way, causes our final justification and salvation. Works are the means through which we come into possession of eternal life, the non-meritorious conditions of final salvation.[89] This idea is not that works are the evidence of our justification, but the condition of it. We will not be justified without our works, which are not merely evidential, but causal in our final salvation. Justification is not just a one-time declaration but is a process that will be completed on the day of judgment.[90] Faith and works are co-instruments in final justification.[91]

Conclusion: Key Doctrines related to Justification by Faith

Several emphases have appeared in this chapter that are signals concerning whether someone might deny the biblical, confessional view of justification by faith. First, the Covenant of Works is foundational for the work of Christ related to the requirement that the law requires perfect obedience. Those who deny the Covenant of Works (mono-covenantal) tend to treat God's relationship with Adam before the Fall and after the Fall in the same way, usually emphasizing grace. However, not everyone who denies a Covenant of Works gets justification wrong because other important doctrines are affirmed.

Second, the law/gospel distinction is important for justification by faith.[92] This is inherent in the bi-covenantal framework of the Covenant

---

89.   Lusk, 'The Tenses of Justification,' 2003 (accessed at hornes.org/theologia/rich-lusk/the-tenses-of-justification). It is also quoted in Waters, *Federal Vision and Covenant Theology*, p. 89.

90.   Waters, *Federal Vision and Covenant Theology*, p. 89. Waters interacts with later statements made by Lusk ('Rome Won't Have Me', 2004) that respond to criticism of his views, but major questions remain.

91.   Lusk, 'Faith, Baptism, and Justification,' 2003.

92.   Lutherans are well-known for their law/gospel distinction as a basis for justification by faith; see 'Formula of Concord, Epitome 5', in *The Book of Concord*, trans. and ed. by Theodore G. Tappert (Philadelphia: Fortress Press, 1959), pp. 477-79; John T. Mueller, Christian Dogmatics (St. Louis MO: Concordia Publishing House, 1934), pp. 44-47; and C. F. W. Walther, *The Proper Distinction Between Law and Gospel* (St. Louis, MO: Concordia Publishing House, 1929 reprint).

of Works over against the Covenant of Grace and is related to the moral requirement of the law that requires perfect obedience (second use of the law).

Third, the imputation of Christ's righteousness related to His active obedience is important to guard the forensic nature of justification; otherwise, it is easy to confuse justification and sanctification.

Fourth, some definitions of union with Christ shift the focus from justification and the necessity of the imputation of Christ's righteousness to our union with Christ in His resurrection as the way we receive the righteousness of Christ.

Fifth, the definition of righteousness in relational terms in key Pauline texts blurs the distinction between our works that condemn us (second use of the law) and our works that are evidence of justification (third use).

Sixth, an implication that follows from the last point is that the role of works in final justification becomes a condition of final justification on the day of judgment. This makes justification a process rather than a one-time declaration of righteousness.

Such teachings are warning signs that someone may end up denying the biblical, confessional view of justification by faith.

CHAPTER 10

Meredith Kline:
Covenants as Administrations
of God's Kingdom

※ ※ ※

MEREDITH Kline has had tremendous influence within Reformed Theology in a number of areas,[1] including covenant theology. The goal in this chapter will be to explain Kline's approach to covenant theology so that his views can be evaluated in the next chapter.[2]

---

1. Kline taught at Westminster Seminary in Philadelphia from 1948 until 1965 and then taught at Gordon-Conwell Seminary until 1993. He also taught at Westminster Seminary in California while he taught at Gordon-Conwell and finished there in 2002. Kline's contributions include the relationship between Deuteronomy and ANE treaty documents (*The Treaty of the Great King: The Covenant Structure of Deuteronomy* [Grand Rapids: Eerdmans, 1963]), the literary framework view of Genesis 1 ('Because It Had Not Rained', *WTJ* 20 [1958], pp. 146-57), and implications related to the canon of Scripture (*The Structure of Biblical Authority* [Grand Rapids: Eerdmans], 1972). For a bibliography of his works, see *Creator, Redeemer, Consummator: A Festschrift for Meredith G. Kline*, eds. Howard Griffith and John R. Muether (Greenville, SC: Reformed Academic Press, 2000); and for a collection of his major articles, see *The Essential Writings of Meredith G. Kline* (Peabody, MA: Hendriksen Publishers, 2017).

2. Kline's view of the covenant is mainly set forth in *Kingdom Prologue: Genesis Foundations for a Covenantal Worldview* (Overland Park, KS: Two-Age Press, 2000). There are a number of different 'editions' of *Kingdom Prologue* and the pagination

Covenant and Kingdom

The kingdom of God is the central, organizing theme of the Old Testament. The divine covenants function as administrations of God's kingly rule. Thus, to follow the course of the kingdom is to trace the series of covenants that administer God's kingship. As the administration of God's kingdom, the covenants are primarily legal arrangements that are ratified by the swearing of oaths with curses included to demonstrate commitment to the covenant. The party that swears the oath of the covenant is used to distinguish the two different types of covenants. If the covenant is ratified by divine oath alone, it is a Covenant of Grace (either saving or common grace) and is called a royal grant. If the covenant includes a human oath of ratification, as in Exodus 24, there is a works principle operative in the covenant according to the form of the treaty covenant.[3] God's commitment to such an arrangement is to enforce the terms of the covenant by rewarding obedience with blessing and disobedience with covenant curse.[4] These distinctions are important for how Kline understands the covenants and their historical administrations.

The Covenant of Creation

Adam had a covenant relationship with God from the moment of being created in the image of God. This relationship was not superimposed on a non-covenantal human state that was already in existence.[5] Thus, the divine act of creation was a covenantal act whereby God, as Lord of the covenant, created Adam and Eve, who were servants of the

---

between them may not match. For an excellent summary of Kline's views, see Jeong Koo Joen, *Covenant Theology: John Murray's and Meredith G. Kline's Response to the Historical Development of Federal Theology in Reformed Thought* (Lanham, MD: University of Press America, 1999). Mark W. Karlburg has also written in support of Kline's views; for a collection of his essays, see *Covenant Theology in Reformed Perspective* (Eugene, OR: Wipf & Stock, 2000).

3. Michael Horton uses the terms 'treaty covenant' and 'royal grant' to describe the law covenant and the promise covenants as developed by Kline (*God of Promise: Introducing Covenant Theology* [Grand Rapids: Baker Books, 2006], pp. 23-50).

4. *Kingdom Prologue*, pp. 1-5. This book is titled *Kingdom Prologue* because even though an earthly kingdom is mentioned in Eden and Noah, the kingdom promised in the Abrahamic Covenant was not established until Moses (p. 1). The book itself focuses on Genesis with comments on the Mosaic Covenant scattered throughout the book.

5. *Kingdom Prologue*, p. 17.

covenant.[6] They were given lordship over God's creation and were to reflect God's rule on the earth. If Adam and Eve had obeyed the Law of God, they would have been given the promised eschatological glory, which would have far exceeded the original covenantal blessings of creation. The promise of eschatological kingdom blessing was offered on the basis of works. Thus, Kline sees this covenant arrangement as a Covenant of Works with a probationary period for Adam as representative of humanity. Adam was able to earn or merit eternal life on the basis of simple justice apart from grace.[7] The Sabbath ordinance represented the blessing sanction of the covenant and shows that the covenant of creation leads toward consummated eschatology.[8]

The failure of the first Adam to keep the Covenant of Works has tremendous implications for his posterity, but it is also foundational for the work of Christ, the second Adam (Rom. 5:19). Adam failed the first Covenant of Works, but Christ fulfilled the second Covenant of Works, an intra-trinitarian, eternal covenant between Christ the Son and His Father. In this covenant Christ is the covenant servant, the second Adam, who represents the elect. The operating principle of this covenant is works because Christ's obedience is the foundation of the gospel. He fulfilled the law on our behalf and secured our salvation.[9] This eternal covenant is also essential for the historical administration of God's redemptive grace to His people, traditionally called the Covenant of

---

6. *Kingdom Prologue*, p. 63. Kline rejects the distinction between Adam in his original created state and Adam in a covenant relationship with God. In this distinction, Adam in his natural, created state owed allegiance to God's commands and then God entered into a covenant relationship with him to set up the probationary test. This distinction is reflected in WCF 7.1 that talks about the distance between God and mankind being so great that God had to voluntary condescend to Adam to enter into a covenant relationship. Kline's rejection of this distinction will have implications for the way he understands merit in humanity's fallen condition.

7. Kline, *Kingdom Prologue*, p. 107. He argues that a 'successful probation would be meritorious' and if obedient, Adam would receive the reward 'as a matter of pure and simple justice'. This is the same kind of merit by which Christ will earn our salvation.

8. Jeon, *Covenant Theology*, pp. 197-200.

9. Kline writes: 'if meritorious works could not be predicated of Jesus Christ as second Adam, then obviously there would be no meritorious achievement to be imputed to his people as the ground of their justification. ... We who have believed in Christ would still be under condemnation' (*Kingdom Prologue*, pp. 108-09).

Grace, that is worked out in the various covenants in the Old Testament and culminates in the New Covenant.[10] In the Covenant of Grace the messianic Son is Lord and mediator of the covenant with the church (the community of the confessors of the faith and their children). The operating principle is grace.[11] Kline uses the term 'Covenant of Creation' to refer to the broader covenantal implications in Genesis 1–3 for Adam, the covenant servant, and his posterity.[12] He reserves the term Covenant of Works to refer to the unique function of the first Adam in the original covenant, separating his role from that of the second Adam who fulfilled the requirement of the Covenant of Works which the first Adam failed to fulfill. Thus, Kline affirms the antithesis between the Covenant of Works and the Covenant of Grace as essential for the gospel.[13]

Common Grace Covenants

When the first Adam failed to keep the Covenant of Works there was the need for a second covenant, typically called the Covenant of Grace, which was inaugurated in Genesis 3:15. Kline generally uses 'Covenant of Grace' as an overarching term to refer to the unity of the various administrations of the covenants in history and refers to each of the various covenants as redemptive covenants.[14] In addition to redemptive covenants there are also common grace covenants that apply to both the elect and the non-elect. A common grace principle controls the world

---

10.   Adam represented all mankind and would have received the Covenant of Conferment if he had fulfilled the requirements of the Covenant of Works ('conferment' refers to the ability to distribute the covenant blessings based on fulfillment of the covenant's requirements). The second Adam represented the elect and did fulfill the requirements of the covenant and so received the Covenant of Conferment as the mediator of the covenant between God and the community formed by His work. Christ is able to confer the blessings of the Covenant of Grace to the elect and thus guarantee the eschatological heavenly kingdom blessings for them (Jeon, *Covenant Theology*, pp. 215-16).

11.   *Kingdom Prologue*, pp. 138-39. Kline also talks about the role of the Holy Spirit in creation and in the making of the covenants throughout *Kingdom Prologue*.

12.   Issues discussed include man as the image of God, dominion, the Sabbath, marriage, and the eschatological focus in Eden.

13.   *Kingdom Prologue*, pp. 20-21.

14.   Ibid., p. 138. Kline is not always consistent in the use of this terminology and at times refers to the Covenant of Grace as the Covenant of Redemption. Jeon frequently uses the phrase Covenant of Redemption in explaining Kline's approach (*Covenant Theology*, pp. 215, 224).

after the Fall. It allows general history to move forward without God's immediate judgment so that God's kingdom program of saving grace can be fulfilled. In the present world both the holy and the common coexist together, yet these two types of covenant operate differently. At the consummation of history common grace will be terminated, along with the antithesis between the holy and the common. Until then, God's eschatological judgment is delayed. The common grace covenant provides the background for redemptive history.[15]

The kingdom before the Fall was a theocratic kingdom of God's lordship where the worship of God and the political rule were indistinguishable. There was no need for a common grace state because everyone was a worshiper of God. God's reign was exhibited in an external realm and in the hearts of the people.[16] The entrance of sin and rebellion into the human world changed this arrangement so that the need developed for both redemptive covenants and common grace covenants. The inauguration of the redemptive covenant occurred in Genesis 3:15 and the inauguration of common grace immediately followed in Genesis 3:16-19. These latter verses do not have in view Adam and Eve's personal identity as elect individuals but all humanity whom Adam represented. Thus, the curse of Genesis 3:16-19 was not the ultimate curse of damnation for those who reject God, but a temporal curse experienced by all people until the separation at the final judgment. This curse will be tempered by common grace which will inform the divine government of the world after the Fall.[17] The positive benefits of common grace include the preservation of the natural order of the world, the continuation of the marriage institution, the continuing importance of dominion and work, and the development of arts and sciences (Gen. 4:19-22). Chaos in the world will be avoided with the social structuring of society through the family, and later the state.[18]

The common aspect of common grace refers to the common benefits shared by both the godly and ungodly and the character of the political, institutional aspect of common grace culture as profane or secular; it

---

15. *Kingdom Prologue*, pp. 153-54 and Jeon, *Covenant Theology*, pp. 217-18.
16. *Kingdom Prologue*, pp. 49-51.
17. Ibid., pp. 134-36.
18. Ibid., pp. 153-55.

should not be considered holy. This is particularly evident in the fact that God did not attach the Sabbath promise to the common cultural order. Thus, the sabbatical time pattern, which gives symbolic promise of the consummation, does not operate in common grace institutions. Also, even though certain provisions of the original cultural mandate are resumed in the common grace order, these have different objectives so that one cannot simply say that it is *the* cultural mandate that is being implemented in the common grace order because they are not part of redemptive grace *per se*.[19] The coexistence of the holy and common is what characterizes the present world. The partial presence of the holy eternal reality is antithetical to the common grace order and is an eschatological intrusion into this order. Such intrusions include the breaking-in of the power of eschatological restoration into the present physical realm, with anticipatory applications of the principle of redemptive judgment in the political life of Israel, including the deliverance from Egypt, the conquest of Canaan, and the governmental and judicial laws of the Mosaic Covenant.[20]

The Noahic Covenant

Kline distinguishes between two types of covenants in the account of the Flood. The covenant before the Flood is a redemptive covenant (Gen. 6:18) that is fulfilled within the Flood episode (see more on this covenant below). The covenant that God made with Noah after the Flood is a common grace covenant (Gen. 8:20–9:17), an administration of common grace, not redemptive grace. This covenant is made not just with Noah, his family, and their descendants, but also with every living creature on the ark and every living creature of all flesh for future generations (9:10, 12, 15-17). This is a universal covenant made with all creation that ensures the continuation of the common grace order so that God's program of redemption can be carried out. However, this covenant does not grant the kingdom of God to the elect. The sign of

---

19. *Kingdom Prologue*, pp. 155-157. Kline comments that it is closer to the truth that the cultural mandate of the original covenant is being carried out in the program of salvation (p. 156).

20. Ibid., pp. 157-58. For a discussion and evaluation of intrusion ethics, see the next chapter.

this covenant, the rainbow, is part of the natural world and is visible to all of God's creation. It is not like other signs, such as circumcision, that are only for the community of God's people. In fact, the Sabbath as the sign of the eschatological cosmic kingdom is not present in the common grace Noahic Covenant because it does not culminate in the new heavens and earth. Instead, it will be terminated by the final act of the judgment of consummation. Thus, Genesis 8:20–9:17 is limited to common grace and the curses which might come on nature itself.[21] The purpose of this covenant is to temper the devastating impact of the common curse and to assure the continuing stability of the natural order and the procreation process. Thus, it serves God's redemptive program only indirectly.[22]

Redemptive Covenants

The Covenant of Genesis 6:18

God's redemptive program after the Fall begins with Genesis 3:15,[23] which sets forth the eschatological struggle between the woman's seed and the serpent's seed, a declaration of holy war that will lead to the final destruction of Satan. Although this battle will culminate in two individuals, this warfare will be manifested between the spiritual community that believes in God and the unbelieving community that persists in their rebellion against God (John 8:44).[24] The translation of Enoch into heavenly glory in Genesis 5:22-24 is a prophetic sign of the eschatological victory of the promised seed of the woman over death.[25] The warfare continues with the increasing wickedness of the

---

21.   The stipulations that regulate the cultural functions and institutions in Genesis 9:1-7 resume the common grace world order in Genesis 3:16-19 and 4:15. Genesis 9:1-7 has many parallels with Genesis 1–2, but it is not a simple reinstitution of the creation ordinances; rather, it is a revision of them in common grace mode (*Kingdom Prologue*, pp. 250-262).

22.   *Kingdom Prologue*, pp. 212-13; 244-50 and Jeon, *Covenant Theology*, pp. 221-22.

23.   Adam's expression of faith comes when he names his wife Eve because she was the mother of all living (Gen. 3:20). God's response is to cover their nakedness by providing them with clothing of garments of skin (Gen. 3:21), a seal of the inauguration of the redemptive covenant and a symbolic investiture with the divine image (*Kingdom Prologue*, pp. 150-51).

24.   *Kingdom* Prologue, pp. 132-33; 143.

25.   Kline, 'Gospel until the Law: Rom. 5:13-14 and the Old Covenant,' *JETS* 34 (1991):' p. 437.

seed of the serpent, but Noah found favor with God (Gen. 6:1-8). God entered into a covenant with Noah (Gen. 6:18) that is fulfilled within the Flood account leaving the way for the common grace covenant to be established in 8:20–9:17. Thus, Genesis 6:18 is a covenant of salvation whose promise of salvation for Noah and his family is realized in the events of the Flood and not in any arrangement afterwards.[26] The covenant of Genesis 9 is not referring back to the covenant of 6:18. These are two different covenants. The covenant of Genesis 6:18 does not refer to any previous covenant promises,[27] such as the promises of kingdom blessings earlier disclosed in the Covenant of Grace. It only refers to the specific promise of salvation given to Noah, but it also allows for a fulfillment of those promises on a typological level. What Noah experienced in the ark was a type of the ultimate fulfillment of salvation.[28] The covenant that God made with Noah and fulfilled in the ark is a part of the series of redemptive covenants.[29]

Kline identifies the covenant with Noah as a grant covenant that ancient rulers would give to individuals for faithful service. Such grants bestowed on a faithful servant special status or other blessings, such as lands with their revenues. Noah is described as a faithful servant of God in 6:8-9 and 7:1 in contrast to the rest of the world. This grant is given to Noah under the Covenant of Grace, an administration of mercy to fallen people deserving covenantal curse because of sin. Genesis 6:18 is consistent with that perspective, but the point is that Noah had demonstrated the loyal service to God that received His approval. The kingdom that was granted to Noah as the reward for his good works was typological of the messianic

---

26. *Kingdom Prologue*, pp. 230-32. Kline's argument, that Genesis 6:18 is fulfilled in the Flood account, is based on several factors, including the fact that the divine remembering of Genesis 8:1 corresponds to the divine covenanting of Genesis 6:18 as fulfillment to promise.

27. Kline understands the phrase 'I will establish my covenant' (*qûm* in the hifil) as not referring to the inauguration of the covenant but to the assurance God gives that He will fulfill the covenant promise of salvation (*Kingdom Prologue*, p. 232).

28. Kline argues that this parallels the relationship between the Abrahamic Covenant and the Mosaic Covenant, with the fulfillment of the land promise in the land of Canaan being a typological figure of the consummated kingdom (*Kingdom Prologue*, pp. 230-33).

29. Ibid., p. 234.

kingdom and thus not in conflict with the redemptive Covenant of Grace. Noah was a typological prefiguration of Christ whose obedience provided the ground for God's gift of redemption to His people.[30]

The Abrahamic Covenant

A new stage is reached in redemptive history with the Abrahamic Covenant, but it stands in continuity with the Covenant of Grace concerning kingdom goals and the purpose and way of salvation. The descendants of Noah after the Flood populated the world, as represented in the Table of Nations (10:1-32), with the line of Shem leading to Abraham. The Abrahamic Covenant represents the culmination of covenant promises not only for Abraham, but also for the future of God's covenantal kingdom, particularly in anticipation of the New Covenant. It is a bridge between the Old and New Covenants so that Paul can explain the New Covenant in light of the Abrahamic Covenant. Thus, the promise of God revealed to Abraham would result in the blessing of all the nations. Paul identifies the Abrahamic Covenant with the promise of God over against the works of the law (Gal. 3:17-22), so that Abraham is an example of someone who is saved by faith alone and not by works (Rom. 4:2-6).[31]

The promises that God gave to Abraham in Genesis 12 are ratified in Genesis 15 in a formal ceremony where God placed Himself under curse if He breaks the covenant. He does this by being the only party, symbolized in the flaming torch, that passes through the slain animals. God swears the oath to keep the promises of the covenant lest He become like the slain animals. Of course, God will keep His covenant promises so that He will not have to undergo the curse as a covenant-breaker; rather, He voluntarily took upon Himself covenant judgment in line with the bruising of the head of the seed of the woman in Genesis 3:15 and the sacrificial, substitute offering for Isaac in Genesis 22. God gave to Abraham a confirmatory oath not to spare His own Son but to give Him as a substitutionary sacrifice.[32]

The sovereignty of God is demonstrated in the Abrahamic Covenant by the fact that God Himself swore the oath to keep the covenant in

---

30. *Kingdom Prologue*, pp. 234-39 and Jeon, *Covenant Theology*, pp. 219-20.
31. *Kingdom Prologue*, pp. 292-94.
32. Ibid., pp. 295-301 and Jeon, *Covenant Theology*, pp. 224-25.

Genesis 15. It is also seen in the divine election of Abraham and in the divine appointment of Isaac and Jacob as his patriarchal successors. Kline argues for a two-level structure of the meaning and realization of the promises of the Abrahamic Covenant.[33] One level is the typological kingdom of Israel under Moses (see below) and the other level is the ultimate, abiding level of meaning that focuses on the spiritual promises of salvation that were realized in the Old Covenant era and come to fulfillment in the antitypical, eternal kingdom of righteousness and peace in the Spirit (the New Covenant).[34]

Although the promised kingdom blessings were guaranteed by God's sovereignty and power, the conditionality of human responsibility is also part of this covenant. Abraham's obedience also partakes of the character of two-levels of meaning. On the level of the spiritual promises of salvation, obedience is essential for the reception of covenant blessings, but not in such a way that it contradicts the gospel principle of grace. In other words, the promised heavenly inheritance was not secured by obedience (the works principle). God's call to Abraham to leave his homeland was a call to discipleship. The promises to God are ratified in the covenant of Genesis 15 and human obligation is the focus in Genesis 17 with the sign of circumcision. Although Genesis 17 uses 'covenant' to refer to the Abrahamic Covenant as a whole (vv. 4, 7, 19), and more specifically, to circumcision itself (vv. 10, 13), it is not a separate covenant because circumcision is the sign of the covenant previously made with Abraham.[35] Kline relates circumcision to the cutting ritual of Genesis 15 as portraying the curse inflicted by the sword of God's judgment. This is explicitly stated in Genesis 17:14 where the one who breaks the covenant by failure to observe circumcision will be cut off. Thus, circumcision symbolized being cut off from the covenant and thus threatened the cutting off of descendants. On the positive side, circumcision marked the entrance of individuals into the community, pointing to redemptive judgment undergone by Christ

---

33. Kline understands the two levels as Paul's answer to the problem of Israel discussed in Romans 9–11 (*Kingdom Prologue*, p. 303).

34. Ibid., pp. 302-03.

35. *Kingdom Prologue*, pp. 309-14. Kline argues that the verb 'give' (*nāṭan*) is not used for making or ratifying covenants but is used for appointing covenantal signs of confirmation (Gen. 9:12-13; 17:2; Exod. 20:12).

(Col. 1:22; 2:11). Thus, it presents the promise of the cross and invites the circumcised to identify by faith with Christ, to undergo the judgment of God in Him, and to experience justification and life. To be circumcised in Christ further involves a dying to sin in the spiritual transformation of sanctification. Baptism takes on the same twofold meaning of circumcision. It symbolizes divine judgment and the curse of death as when John the Baptist used baptism to refer to the Messiah's impending judgment of the covenant community (Matt. 3:11) and when Jesus used baptism to refer to His death on the cross (Luke 12:50). Also, Christian baptism is seen as a participation with Christ in the judgment ordeal of his death, burial, and resurrection (Rom. 6:3-6; Col. 2:11-12). According to its redemptive purpose, baptism speaks of justification, reception of the Spirit, resurrection and everlasting life. It also functions as a sign of separation from the world and incorporation into the holy covenant community.[36]

There is another level to Abraham's obedience that has a specific historic significance as the basis of future, favorable actions toward his descendants and that anticipates the meritorious works principle of the Mosaic Covenant. In Genesis 26, Isaac is tempted to go down to Egypt because of a famine, but God tells him not to go to Egypt, and gives him the assurance that God will bless him and his offspring because of the obedience of Abraham (referring to Genesis 22). In fact, Genesis 26:5 describes Abraham's obedience in language used of the laws of the Mosaic Covenant. Based on the Hebrew word 'because' ('ēqeḇ) and the use of covenant stipulations from the Mosaic Covenant that operates according to a meritorious works principle, Abraham's obedience was meritorious as the ground of the reward enjoyed by his descendants. Abraham's meritorious obedience functioned as a type of the obedience of the coming Messiah. Thus, Abraham's faithfulness in keeping the covenant obtained a reward that was enjoyed by others. His obedience was the meritorious basis for Israel's inheritance of Canaan.[37]

The Mosaic Covenant

The typological aspects of the works principle are fully worked out in Kline's view of the Mosaic Covenant. This is one of the more difficult

---

36. *Kingdom Prologue*, pp. 314-18.
37. Ibid., pp. 324-26.

aspects of Kline's thought.[38] Not only are there a variety of ways that Reformed theology has understood the Mosaic Covenant, but Kline has been understood in different ways on this issue.[39] The Mosaic Covenant, according to Kline, is not a royal grant like the Abrahamic Covenant, but is a law covenant formulated according to treaty covenants in the ANE.[40] The key aspect of the covenant ratification ceremony is that the people of Israel, not the Lord, swear the oath to keep the terms of the covenant (Exod. 24:7). If the covenant is ratified by divine oath alone, it is a Covenant of Grace, either a redemptive covenant (Abraham) or a common grace covenant (Noah). If the covenant includes a human oath of ratification (Exodus 24), then the arrangement is informed by a works principle.[41]

There is both continuity and discontinuity between the Abrahamic Covenant (a promise covenant synonymous with the gospel of grace) and the Mosaic Covenant (a law covenant). Kline sees continuity primarily in

---

38. For an explanation of Kline's view of the relationship between the Covenant of Works and the Mosaic Covenant, see *The Law is Not of Faith: Essays on Works and Grace in the Mosaic Covenant*, eds. Bryan D. Estelle, J. V. Fesko, and David VanDrunen (Phillipsburg, NJ: P&R, 2009). Not all the chapters in this book deal specifically with this question and not all the authors would argue for Kline's republication view.

39. For the variety of views related to the unique function of works in the Mosaic Covenant, see Brenton C. Ferry, 'Works in the Mosaic Covenant: A Reformed Taxonomy' in *The Law is Not of Faith*, pp. 76-108. He understands Kline's view of the Mosaic Covenant as an administration of the Covenant of Grace and as a typological, formal republication of the Covenant of Works aligned with the national principle of works inheritance (pp. 96-97, 102). Some argue that Kline's view is the Subservient Covenant view (see D. Patrick Ramsey, 'In Defense of Moses: A Confessional Critique of Kline and Karlburg,' *WTJ* 66 (2004): pp. 373-400) and an unpublished paper by Lee Irons, 'The Subservient Covenant: A 17th Century Precursor of Meredith Kline's View of the Mosaic Covenant', accessed at upper-register.com/papers/subservient_cov.pdf). Two views of Kline on the Mosaic Covenant are set forth in 'The Report of the Committee to Study Republication: Presented to the Eighty-third (2016) General Assembly of the Orthodox Presbyterian Church' (hereinafter 'The OPC Report') accessed through the OPC website (opc.org/GA/republication.html). The two views are the substantial republication view and the administrative republication view (see below).

40. See Appendix 1 for a discussion of covenants in the ANE.

41. *Kingdom Prologue*, pp. 5, 323. Kline argues that a divine oath in a works covenant is a commitment by God to enforce the sanctions of the covenant appropriately by rewarding obedience with the promised blessing and disobedience with the threatened curse.

terms of the individual application of redemption.[42] Salvation is received by individual Israelites through faith. Thus, on its foundational level, having to do with the personal attainment of the eternal kingdom of salvation, the Mosaic Covenant is continuous with the Covenant of Grace.[43] The principle of works, on the other hand, operates on a different secondary level. In the national election of Israel, the nation's enjoyment of the theocratic kingdom was based on her national faithfulness to the Lord. She would experience the blessings or the curses of the covenant based on her obedience according to the do-and-live principle of inheritance in Leviticus 18:5. This principle is limited to the temporary, typological phase of the Old Covenant. As Kline states: 'The works principle in the Mosaic order was confined to the typological sphere of the provisional earthly kingdom which was superimposed as a secondary overlay on the foundational stratum.'[44] If the people broke the covenant they would suffer exile and the loss of their national, typological election. Also, individual Israelites who were elect in terms of eternal salvation could be cut off from the temporal, typological realm as being part of the nation that broke the covenant. At this secondary, typological stratum, kingdom blessings were not guaranteed by sovereign grace on the basis of Christ's meritorious accomplishments, but they could be merited by the Israelites' works of obedience to the law.

There are several reasons that the Mosaic Covenant should be understood as a substantial republication of the Covenant of Works.[45] It makes the reception of the inheritance to be by works according to the law and not by faith according to promise. It operates according to a similar probationary-works principle as the Covenant of Works.[46]

---

42. Kline also sees continuity with the initial fulfillment of the kingdom promise to Abraham in the promised land (*Kingdom Prologue*, p. 320).

43. Ibid.

44. Ibid., p. 321.

45. 'The OPC Report,' pp. 50-54. Included under substantial republication are the views of the Mosaic Covenant as a mixed covenant and a subservient covenant, which are summarized in the report (pp. 33-39).

46. Ibid., pp. 306-07; Kline writes that 'Israel's situation was like Adam's in the creational covenant of works, Israel's probation, however, being corporate and continuing through their generations' (*God, Heaven, and Har Magedon* [Eugene, OR: Wipf & Stock, 2006], p. 127). See also David VanDrunen, *Divine Covenants and Moral*

Obedience functions as the meritorious ground of how kingdom blessings are received. On this basis, Kline argues that Israel's obedience not only functioned like Adam's obedience in his probation, but also served as a type of Christ's obedience.[47] The contrasting conditions of works versus grace indicates there is a substantial contrast between the Mosaic Covenant and the Covenant of Grace. The Mosaic Covenant is governed by a principle of works on the typological level which is not gracious.[48] This is over against the principle of grace on the foundational level that governs reception of the eternal kingdom promised as a gift of grace. Because works and grace operate on two different levels, they operate simultaneously without conflict. Finally, it is important to note that the typological kingdom of the Mosaic Covenant anticipates the coming final, theocratic kingdom of the new heavens and earth.[49]

Another understanding of Kline's view of the Mosaic Covenant is that it is not a substantial republication of the Covenant of Works but that it is an administrative republication of it. The Abrahamic and Mosaic Covenants are viewed as distinct administrations of the Covenant of Grace, but both covenants feature a typological works principle adapted from the garden of Eden. This works principle connected the inheritance of blessings to obedience but is restated with substantial modifications in Abraham (Gen. 22:16-18; 26:5). Abraham's imperfect, Spirit-wrought obedience operates in a way that emphasizes the redemptive character of Israel's obedience and supplies a prophetic type of the perfect obedience of Christ. The works principle that passes into Israel's theocracy at the national level is adjusted to the realities of sin and redemption. The situation of Israel in the land is thus different from the situation of Adam in the garden because Adam could inherit eternal life through perfect obedience whereas Israel's obedience does not need to be perfect

---

Order: A Biblical Theology of Natural Law (Grand Rapids: Eerdmans, 2014), pp. 326-29, who argues that Israel recapitulates Adam's experience based on the parallels between the garden and Canaan, the periods of probation of Adam and Israel, and the loss of land because of disobedience.

47. Kline, *Kingdom Prologue*, pp. 352-53.

48. 'The OPC Report,' p. 54. The report at this point comments that the Mosaic economy is itself a covenant of works in contrast to the Covenant of Grace, a form of substantial republication.

49. *Kingdom Prologue*, pp. 320-23.

to keep the land inheritance. Adam's situation was non-redemptive, but Israel's situation is redemptive so that the requirement of her obedience is the imperfect obedience of those graciously redeemed by blood from sin and bondage. This explains why God is longsuffering with Israel and does not remove her from the land at the first instance of disobedience.[50]

Those who contend for an administrative republication view of Kline argue that readings of him that do not take into account that the nature of the works principle with Abraham and national Israel is different than with Adam will not acknowledge the role of redemptive grace in relation to typology in Kline's thought. Kline is seen as offering an advancement of covenant theology within the tradition of the reformed biblical theology movement pioneered by Geerhardos Vos.[51]

The New Covenant

A few words concerning the Davidic Covenant are in order before discussing the New Covenant. Kline's comments on the Davidic Covenant are scattered throughout *Kingdom Prologue*. He identifies the Davidic Covenant as a royal grant because God swore the oath. In response to dispensationalism, he discusses the nature of the kingdom and the role of the king in relationship to Christ and the New Testament. The Davidic Covenant was the covenant of the kingdom with the Davidic kingdom serving as a type of the everlasting kingdom. Jesus Christ, the son of David, is the Davidic king who at His resurrection and ascension sits on David's throne as King of kings and Lord of lords.[52]

Kline's comments on the New Covenant arise in his discussions on Paul's view of the works principle in the Mosaic Covenant scattered throughout *Kingdom Prologue* and in various other books and articles. The key New Testament texts that he examines are Romans 5:13-14;

---

50. 'The administrative republication view is explained in 'The OPC Report,' pp. 54-71; see also Kline, *Kingdom Prologue*, pp. 107-10; 118; 324-26 and *Treaty of the Great King*, p. 65.

51. 'The OPC Report,' p. 55. This report also gives a brief summary of Vos to show how he relates to Kline (pp. 77-79).

52. *Kingdom Prologue*, pp. 15, 332-55. For further discussions of Kline's view of the Davidic Covenant, see Jeon, *Covenant Theology*, pp. 233-34; Jeon, *Biblical Theology: Covenants and the Kingdom of God in Redemptive History* (Eugene, OR: Wipf & Stock, 2017), pp. 131-71.

10:5-8, and Galatians 3:15-18. In these discussions he also comments on the New Covenant passage in Jeremiah 31. Paul in Galatians 3 identifies the Abrahamic Covenant with promise (3:17), sets over against it the principle of works operative in the law (3:18), and argues that salvation is received by faith in Jesus Christ (3:22). The inheritance of the promise comes through faith as demonstrated in Abraham's faith (Gen. 15:6; Rom. 4:1-3).[53] Paul argues in Romans 10 and in Galatians 3 that there is a principle of works operative in the Mosaic Covenant as expressed in Leviticus 18:5. There is a righteousness which is of the law that is antithetical to the righteousness that is by faith (Rom. 10:5-6). This works principle, however, did not annul the promise arrangement given to Abraham by faith (Gal. 3:17) because the works principle was confined to the typological sphere of the provisional earthly kingdom that was superimposed as a secondary overlay on the foundational stratum of individual salvation by faith (see the discussion above). Paul's thinking agrees with Jeremiah's analysis of the New Covenant as contrasted with the Old Covenant, at least the part of it that is restricted to the typological dimension. The Old Covenant was breakable (Jer. 31:32), but the New Covenant cannot be broken as it is founded on God's sovereign, forgiving grace in Christ. The Old Covenant's typological kingdom order lacked the guarantee afforded by the grace principle because it was based on the works principle. The continuity between the Old and New Covenants is found in the underlying, foundational stratum of gospel-grace as the way to heavenly hope in Christ.[54]

---

53. *Kingdom Prologue*, pp. 294-95. At the level of individual salvation, the principle of redemptive grace is operative in the Old Covenant that shows its continuity with the New Covenant (Jeon, *Covenant Theology*, p. 234).

54. *Kingdom Prologue*, pp. 321-22, 345.

CHAPTER 11

Evaluation of Kline's Views of the Covenant

✳ ✳ ✳

KLINE is not the easiest to read and there are a variety of ways his views have been understood, particularly concerning the Mosaic Covenant. The previous chapter set forth his views on the different covenants. After an evaluation of his views, the end of this chapter will give a comparison of Kline and Murray to see how they differ from each other.

The Covenant of Works

Kline is very clear on the differences between the Covenant of Works and the Covenant of Grace (a bi-covenantal framework). The Covenant of Works is the necessary foundation for justification by faith so that if someone denies the Covenant of Works his understanding of justification by faith can be impacted. The obligation for someone to fulfill the Covenant of Works continues and for salvation to be accomplished someone must keep the law on our behalf. In fact, without the Covenant of Works, there is no imputation of Adam's sin or of Christ's righteousness. If there is no probationary period for Adam as our representative, there is no imputation of his sin to his descendants. Likewise, if Christ as the second Adam does not fulfill the Covenant of Works on our behalf, there is no imputation of His righteousness.

Without the Covenant of Works as background, Christ's work hangs in the air without any foundation. Christ in His obedience fulfills the law on our behalf so that we who are sinners can be declared righteous. To deny the Covenant of Works is to pervert the gospel because imputation and the active obedience of Christ are downplayed or denied.[1]

Kline also argues that Adam had a covenant relationship with God from the moment of being created in the image of God. The covenant relationship was not superimposed on a non-covenantal human state that was already in existence. Thus, the divine act of creation was a covenantal act whereby God was Lord of the covenant and Adam and Eve were servants of the covenant.[2] Kline rejects the distinction between Adam in his original created state and Adam in a covenant relationship with God. In this distinction, Adam owed allegiance to God's commands in his natural, created state and then God entered into a covenant relationship with him to set up the probationary test. This view is reflected in WCF 7.1 that mentions the distance between God and mankind being so great that God had to voluntary condescend to Adam in order to enter into a covenant relationship. Kline wants to avoid this distinction because some have used voluntary condescension to import grace back into the covenant relationship between God and Adam.[3] Lee Irons argues that the WCF's overall system of doctrine supports the covenantal nature of creation when it speaks of the eternal moral law reflecting 'the holy nature and will of God' as a Covenant of Works (WCF 19.1-3; WLC 93, 95) and that as image-bearers Adam and Eve had 'the law of God written on their hearts' (WCF 4.2). If the law was written on Adam's heart as a Covenant of Works, then the Covenant of Works cannot be viewed as a voluntary condescension in addition to creation.[4]

---

1. For a negative evaluation of Norman Shepherd's views of justification due to his denial of a Covenant of Works, see Kline, 'Of Works and Grace,' *Presbyterion* 9 (1983): pp. 87-92.

2. *Kingdom Prologue*, pp. 17, 63, 107.

3. Kline was very concerned about this problem as manifested in Norman Shepherd and Daniel Fuller, among others (see Kline, 'Of Works and Grace,' *Presbyterion* 9 (1983): pp. 87-92).

4. Lee Irons, 'Redefining Merit: An Examination of Medieval Presuppositions in Covenant Theology' in *Creator, Redeemer, Consummator: A Festschrift for Meredith G.*

Although one can appreciate the concerns of Kline to correctly define the probationary arrangement between God and Adam in the Covenant of Works, the consequences he fears do not necessarily follow from affirming the voluntary condescension of God (WCF 7.1). First, the WCF itself emphasizes both God's voluntary condescension and that the Covenant of Works promised life to Adam on the basis of his perfect and personal obedience (WCF 7.2). These two things do not have to be seen as contrary to each other. Second, God's voluntary condescension can be defined in such a way as to emphasize God's benevolence apart from redemptive grace.[5]

Third, it is possible to define Adam's natural relationship with God and his covenant relationship as logical and judicial, not temporal. Vos, who accepts this distinction, argues that Adam did not exist for a single moment outside of the Covenant of Works but was created to be under it.[6] It is thus appropriate to argue that human beings are covenant beings.

Finally, one of the consequences of Kline's rejection of voluntary condescension is the way he defines merit.[7] Traditionally, merit has been defined in relationship to ontology (the state of one's being). The great distance between the Creator and the creature meant that Adam in his natural condition could not merit anything before God. It was only through a covenant arrangement established by God whereby God in His benevolent freedom would reward Adam's obedience (called 'covenant' merit).[8] If Adam would fulfill the condition of the covenant, which was perfect and personal obedience, he would merit the reward according to the terms of the covenant. The merit of Christ, who fully satisfies the justice of His Father, is different. For Christ to accomplish this as our Mediator, He must be God (WLC 38), full of the Spirit (WCF 8.3), and perfectly obedient (WCF 8.4 and 8.5). This is called 'strict' merit and is based on the ontological status of Christ.[9]

Kline, eds. Howard Griffith and John R. Muether (Greenville, SC: Reformed Academic Press, 2000), pp. 266-67. He comments that voluntary condescension is incorrect and its removal would not jeopardize the continued vitality of the larger system.

5. See the discussion on the role of grace in the Covenant of Works in Chapter 2.

6. Vos, *Reformed Dogmatics*, pp. 2:31-32.

7. Irons, 'Redefining Merit,' p. 267, makes this connection.

8. Turretin, *Institutes, Volume Two*, p. 712.

9. 'The OPC Report,' pp. 29-30; Andrew M. Elam, Robert C. Van Kooten, and Randall A. Bergquist, *Moses and Merit: A Critique of the Klinean Doctrine of Republication*

Kline argues that merit is a matter of pure and simple justice based on the way merit is defined by the terms of the covenant.[10] This means that both Adam and Christ are governed by the principle of simple justice and equally earn the rewards of their respective covenants.[11] Kline not only uses merit to refer to an innocent Adam before the Fall and a sinless Christ, but he also uses merit in a typological way to refer to the work of human beings who are fallen and sinful, such as Noah and Abraham, whose righteousness points to the righteousness of the Messiah.[12] No doubt Kline would affirm that apart from merit understood in a typological way, sinful human beings are not able to merit anything before God (WLC 193).[13]

The Covenant as Treaty

Kline's work on the structure of the treaty covenants has several implications. In the *Treaty of the Great King* he argues that the treaty structure in Deuteronomy fits the structure of the second millennial Hittite treaties rather than the structure of the seventh century Assyrian treaties. He uses this parallel to support the Mosaic authorship of Deuteronomy against the critical view that Deuteronomy was written in 621 B.C. to support the reforms of Josiah.[14] He also argues that when a treaty is made it produces written documents that are important to define the community's life and obligations. These documents stand as witnesses to what was agreed to by oath. Normally, two covenant documents were produced to be placed in both the suzerain's

---

(Eugene, OR: Wipf & Stock, 2014), pp. 52-56. For a negative review of this book from someone committed to Kline's views, see Charles Lee Irons, 'A Response to *Merit and Moses: A Critique of the Klinean Doctrine of Republication*,' accessed at www.monergism. com/merit-and-moses-response-charges-against-republication-covenant-works; for an appreciative review of the book, with some critical analysis, see Stephen Myers, 'Critiquing the Klinean Doctrine of Republication: A Review Article,' Reformation 21, March 2015.

10. *Kingdom Prologue*, pp. 17, 107, 111, 115.

11. Elam, Van Kooten, and Bergquist, *Merit and Moses*, p. 68.

12. *Kingdom Prologue*, p. 240 (Noah), and p. 325 (Abraham).

13. For further discussion of this issue, see the evaluation of Kline's view of the Mosaic Covenant below.

14. *Treaty of the Great King*, pp. 27-49; see also *The Structure of Biblical Authority*, 2nd ed. (Grand Rapids: Eerdmans, 1972), pp. 131-53.

(conquering king) temple and the vassal's (conquered people) temple.[15] These documents were carefully guarded and periodically read publicly. Curses are offered against those who would change the terms of the covenant (Deut. 4:2). The fact that covenants produce written documents mean that the idea of canon is inherent in the making of covenants. This has implications for the New Covenant.[16]

The Administration of the Covenant

Kline's analysis of the administration of the covenant has implications for the New Testament. The function of the curse in the covenant has consequences not only for the work of Christ, but also for the members of the covenant community and the role of curse in the sacraments of baptism and the Lord's Supper. Kline argues for institutional continuity in the way the covenant is administered in moving from the Old Testament to the New Testament based on the image of the olive tree in Romans 11:16-24. The root of the tree, along with the branches, is holy. This holiness can only refer to a formal state of holiness in relationship to membership in the covenant because some of the holy branches are broken off. Paul earlier states that 'not all who descended from Israel belong to Israel' (Rom. 9:6). In other words, the olive tree not only represents the inward spiritual holiness that is the fruit of election, but also a formal holiness related to being members of the covenant. There is a parallel aspect to baptism and circumcision in relationship to covenant curse. If

---

15. Thus, Kline argued that the two tablets of the law each contained the Ten Commandments rather than half of the law on one tablet and half of the law on the other tablet. Both tablets were placed in the ark of the covenant (Deut. 10:5) as a testimony to what God's people agreed to and as a witness against them if they disobeyed (*Structure of Biblical Authority*, p. 121-25).

16. Michael Kruger has developed these implications for canon in *Canon Revisited: Establishing the Origins and Authority of the New Testament Books* (Wheaton, IL: Crossway, 2012), p. 162-70. There are statements in *The Structure of Biblical Authority* that some may find troubling or confusing. Kline writes that 'the Old Testament is not the canon of the Christian church' (p. 99). He believes that the Old Testament is the Scripture of the Christian church but not the canon of the Christian church because of the close relationship between covenant, canon, and community. He also states, 'the treaty canon that governs the church of the new covenant as a formal community is the New Testament alone, while Scripture is the broader entity consisting of the canonical oracles of God' (p. 100). In whatever way these remarks are understood, they do not take away from the beneficial relationship Kline draws between covenant and canon.

someone who receives circumcision or baptism does not live up to the vow of consecration, the covenant breaker is threatened with ultimate exclusion from the covenant community.[17] Although Kline emphasizes the legal aspect of the covenant, he understands the importance of both a personal relationship and a legal relationship in the covenant.

The Mosaic Covenant

One of the major controversies surrounding Kline's view of the covenant is that the Mosaic Covenant is a republication of the Covenant of Works. The nature of the Mosaic Covenant is a difficult issue that Reformed scholars have understood in a variety of ways, but there are several problems with Kline's formulation of the Mosaic Covenant.

First, he argues that the condition of the Mosaic Covenant is works, and not grace. It is a covenant governed by the legal principle of works, not the principle of grace, so that it differs in kind or substance from the Covenant of Grace. It is thus difficult for Kline to account for passages that stress the gracious substance of this covenant, such as the preface to the Decalogue. The fact that the Mosaic Covenant has a mediator speaks to its redemptive, gracious character. The idea that the Mosaic Covenant is in substance a kind of 'works' covenant, but at the same time an administration of the Covenant of Grace, seems to create a hybrid position that combines elements that are opposed to one another.[18]

Second, Kline places faith and works on two different levels that leads to a bifurcation or separation of the role of faith and works (or grace and law). The legal aspects of the covenant are emphasized which leads to a priority of the principle of works and the second use of the law.[19] It is difficult to talk about the third use of the law when the works principle

---

17. Circumcision symbolized curse on the covenant breaker and referred to cutting off one's descendants, which means that one's name and future place in the covenant community are cut off. It is also an image for the redemptive judgment undergone by Christ. Baptism symbolizes the curse of death in a divine judgment ordeal as seen in the description of the death of Christ in Luke 12:50 as a baptism (*Kingdom Prologue*, pp. 316-17, 361-62 and *By Oath Consigned* [Grand Rapids: Eerdmans, 1968], pp. 45-47, 71; 65-83).

18. 'The OPC Report,' pp. 82-83, 87.

19. Kline defines the covenant as 'primarily a legal disposition, characteristically established by oath and defined by the terms specified in oath-bound, divinely sanctioned commitments' (*Kingdom Prologue*, p. 1).

of the Mosaic Covenant is seen as overlaid on top of the foundational stratum of salvation by grace through faith.[20] The two different stratum of the Mosaic Covenant separates the function of faith and works.

Third, Kline also finds the works principle operative in a typological way in both the Sinai Covenant and the Abrahamic Covenant. In the Sinai Covenant the personal attainment of salvation is continuous with the Covenant of Grace on the foundational level.[21] The principle of works, on the other hand, operates on a different, secondary level that is laid over the top of the foundational level. In the national election of Israel, the nation's enjoyment of the theocratic kingdom was based on her national faithfulness to the Lord. She would experience the blessings or the curses of the covenant based on her obedience according to the do-and-live principle of inheritance in Leviticus 18:5. Two radically opposed principles of inheritance operate at different levels of Israel's life, works in the case of the temporal blessings and faith in the case of spiritual salvation. This creates tension in the life of an Israelite believer because obedience according to these two principles arise from completely opposite mindsets. The mindset of grace is characterized by unworthiness and gratitude, but the mindset of works is characterized by demanding just payment for work performed.[22]

Fourth, in the Abrahamic Covenant the requirement of human obedience is not the meritorious basis for obtaining the blessing of the covenant because that is found in the obedience of Christ. Abraham was justified by faith, not by works. Human obedience is the result of grace and is a confirmatory witness of the presence of genuine faith.[23] And, yet,

---

20. The question is, if the Mosaic Covenant is substantially a Covenant of Works, how can it function as a rule of life for those in the Covenant of Grace? This seems to weaken the third use of the law ('The OPC Report,' p. 88). The New Testament, on the other hand, treats the same law as either second or third use (Cara, *Cracking the Foundation*, pp. 49-51; 'The Use of the Old Testament in the New: Trusting the New Testament's Hermeneutic,' in *A Biblical-Theological Introduction to the New Testament*, ed. Michael J. Kruger [Wheaton, IL: Crossway, 2016], p. 595, n. 8). He gives examples of how the New Testament can use one of the Ten Commandments for first, second, or third uses of the law.

21. *Kingdom Prologue*, p. 320.

22. Elam, Van Kooten, and Bergquist, *Merit and Moses*, p. 142. They use the term 'spiritual schizophrenia' to describe the Old Testament Israelite.

23. *Kingdom Prologue*, pp. 319-20. The obedience Kline talks about is in line with the meaning of the third use of the law, but he does not use this phrase in this passage.

Kline also sees Abraham's obedience as the meritorious ground for Israel inheriting the land of Canaan (based on the description of Abraham in Genesis 26:5 as a law keeper). Abraham's works were accorded by God a value analogous to the typological stage represented by the Mosaic Covenant. In this way the principle of grace is incorporated into the Mosaic Covenant in relationship to Israel's inheritance of the land. In other words, Israel is not required to fulfill the condition of perfect obedience to keep the land.[24] But, wouldn't an imperfect obedience weaken the requirements connected to the second use of the law? Obedience under the Covenant of Grace operates differently because sinners are unable to merit anything from God (either eternal life, the forgiveness of sins, or the temporal blessings of life).[25] Salvation is by grace through faith (justification) that leads to a life of obedience (sanctification) where the law is the rule of life given to believers to show them how God wants them to live (third use).[26] It is clear that the Covenant of Works cannot be renewed with the sinner and that the requirement of faith for the Covenant of Grace separates it from the Covenant of Works.

Fifth, there are problems with understanding the meritorious obedience of works as typological. The Westminster Standards do not talk about the works principle in a typological way.[27] It is difficult to see how Israel's imperfect obedience can ever be a type of Christ's perfect obedience. For a type to work, there must be a degree of correspondence between the type and the reality, but there are absolute differences between the obedience of Israel and the obedience of Christ. Also, if the

---

24. On this basis some argue that Kline's view is not a substantial republication view but an administrative republication view ('The OPC Report,' pp. 54-73).

25. Kline's use of merit to refer to sinners is difficult because the WCF uses merit to refer to the work of Christ (pp. 17.2; 19.1-2), and not to the work of sinners (p. 16.5), who are unable to merit anything ('The OPC Report,' p. 81).

26. 'The OPC Report,' p. 80. The strong contrast between the way works operate in the Covenant of Works and the Covenant of Grace argues against a substantial republication view. It is not clear that the typological use of meritorious obedience that comes into the Mosaic Covenant through Abraham salvages an administrative republication view of Kline.

27. 'The OPC Report,' p. 88-89. This report also states that the WCF is very modest in its use of typology and that it sticks to well-established types, most of them confirmed by the New Testament (p. 29). This is not to deny that there might be types that the New Testament does not explicitly identify as types.

land is typological of heaven, and the way to receive blessing in the land is through Israel's works, how does that teach that the way to heavenly, eternal blessing is by grace through faith?[28] The promises and demands of the Mosaic economy are typical of the promises and demands of the New Covenant (WCF 19.5-6) and are received by grace through faith.[29]

Sixth, Kline's view of the typological, theocratic kingdom under the Mosaic Covenant refers primarily to the consummation and makes it difficult to see the blessings and curses of the covenant as having relevance to believers today. He argues that the typological, theocratic kingdom under Moses looks both backward and forward. It looks backward to the pre-fall sanctuary in Eden so that Israel's situation in the land parallels Adam's situation in the garden. Israel can continue in her inheritance of the land by obedience to the law. The kingdom blessings on this typological level were not guaranteed by sovereign grace on the basis of Christ's meritorious accomplishments. Israel's disobedience led to the loss of the typological kingdom through exile and the loss of their identity as God's people in the corporate, typological sense. Israel's retention of blessing was governed by a principle of works on a national scale.[30] Such parallels between Adam and Israel is part of the reason that the Mosaic Covenant is seen as a republication of the Covenant of Works. But the Mosaic Covenant also looks forward as a preview to the heavenly eschatological kingdom of the new heavens and earth. The kingdom under the Old Covenant is a type of the coming eternal kingdom pointing to cosmic eschatological restoration and redemptive blessings.[31] The first level fulfillment of the land promise is the taking of the land of Canaan by the Israelites and the second level of fulfillment, looking forward to the consummation, is the way the New Testament understands the land promise.[32] Such a scenario makes it difficult to see the blessings and curses of the Mosaic Covenant having any meaning for God's people today, other than pointing toward the

28. Elam, Van Kooten, and Bergquist, *Merit and Moses*, p. 130.

29. Venema, *Covenant Theology*, pp. 128-29 and O. Palmer Robertson, *The Christ of the Prophets* (Phillipsburg, NJ: P&R Publishing, 2004), pp. 264-365, n. 6.

30. *Kingdom Prologue*, pp. 322-23.

31. Jeon, *Covenant Theology*, pp. 235-37.

32. *Kingdom Prologue*, pp. 398-99.

blessings and judgments of the consummation. This seems to weaken the third use of the law because the law as the meritorious ground for keeping the land cannot be applied to New Testament believers. And, yet, the WCF 19.6 sees that the blessings and curses of the covenant have great benefit for the church, informing them of the will of God and their duty, the threatenings that their sin deserves, the afflictions they may experience in life apart from the curse of the law, and the blessings they may experience in faithful obedience, although not being under the law as a Covenant of Works. The continuing obligation to keep the law is recognized in WCF 19.6 in the Scripture proofs that refer to the curse that falls on anyone who fails to keep it (Gal. 3:13, 24; 4:4-5). The relevance of the blessings of the covenant in relationship to obedience, even for believers today, is seen in the reference to Leviticus 26:1-14. Believers experience temporal afflictions and blessings now, but they look forward to a day when there will be no curse and the blessings will be experienced in their fullness at the consummation.

Common Grace Covenants and Two Kingdoms

Kline distinguishes between redemptive and common grace covenants in Genesis 3 and Genesis 6–9. The common grace covenants focus on the common benefits shared by the godly and the ungodly. Kline views the common political and institutional aspects of the common grace culture as being secular, not holy. The coexistence of the holy and common is what characterizes the present world. The partial presence of the holy, eternal reality is antithetical to the common grace order and is an eschatological intrusion into this order. There are several implications of this view. Although the idea that there are two kingdoms at work in the world that operate differently is not unusual,[33] Kline's view that the common grace kingdom is secular, not holy, leads to a particular version of the two-kingdom view. The common grace covenants do not operate under the authority and obligation of the revealed will of God in Scripture but under the authority and obligation of natural law. The

---

33. See *Kingdoms Apart: Engaging the Two Kingdoms Perspective*, ed. Ryan C. McIlhenny (Phillipsburg, NJ: P&R Publishing, 2012). Although this book is negative toward the two-kingdom view of VanDrunen, it discusses other views of the two-kingdoms.

development of Kline's views has been taken up by David VanDrunen who has written extensively on this issue.[34]

VanDrunen defines natural law as the content of God's moral law made known to every human being through natural revelation that is engraved on their hearts as God's image bearers and is perceived through the judgments of conscience. It has the negative function of condemning people because of their sin, thus showing them their need of a Savior. It has the positive function of being the standard for the development of civil law in the common grace kingdom. He also argues that the natural law imparts both the moral will of God and the consequences that come from doing that will. In other words, the natural law makes clear that obedience leads to blessing and disobedience leads to curse.[35] Thus, when God gave to Adam the probationary command in Genesis 2:17, threatening death for disobedience, He was not giving to Adam any new information but was focusing on what he already knew by nature.[36] The fact that natural law discloses not only the obligation but also the penalties and rewards of the moral law leads to the conclusions that natural law proclaims the same works principle that is embedded in the Mosaic Covenant and that the natural law and the moral law express identical moral

---

34. David VanDrunen, *A Biblical Case for Natural Law* (Grand Rapids: Acton Institute, 2006); 'Natural Law and the Works Principle under Adam and Moses' in *The Law is Not of Faith*, pp. 283-314; *Natural Law and the Two Kingdoms: A Study of the Development of Reformed Social Thought* (Grand Rapids: Eerdmans, 2010); *Living in God's Two Kingdoms: A Biblical Vision for Christianity and Culture* (Wheaton, IL: Crossway, 2010); and *Divine Covenants and Moral Order: A Biblical Theology of Natural Law* (Grand Rapids: Eerdmans, 2014). He wants to clarify the relationship between Christianity and culture and offers a 'biblical corrective' against the following views: God is redeeming all legitimate cultural activities, Christians can build the kingdom of God through the transformation of culture, and redemption will lead to the transformation of culture. The two-kingdom view argues that God preserves the common kingdom of honorable but temporary institutions through the Noahic Covenant. Believers are called to live in two kingdoms, but the heart and life of the church is in the redemptive kingdom, a culture distinct from the world whose authority, unlike the institutions in the common kingdom, derives from Scripture alone (*Living in God's Two Kingdoms*, pp. 25-31, 78-81). He argues against the transformation of culture as represented by Dooyeweerd, Wolters, Plantinga, and their followers, who are called neo-Calvinists.

35. VanDrunen, 'Natural Law and the Works Principle', pp. 284-86.

36. Ibid., p. 291, n. 17.

conduct.[37] In this way the works principle of the Covenant of Works is republished in the Mosaic Covenant to expose Israel's sinful inability to procure life on the basis of obedience to God's law, which is the basic predicament of all humanity.[38]

Although VanDrunen recognizes that there are limits to natural law, he gives natural law a major role in the common grace kingdom and in the Mosaic Covenant. He argues that the natural law is the standard for the development of civil law by appealing to the similarities between the ancient Near Eastern laws and the laws of the Mosaic Covenant, including specific collections of laws, the way judicial disputes were resolved, and the variations of the *lex talionis* principle (eye for an eye, tooth for a tooth).[39] Although the Mosaic law was divine revelation and a protological moral standard,[40] the civil laws of other nations were in a certain sense 'a model for the Mosaic civil law' because many of the ancient Near Eastern law codes came into existence prior to the time of Moses. Both were based on natural law.[41] The role of natural law is key to the works principle in the Covenant of Works and the Mosaic Covenant and it functions as the basis of civil law in the common grace kingdom and the kingdom under Moses. This view of the natural law gives it a major role in redemptive history which leads to several problems.

First, the little we know of natural law is revealed in Scripture. VanDrunen bases his discussions of natural law in extensive expositions of the pertinent chapters in Genesis related to creation (Gen. 1–2) and the Noahic Covenant (Gen. 6-9), as well as in Paul's discussion in Romans 1–2.[42] He gives so much attention to natural law that it seems

---

37. Ibid., p. 302. According to VanDrunen, for Paul's argument in Romans 2:12-13 to stand, natural law must be substantially identical to the Mosaic law (p. 304).

38. Ibid., p. 309.

39. Ibid., pp. 303-07.

40. Protological means that the Mosaic law was designed for people living in the present, nonconsummated creation who are under a state of probation, and so will be judged on the basis of their obedience or disobedience to the law (*Divine Covenants*, p. 283).

41. VanDrunen comments that it is not demeaning to God to make Him a copycat of pagan nations because it was God Himself who wrote the natural law on human hearts and preserved their significant resemblances to and commonality with the sea of humanity around Israel ('Natural Law and the Works Principle,' p. 308).

42. VanDrunen, *Divine Covenants*, has extensive discussions of each of the covenants in Scripture and how natural law relates to them.

to take precedence over special revelation. Natural law is foundational to the moral law in the Covenant of Works, as well as to the civil laws of the Mosaic and common grace kingdoms. Without special revelation, however, we would not really know very much about natural law and how it functions. If natural law has a role to play in redemptive history, it must be subordinate to special revelation. Natural law is not meant to function in isolation from special revelation, but functions together with it from creation to the consummation. This is true even before the Fall because there was non-redemptive special revelation in the pre-fall situation.[43] Just as natural law was not meant to function apart from special revelation, so common grace is not meant to function on its own but to further the interests of special grace.[44]

A second difficulty is that natural law is the governing principle for unbelievers and believers in the common grace kingdom. Although Christ rules over the common kingdom through the Noahic Covenant, natural law seems to make Scripture irrelevant to the secular sphere of the common order. VanDrunen writes:

> Why should Christians, even Protestant Christians, deem natural law to be an important issue? Perhaps chiefly, they should do so because Scripture itself teaches that *all* human beings, made in God's image and situated within a broader created order, know their basic moral obligations before God and their accountability to him as their ruler and judge. And because these obligations are universal, Scripture also presents them as foundational for *Christians'* understanding of their moral responsibilities, both as citizens of the broader civil societies and as members of the church of Jesus Christ (emphasis original).[45]

The common grace kingdom has its own existence separate from special revelation and, in this kingdom, unbelievers can fulfill God's

---

43.   Jeffrey C. Waddington, '*Duplex in Homine Regimen*. A Response to David VanDrunen's "The Reformed Two Kingdoms Doctrine: An Explanation and a Defense",' *The Confessional Presbyterian* 8 (2012), p. 192; he references Vos, *Biblical Theology*, pp. 28-36 and Cornelius Van Til, 'Nature and Scripture,' in *The Infallible Word*, ed. N. B. Stonehouse and Paul Wooley (Phillipsburg: P&R Publishing, 1967), pp. 263-301.

44.   Waddington, 'Response to VanDrunen,' 193. He comments that the reason for common grace is for the calling out of the elect in time and space throughout history until the consummation (p. 194).

45.   VanDrunen, *Divine Covenants*, p. 3.

will related to politics and culture with respect to penultimate ends. In other words, in the redemptive kingdom, believers fulfill God's will as it relates to the ultimate, or final, end of eternal life; and in the common grace kingdom, unbelievers fulfill God's will related to secondary purposes of God focused on living life in this world.[46] This approach separates the activities of unbelievers in the common grace kingdom from the religious bent of all human beings either toward God or away from God. It is impossible to be social or political without being oriented by the worship of something ultimate. Modern politics tells 'a pseudo-soteriological' tale in which the liberal state is the answer to all of life's problems.[47] Confidence in what fallen humanity can accomplish is misguided. Even though the ethic of the moral law and the natural law are the same, it is not evident in Scripture that natural law is perceived clearly enough to build upon it a full-fledged ethic for the common kingdom.[48] Although as unbelievers interact with God's created order they are able to understand how the world operates to some degree (common grace insights), they are limited in their understanding without special revelation.[49] The knowledge that

---

46. VanDrunen, *Natural Law and the Two Kingdoms*, pp. 305-06, 367-70. See also VanDrunen, 'The Importance of the Penultimate: Reformed Social Thought and the Contemporary Critiques of the Liberal Society,' *Journal of Markets and Morality* 9/2 (Fall 2006), pp. 219-49, which offers a tempered and indirect theological defense of liberalism in the common grace kingdom.

47. Branson Parler, 'Two Cities or Two Kingdoms? The Importance of the Ultimate in Reformed Social Thought,' in *Kingdoms Apart: Engaging the Two Kingdoms Perspective*, ed. Ryan C. McIlhenny (Phillipsburg, NJ: P&R, 2012), pp. 176-86. Parler speaks about the doxological nature of politics which tends to become god-like in nature 'as the one by whom, through whom, and in whom all things hold together'.

48. VanDrunen acknowledges that the natural order does not provide comprehensive knowledge of human behavior (*Divine Covenants*, p. 392), but he emphasizes what can be understood through natural law, as when he says that the book of Proverbs grounds the moral life in the natural order created by God (p. 375) and presents wisdom as gained primarily through natural revelation (p. 399).

49. Even the best examples of societal ethics apart from God's revelation fall very short of God's standards for the institutions of society. The different values expressed in the ANE laws as compared to the Mosaic law are fundamental and show the superiority of biblical law. For a discussion of creation order, common grace insights, and the necessity of special revelation, see Belcher, *Finding Favour with God: A Theology of Wisdom Literature* (NSBT; Downers Grove, IL: IVP Academic, 2018), pp. 55-67.

unbelievers have of God is a suppressed and distorted knowledge. They have taken the knowledge of God and exchanged it for idolatry (Rom. 1:18-23). Unbelievers will always misuse the knowledge they have for their own benefit.[50]

Finally, the common grace covenants represent the normal way that the world operates day-by-day according to the customary application of the law. It allows for a delay of judgment so history can move forward toward consummation where there will be eschatological blessing and judgment. But sometimes the ethics of eschatological judgment, called the ethics of consummation, intrude into this age and suspend the normal way that the common grace covenants operate. Intrusions include both matters of judgment and salvation. Intrusions of salvation include the relationship of Israel's theocracy to the nations, the sacrifice of Isaac, and the marriage of Hosea. Intrusions of judgment include the curses of the Psalms, the conquest of Canaan, and instances of deception toward civil authority (Rahab's lie, the midwives' deception of Pharaoh, and Samuel's not giving the whole truth to Saul when going to anoint David). Kline argues that the common grace order operates in a way that is mutually exclusive and antithetical to the principles of consummation. For example, the holy war that Israel waged is not like normal war because it ends in the complete destruction of the enemy, which is a suspension of the 'love your neighbor' commandment. The extermination of the Canaanites is a type of the judgment of consummation.[51] It is helpful to see this event as a type of eschatological judgment, but does that limit its focus solely to the consummation? In other words, do such events have anything to say to the church today? In places where Kline discusses intrusion ethics and mentions the destruction of the Canaanites, he does not discuss any New Testament implications for how God's people today wage holy war (Eph. 6:10-20).

---

50. Calvin discusses the impact of sin for human knowledge and for natural law in the *Institutes of the Christian Religion*, ed. John T. McNeill (Philadelphia: Westminster Press, 1960), pp. 2.1.3; 2.1.8; 2.2.22-24. For a general analysis of the two-kingdom view, see *Kingdoms Apart*, including the article by Gene Haas, 'Calvin, Natural Law, and the Two Kingdoms,' *Kingdoms Apart*, pp. 33-64.

51. Kline, 'The Intrusion and the Decalogue,' *WTJ* 16 (1953/54): pp. 2-3, 13-22. This article is virtually reproduced in *The Structure of Biblical Authority*, pp. 154-71, although it is shorter than the original article.

Admittedly, this is an argument from silence and there may be places where Kline makes this connection,[52] but intrusion ethics are limited to the consummation and are not meant for the church today. One implication of this view is that the imprecatory psalms cannot be used by the church today to sing about or pray for serious instances of injustice and persecution of God's people.[53] The pattern of conduct in these psalms reflects the ethics of consummation and not the ethics of common grace. Concerning the instances of deception of civil authorities, Kline offers no guidance on what a Christian should do if confronted by a civil authority who wants information that will lead to the death of other believers. In fact, he states that Rahab owed obedience to the civil authorities of Jericho and so it was her duty to give them the information they requested.[54] Is it not possible for civil authorities to forfeit the right of information in the common grace order? Intrusion ethics tends to leave the church without guidance in certain difficult areas of ethical decisions related to the common grace order.

Conclusion: A Comparison of Murray and Kline

It is not uncommon for Murray and Kline to be set over against one another as representing different approaches to covenant theology. Of course, they disagree on a number of things and approach covenant theology from different perspectives. It is helpful to recognize the differences between them, but it is also necessary to affirm where they agree.

The differences between Murray and Kline are many. Kline affirms the existence of a Covenant of Works between God and Adam. Although Murray denies such a covenant, he recognizes the basic elements of that

---

52. Kline does mention the variableness of the sanctions of the covenant so that a covenant member in the New Testament dispensation is subject to ecclesiastical discipline and not the sword ('Intrusion and the Decalogue', p. 9).

53. Elmer Smick, 'The Psalms as Response to God's Covenant Love: Theological Observations' in *Creator, Redeemer, Consummator: A Festschrift for Meredith G. Kline*, eds. Howard Griffith and John R. Muether (Greenville, SC: Reformed Academic Press, 2000), pp. 77-86. For the argument that the imprecatory psalms can be used by God's people today, see James Adams, *War Psalms of the Prince of Peace: Lessons from the Imprecatory Psalms*, 2nd ed. (Phillipsburg, NJ: P&R, 2016), John N. Day, *Crying for Justice* (Grand Rapids: Kregel, 2005), and Belcher, *Messiah and the Psalms*, pp. 76-83.

54. 'Intrusion and the Decalogue,' p. 16; *Structure of Biblical Authority*, p. 164.

covenant in his explanation of the Adamic Administration. Kline wants to be sure that redemptive grace is not brought into the relationship between God and Adam before the Fall. Murray sees the relationship between God and Adam before the Fall as based on God's grace. Kline pushes for discontinuity between the nature of the covenants with some covenants emphasizing grace and some covenants, like the Mosaic Covenant, emphasizing works as a way to attain the blessings of the covenant (on a typological level). He highlights the distinctive nature of each covenant and understands the role that covenant curse plays in the covenants. Murray stresses the continuity of the covenants in the unfolding Covenant of Grace and defines each covenant as a sovereign administration of grace and promise. He has little discussion of the continuing validity of the requirement of the law as expressed in the Covenant of Works. Kline emphasizes the legal aspect of the covenant so that he emphasizes the second use of the law with little discussion of the third use of the law. Murray emphasizes the relationship established by the covenant, expressed in the idea, 'I will be your God and you will be my people,' so that he emphasizes the third use of the law.

Kline and Murray agree on justification by faith apart from the works of the law, the necessity of the obedience of Christ to fulfill the law for us, and the imputation of the righteousness of Christ to those who believe in Him. This agreement is very significant and should not be overlooked in light of the discussion today concerning justification by faith. Kline and Murray could be brought even closer together with the recognition that any law in the Old Testament can function as either second or third use. A bifurcation between the second use and the third use is unnecessary. These two uses are very different, but the second use shows us our failure to keep the law, that we are condemned by it, and we need someone to undergo it's curse. The second use of the law drives us to Christ, whereby we are justified by faith. The law then functions as a rule of life for believers in Christ (third use). Without denying the differences between Murray and Kline, we can celebrate the fact that they both affirm that the basis of our salvation is the work of Christ.

CHAPTER 12

Confessional Baptists

Introduction

UNKNOWN to many Baptists, they have a confessional heritage that goes back to the seventeenth century expressed in the Second London Confession of 1689 (hereafter 2LCF).[1] This confession became the standard for Baptists in Colonial America, and recently it has gained greater attention among Baptists in the United States and around the world as more churches identify the 2LCF as their confessional standard.[2]

Renihan writes about the historical background of both the First London Confession of 1646 (1LCF) and the 2LCF of 1689. The 2LCF became the standard of Calvinistic Baptist orthodoxy. It was largely dependent on statements of earlier Reformed Confessions, especially

---

1. For a brief history of Baptists and covenant theology, see Ken Fryer, 'Covenant Theology in Baptist Life,' in *Covenant Theology: A Baptist Distinctive*, ed. Earl M. Blackburn (Birmingham, AL: Solid Ground Christian Books, 2013, pp. 145-59). The demise of Baptist covenant theology has been related to the revival movement with new forms of evangelism that led people to turn from a thoughtful and theological faith to an experience-oriented belief and the rise of the popularity of Dispensationalism (James M. Renihan, 'Introduction', in *Recovering a Covenantal Heritage: Essays in Baptist Covenant Theology*, ed. Richard C. Barcellos [Palmdale, CA: RBAP, 2014], pp. 14-16).

2. These statements come from the Series Preface of *Recovering our Confessional Heritage* in the book by Richard C. Barcellos, *The Covenant of Works: Its Confessional and Scriptural Basis* (Palmdale, CA: Reformed Baptist Academic Press, 2016), pp. 1-2.

the WCF, except it was closer to the revision of the WCF in the Savoy Declaration concerning church polity.[3] The Particular Baptists were confident in their doctrinal distinctives but also wanted to establish their legitimacy among Presbyterians and Independents in order to distance themselves from the Arminians and Anabaptists.[4] There are different emphases in the 2LCF in comparison to the WCF, particularly its framing of covenant theology in a more historical cast. This may explain why the phrase 'Covenant of Works' does not occur early in chapters 6 and 7 of the 2LCF. These chapters are forward looking and positive in their development of the plan of salvation.[5]

Particular Baptists distinguished themselves from paedobaptists in the way they defined the covenant of grace.[6] The 2LCF discusses 'God's Covenant' in Chapter 7. It is called the Covenant of Grace in 7.2 and is described in 7.3 in the following way:

> This covenant is revealed in the gospel; first of all to Adam in the promise of salvation to the seed of the woman, and afterwards by further steps, until

---

3. The Savoy Declaration is also much closer to the WCF in its statement on covenant theology than the 2LCF (compare Chapter 7 in each confession); for historical background to the Declaration and easy to see comparisons with the WCF, see *The Savoy Declaration of Faith and Order 1658*, ed. A. G. Matthews (London: Independent Press, 1959). Another resource is Philip Schaff, *The Creeds of Christendom*, Volume 3: *The Evangelical Protestant Creeds* (Grand Rapids: Baker Books, 1996), pp. 707-29.

4. Samuel D. Renihan, *From Shadow to Substance: The Federal Theology of the English Particular Baptists (1642-1704)* (Oxford: Regent's Park College, 2018), p. 14. This work seeks to fill in the gaps in the present research in Baptist covenant theology by conducting a study of the primary sources of the covenant theology of the Particular Baptists between 1642 and 1704. He shows how the law/gospel distinction was foundational to both Reformed covenant theology and Particular Baptist covenant theology (pp. 66-67).

5. J. Renihan, 'Covenant Theology in the First and Second London Confessions of Faith', in *Recovering a Covenantal Heritage*, pp. 45-70. S. Renihan shows on the basis of the historical context that the 2LCF was not a polemical document seeking to distance Baptists from Presbyterians and Independents but was a declaration of agreement on the fundamentals of the faith (*From Shadow to Substance*, p. 181).

6. This author writes with fondness for his Baptist friends as my father, Richard P. Belcher, Sr., was a Southern Baptist pastor who had a 'conversion' to Calvinism (see *Journey in Grace* [Columbia SC: Richbarry Press, 1990] and then taught for almost thirty years at Columbia International University, Columbia, SC. He was involved in the Founders Movement and had a small part in bringing the doctrines of grace to many students and churches throughout his life.

the full discovery thereof was completed in the New Testament ... and it is alone by the grace of this covenant that all the posterity of fallen Adam that ever were saved did obtain life and blessed immorality....[7]

S. Renihan argues that from a dogmatic standpoint the Particular Baptists[8] had no disagreement with the term Covenant of Grace as the covenant through which the elect obtained salvation, but they used the underlying dogmatic unity of the covenant to argue against the idea that it included the non-elect. They avoided putting the Covenant of Grace into two historical administrations and rejected the idea that the Old Covenant was the Covenant of Grace in a different form. They also rejected the terminology of 'different administrations but one substance', even though the Covenant of Grace was appropriated by the elect through the Old Testament and its ordinances. Renihan summarizes their approach in this way:

In the Confession, by expressing the doctrine of the covenant of grace with direct reference to the gospel, a dogmatic move, and by expressing the continuity of salvation by this covenant in history, a historical move, the Particular Baptists avoided the standard paedobaptist model of covenant theology, but expressed the same core beliefs.[9]

Thus, although the 2LCF 7.3 reflects their model of the Covenant of Grace, this chapter of the confession was written broadly. They wanted to avoid unnecessarily distancing themselves from Presbyterian and Congregational allies, but they also wanted to allow varying thoughts on the subject that existed among Baptists.[10] The result is that there are different ways that the unity of the Covenant of Grace is discussed among Confessional Baptists today, particularly the character of the Abrahamic and Mosaic Covenants. One approach is much closer to the WCF in its formulation of covenant theology even though it differs in its

---

7. Samuel E. Waldron, *A Modern Exposition of the 1689 Baptist Confession of Faith* (Darlington, Evangelical Press, 1989), p. 105.

8. Particular Baptists are defined as those who dissented from the more prevalent views of paedobaptism (infant baptism) and the nature of the church by an appeal to covenant theology in books, pamphlets, and confessions of faith (S. Renihan, *From Shadow to Substance*, p. 1).

9. S. Renihan, *From Shadow to Substance*, p. 189.

10. Ibid., p. 190.

view of ecclesiology and baptism. The second approach is different than the WCF in the explanation of the nature of the covenants, particularly the Abrahamic and Mosaic Covenants. Each approach will be described, focusing on their distinctive emphases.

Confessional Reformed Baptist Covenant Theology[11]

The Covenantal Structure of Scripture

Covenant theology among Baptists has had three basic divisions that are foundational for the outworking of God's salvation in redemptive history. The Covenant of Redemption is specifically mentioned in the 2LCF, 'The salvation of the elect is based upon a covenant of redemption that was transacted in eternity between the Father and the Son' (7.3; see also 8.1). This covenant is called by Blackburn 'the chief and greatest of all covenants'.[12] It is the basis for the historical manifestation of the work of Christ through His life and ministry whereby He accomplishes redemption. The Covenant of Redemption shows that salvation is carefully planned by the triune God to save undeserving sinners.[13] The other two covenants in Scripture are the Covenant of Works and the Covenant of Grace. These two covenants are very different in how they operate. In the Covenant of Works, Adam must do what he is commanded in order to continue in a state of blessedness. In the Covenant of Grace, a sinful human being receives the blessing of life and communion with God on the basis of what God does for him. As Walt Chantry writes:

> In the entirety of Scripture there are only two divinely instituted arrangements by which man could be blessed: The Covenant of Works for sinless man and the Covenant of Grace for fallen man.[14]

---

11. The names used to describe each approach are very general and could apply to either approach, but some name had to be used to distinguish them. This approach is closer to the WCF in its discussion of the nature of the Abrahamic and Mosaic Covenants.

12. Blackburn, 'Covenant Theology Simplified,' in *Covenant Theology: A Baptist Distinctive*, 25. He briefly lays out the evidence for this covenant (pp. 26-30).

13. Blackburn, 'Covenant Theology Simplified,' p. 30. In the 2LCF 7.3 the Covenant of Grace is founded on the Covenant of Redemption. This closely connected the historical application of salvation of the Covenant of Grace to the decree of salvation in the Covenant of Redemption (S. Renihan, *From Shadow to Substance*, p. 192).

14. Walter J. Chantry, 'The Covenants of Works and of Grace,' in *Covenant Theology: A Baptist Distinctive*, pp. 91-93, with the quote on p. 93.

This view clearly expresses a bi-covenantal framework for Scripture with recognition of the ongoing obligations of the Covenant of Works that must be fulfilled by the obedience of Christ for sinners to be saved by grace through faith in Christ. There are two covenants with two representatives whose actions are imputed to all who were united to each representative.[15]

The Covenant of Works

Chapter 6 on the covenant in 2LCF is much shorter than Chapter 7 in the WCF. Both chapters begin with God's voluntary condension in order for Him to enter into a covenant with Adam, apart from which he could never have attained life as a reward from God.[16] The WCF immediately mentions the Covenant of Works, which is not explicitly mentioned in the 2LCF until 19:6, in reference to the Law of God, and in 20:1, where the breaking of the Covenant of Works meant that it was unable to confer life. There is no doubt that the 2LCF affirms the Covenant of Works as a way for Adam and his descendants to attain life if Adam had obeyed.[17]

---

15. Walter J. Chantry, 'Imputation of Righteousness & Covenant Theology (An overview of Romans 5:12-21),' in *Covenant Theology: A Baptist Distinctive*, p. 119.

16. For a paragraph-by-paragraph comparison of the 2LCF and the WCF, see Waldron, *The 1689 Baptist Confession of Faith*, pp. 111-12. Both confessions find the need for the divine covenant in the Creator/creature distinction. Nehemiah Coxe writes, '... none can oblige God or make him their debtor until he condescends to oblige himself by covenant or promise' ('A Discourse of the Covenants that God Made with men before the Law,' in *Covenant Theology: From Adam to Christ*, ed. James M. Renihan [Palmdale, CA: Reformed Baptist Academic Press, 2005], p. 36).

17. Greg Nichols states that he cannot explain why the 2LCF left the phrase 'Covenant of Works' in Chapter 20 but omitted it from Chapters 7 and 19:1, but it seems mysterious and inconsistent to him (*Covenant Theology: A Reformed and Baptistic Perspective on God's Covenants* [Birmingham, AL: Solid Ground Christian Books, 2011], p. 8). In an Appendix where he discusses the Adamic covenant, he says that these omissions express distance from the WCF. Although the 2LCF affirms a Covenant of Works, it does not have the same prominence in the 2LCF as in the WCF (p. 325). He goes on to give a full exposition of the Adamic covenant, both from a confessional standpoint and a Scriptural standpoint. S. Renihan argues that it was redundant for the Particular Baptists to copy the WCF in every regard when the basic elements of the Covenant of Works was taught in the 2LCF, including the federal headship of Adam, the promise of life, and the threat of death (*From Shadow to Substance*, pp. 183-85). See also Barcellos, *Getting the Garden Right: Adam's Work and God's Rest in Light of Christ* (Cape Coral, FL: Founders Press, 2017), pp. 38-52.

Before sin entered the world Adam lived a blessed life that included communion with God and intimate, personal fellowship with his Maker.[18] This relationship was not cold but warm and loving. Adam is tested by God during a period of probation when God gives him a negative commandment related to the tree of knowledge of good and evil. His obedience impacts not only himself, but also his descendants because he is their representative. The warning of death for disobedience implies that there would be a reward of eternal life for obedience.[19] Barcellos affirms that the reward of life for obedience was not the life Adam possessed in the garden. He argues this on the parallels between Adam and Christ and that Adam sinned and fell short of the glory of God. What Adam failed to do, the last Adam accomplished by His death, burial, resurrection, and then He entered into glory.[20]

The arrangements of the Covenant of Works are in force today because the curse of sin still impacts the world and the obligations of personal and perpetual obedience still need to be met. It is impossible for sinful human beings to meet the righteous requirements of the Covenant of Works. The descendants of Adam have inherited his sin by imputation, but they also commit their own sins; therefore they stand condemned. The second Adam has fulfilled the requirements of the Covenant of Works so that His righteousness can be imputed to those whom He represents (Rom. 5:12-21), who are saved by faith in His work.[21]

The Covenant of Grace

Once sin entered into the world, 'the terms of blessing which applied to Adam in his state of innocencey have no application to his posterity

---

18. Chantry, 'Covenants of Works and of Grace,' p. 90.

19. Justin Taylor gives good arguments for a limited probationary period over against a perpetual probationary period. The latter does not fit well with Adam's representative role, and the parallels between Adam and Christ suggests a limited probationary period ('Was There a Covenant of Works?' in *Covenant Theology: A Baptist Distinctive*, pp. 138-39).

20. Barcellos, *Getting the Garden Right*, pp. 48, 76.

21. Blackburn, 'Covenant Theology Simplified,' p. 33; Chantry, 'Covenants of Works and of Grace,' p. 103; and Chantry, 'The Imputation of Righteousness & Covenant Theology,' p. 119.

to render them acceptable to God' (2LCF 7:3).[22] When Adam became a covenant breaker, a different basis was needed for him and his descendants to relate to God, commonly called the Covenant of Grace, whereby God offers to sinners salvation by Jesus Christ (2LCF 7.2). When the Covenant of Works was broken, the promises of the Covenant of Grace are announced in Genesis 3:15, the first gospel proclamation, even before the curses of the first covenant are applied in Genesis 3:19. Adam responds in faith by naming his wife Eve, the mother of all living (Gen. 3:20).[23] There is one Covenant of Grace but there are different methods of administering it, culminating in the New Covenant. There is both unity and diversity in the outworking of the covenants which are coequal and codependent upon each other.[24] Thus, each of the covenants in the Covenant of Grace is subservient to the first manifestation of it (Gen. 3:15) and they build upon it (the Noahic, Abrahamic, Mosaic, and Davidic Covenants), culminating in the New Covenant. The several administrations of the covenants in the one Covenant of Grace is to reveal the knowledge of God in Christ and to reveal God's plan to bring forth the seed of the woman through the line of Abraham and David to be the only mediator between God and man.[25]

The Noahic Covenant is a part of the Covenant of Grace which progressively reveals God's overall plan. It was necessary to ensure that the seed of the woman would come for redemption.[26] The Abrahamic Covenant should not be identified with *the* Covenant of Grace because

---

22. *A Faith to Confess: The Baptist Confession of Faith of 1689* (Sussex: Carey Publications, 1975).

23. Chantry, 'Covenants of Works and of Grace,' p. 90. Although Nichols sees the Covenant of Grace in Genesis 3:15 as implicit, it still has the force of a solemn pledge to redeem Eve and her seed (*Covenant Theology*, p. 123).

24. For a defense of the use of the term 'Covenant of Grace' based on the organic and thematic unity of the covenants, see Waldron, *The 1689 Baptist Confession*, 108-09. Although Paul K. Jewett does not reference the 2LCF, he affirms the unity of the Covenant of Grace (*Infant Baptism and the Covenant of Grace* [Grand Rapids: Eerdmans, 1978], pp. 84-85).

25. Blackburn, 'Covenant Theology Simplified,' pp. 34, 35, 58; see also Chantry, 'Covenants of Works and of Grace,' p. 108.

26. Fred A. Malone, 'Biblical Hermeneutics and Covenant Theology,' in *Covenant Theology: A Baptist Distinctive*, p. 75). Part of its purpose was to allow God's plan of redemption to move forward (Blackburn, 'Covenant Theology Simplified,' p. 39).

it is just one covenant in the unfolding administration of it. The particular promises of the Abrahamic Covenant are that Abraham would have numerous offspring who would inherit the land of Canaan and from his general seed a particular seed would come through whom all the nations of the earth would be blessed (Gal. 3:16). The Abrahamic Covenant does not have to be divided into two covenants to show that it has a carnal element because it includes both earthly and heavenly blessings.[27] Circumcision was the sign of this covenant which distinguished Abraham's descendants from all other peoples on the earth. Circumcision is not fulfilled in baptism but in the circumcision of the heart, the inward seal of divine regeneration, out of which flows justification.[28] Abraham's children are the true children of Abraham who express faith (Gal. 3:7, 26, 29) and baptism should only be given to those who believe.[29]

The Mosaic Covenant is the next stage of the Covenant of Grace where God enters into a covenant with Israel at Mt. Sinai and gives them the law. Although this covenant is the most controverisal aspect of covenant theology, it is very important that the law is understood correctly. The work of the law has been written on the heart since creation to either excuse or accuse the conscience (Rom. 2:14-15). This law was given to Israel as a means of administering God's covenant more effectively to a redeemed community.[30] This covenant should not be seen as a republication of the

---

27. David Kingdon, *Children of Abraham: A Reformed Baptist View of Baptism, the Covenant, and Children* [Sussex: Carey Publications, 1973], p. 32. Jewett also sees a twofold reference to spiritual and physical blessings in the Abrahamic Covenant (*Infant Baptism*, p. 236).

28. Kingdon sees an analogy between circumcision and baptism so that baptism deepens the spiritual and ethical significance of Old Testament circumcision, but baptism is only for the spiritual seed of Abraham. Baptism does not take over the national and fleshly meaning of circumcision. The counterpart to physical circumcision is spiritual circumcision (*Children of Abraham*, pp. 34, 51-54).

29. Kingdon, *Children of Abraham*, pp. 55.

30. Blackburn, 'Covenant Theology Simplified,' pp. 41-42. He also states that this redeemed community should not be regarded as redeemed in the same sense as the church because there are typological relations between Israel and the church. In the Old Testament this may simply refer to God's deliverance of the nation of Israel from Egypt without the full New Testament sense of redemption from sin (he quotes Wellum, 'Baptism and the Relationship between the Covenants' in *Believer's Baptism: Sign of the*

Covenant of Works.[31] There was no need to renew the Covenant of Works because all human beings are already under its obligation to obey the law perfectly. The conditional obedience to God's law in the Mosaic Covenant as a means to possess the land was also a proclamation of the needed righteousness that was broken in the Covenant of Works. The giving of the law restrained Israel's behavior, condemned their sins, and showed the people the need for grace and faith. Although this covenant was added because of transgressions, it also proclaimed the promised grace announced in Genesis 3:15. Thus it was conditional in the form of works only in regard to the possession of the land and the blessings related to the land. The demand for obedience showed the necessity of repentance and faith. In this way the law was a schoolmaster to show us our need of Christ. But the law was also given to show God's people how they were to live as an expression of their faith in God.[32]

The New Covenant

The covenants of promise (Eph. 2:12) in the Old Testament adminis-tration of the Covenant of Grace were limited in what they could do. Hebrews 8:7-13 finds fault with the Mosaic Covenant, the paradigm and representative covenant that incorporated all the former covenants in a prototypical manner, showing that all the Old Covenant administrations were outmoded. Although the Holy Spirit was at work and people were saved in the Old Covenant, not everyone knew God in a saving way. Thus, there was the need for a better, New Covenant, the final stage of the Covenant of Grace. The New Covenant is not administered like the Old Covenant.

Firstly, children are handled differently based on the statements of Jeremiah 31:29-30 and Ezekiel 18:1-32. In the Old Covenant, God dealt with children according to the status of their fathers, but this would not be the case in the New Covenant. God will deal with each person

---

New Covenant in Christ, Thomas R. Schreiner and Shawn D. Wright, eds. [Nashville: B&H, 2006], p. 127).

31. Chantry, 'Covenants of Works and of Grace,' pp. 106-08; Waldron argues that the Mosaic Covenant is not unique in its requirement of obedience (*The 1689 Baptist Confession*, p. 118).

32. Blackburn, 'Covenant Theology Simplified,' pp. 43-47. His explanation expresses both the second and third use of the law, although that terminology is not used.

individually regardless of whether their father was a believer or not. Thus a child will not be included automatically in the covenant by birth or baptism simply because the father is a covenant member.

Secondly, God promises certain things to each member of the covenant that He did not promise to each covenant member in the former administrations of the covenant. These promises are laid out in Jeremiah 31:31-34. The law will be written on the heart, God will be their God, everyone will savingly know God, and their sins would be forgiven. These were possessed by some members of the Old Covenant, but they were not possessed by every member as they are in the New Covenant.[33]

The newness of the covenant includes a new way to administer it. This includes a change of worship related to the temple and a change of the place of children in the covenant. The Law of God will be written on the heart of every covenant member as a result of regeneration (Rom. 8:1-4; Heb. 8:10-13). The New Covenant cannot be broken. Unlike the Old Covenant, where genuine members could become apostate, this is not a possibility in the New Covenant. A false member of the New Covenant can turn and apostasize, but this is impossible for a true member. Membership in the visible church should not be equated with membership in the covenant because a member of the church may not actually be a member of the New Covenant.[34]

Both Reformed Baptists and Presbyterians believe that the New Testament takes priority in how the Old Testament is fulfilled in it.[35] Reformed Baptists believe that they follow this principle more consistently than Presbyterians, which results in a different under-

---

33. Ibid., pp. 49-51.

34. Ibid., pp. 53-54.

35. Malone shows how dispensationalists tend to reject this principle ('Biblical Hermeneutics,' in *Covenant Theology: A Baptist Distinctive*, pp. 75-76). It is interesting to compare Malone's hermeneutical discussion with Barcellos. The latter agrees that the Old Testament should be understood in light of the New Testament, but he also wants the Old Testament to be understood in light of itself (*Getting the Garden Right*, p. 17). He also argues that theology should be done at the concept level, not just at the word level (*Getting the Garden Right*, p. 54), which seems to agree with the principle in the WCF 1.6 that all things necessary for salvation, faith, and life are either expressly set down in Scripture or 'by good and necessary consequence may be deduced from Scripture', a principle denied by Malone (p. 81).

standing of the fulfillment of the New Covenant. This leads to their view of the local church as a body of professing believers, rather than a body of believers and their children, so that baptism should be given only to disciples. The inclusion of children in the New Covenant violates the hermeneutical principle of relying on the New Testament to interpret how the Old Testament is fulfilled in it (Gal. 3:16; 26-29). Each New Covenant member is born again by the Holy Spirit and is justified by faith unto the forgiveness of sins (these are members of the church of the firstborn who are enrolled in heaven). A consistent application of the principle of the priority of the New Testament in how the Old Testament is fulfilled leads to a confessional church, a confessor's baptism, and a confessor's Lord's Supper. Those who express faith should become part of the New Covenant, local (visible) church, but there may be unregenerate members in a local church even though the goal is to build a church of regenerate New Covenant members.[36] John's description of apostates in 1 John 2:19 shows that although they were members of the local church by profession, they were not members of the New Covenant.[37]

The basis of baptism is not primarily tied to covenant theology, but to the exegesis of New Testament texts. Chantry agrees with the definition of baptism given in WCF 28.1, but on the basis of the New Testament, every person baptized made a credible confession of faith in Christ prior to being baptized. Acts 2:39 does not support infant baptism because the phrase 'as many as the Lord our God shall call' (NKJV) qualifies 'you and your children'. Only those children who are effectually called become heirs of the spiritual promises in this passage.[38] The household baptisms

---

36. Nichols recognizes that the New Covenant community on earth will contain hypocrites and apostates because only God can judge whether a profession of faith is genuine. The New Covenant community will not be completely pure until Christ comes again. He gives a long quotation from Bavinck (*Our Reasonable Faith* [Grand Rapids: Baker, 1977], pp. 278-279) who argues that there is not an internal covenant and an external covenant but two sides to the one Covenant of Grace (*Covenant Theology*, pp. 262-263).

37. Malone, 'Biblical Hermeneutics,' pp. 78-84. He also shows how baptism was connected to the regulative principle of worship among Baptists in the past.

38. Most of the material in this paragraph comes from Walter J. Chantry, 'Baptism and Covenant Theology,' in *Covenant Theology: A Baptist Distinctive*, pp. 125-26; see also Fred A. Malone, *The Baptism of Disciples Alone: A Covenantal Argument for Credobaptism Versus Paedobaptism* (Cape Coral, FL: Founders Press, 2003), pp. 137-41.

do not mean that infants were baptized. In the account of the Philippian jailor it is emphasized that all were baptized and after the baptism all rejoiced believing in God. It is also unlikely that the businesswoman Lydia would be nursing an infant. It is not clear that she has a husband, let alone children.[39] 1 Corinthians 7:14 uses the word 'holy' for both the unbelieving spouse and the children, so it cannot support infant baptism. The children are holy because they are born in wedlock.[40] It is clear from New Testament passages, such as Romans 4 and Galatians 3 and 4, that the seed of Abraham are believers alone. The promises are spiritual promises that do not apply to a physical seed.[41]

Confessional Historic Baptist Covenant Theology

A rich history of Baptist covenant theology has been made available through several recent reprints and publications. One of the leading figures of early Baptist covenant theology was Nehemiah Coxe (died 1689). He is considered one of the most significant Baptist theologians in the area of covenant theology, particularly because he was the 'principle artisan' of the 2LCF adopted by the Baptist churches of England in 1689.[42] His work on the covenant was also foundational for other Baptists because it impacted later authors.[43] With good reason his views of covenant theology are considered the standard of Calvinist Baptists.[44] His writing on covenant theology was distinctive in several ways. He intentionally avoided the polemical style of earlier Baptist writings on this topic, not to avoid the controversy surrounding covenant theology,

---

39. Chantry, 'Baptism and Covenant Theology,' p. 127; see also Malone, *Baptism of Disciples Alone*, pp. 127-36.

40. Chantry, 'Baptism and Covenant Theology,' pp. 127-28; see also Malone, *Baptism of Disciples Alone*, pp. 141-49 for a discussion of this passage.

41. Chantry, 'Baptism and Covenant Theology,' p. 133.

42. Pascal Denault, *The Distinctiveness of Baptist Covenant Theology: A Comparison between Seventeenth-Century Particular Baptist and Paedobaptist Federalism* (Birmingham, AL: Solid Ground Christian Books, 2013), p. 17.

43. S. Renihan shows Coxe's influence on 'The Second Confessional Writers (1680-1704),' including Philip Cary, Hercules Collins, and Benjamin Keach (*From Shadow to Substance*, pp. 265-317).

44. Denault, *Baptist Covenant Theology*, p. 18. S. Renihan states that Coxe's writings represent a systematization of covenant theology that no other Particular Baptist had attempted (*From Shadow to Substance*, p. 239).

but to avoid the style of it.[45] He focused on what he considered 'the main hinge' of the controversy, the Covenant of Circumcision in Genesis 17.[46] His views on covenant theology will be the focus of this section.

The Covenant of Works

There was little difference between the Particular Baptists and the Presbyterians on the Covenant of Works (see the discussion earlier in this chapter). Before he addressed God's covenant with Adam, Coxe examined covenant relationships to God in general. Covenants derive exclusively from God who condescends to oblige Himself by way of covenant or promise (stipulation), to which man must respond accordingly (restipulation). In the Covenant of Works, restipulation is doing the things required in the covenant. God's condescension to mankind means that obedience is meritorious because of the terms of the covenant, not meritorious in an absolute way. All covenants are transacted through a federal head, whether it be Adam, Noah, Abraham, or Christ. The only way to belong to a covenant was to belong to the federal head of that covenant, with the implication that believer's children can only lay claim to the Covenant of Grace through Christ, not their parents. Also, an understanding of covenants must be based on divine revelation, not errors that 'strangely perplexes the whole system or body of divinity and entangles our interpretation of innumerable texts of Scripture'.[47]

The Covenant of Redemption and the Covenant of Grace

In a section covering God's mercy to fallen man, the Covenant of Redemption is affirmed as the basis for God to redeem and save a

---

45. Denault highlights that Baptists, including Nehemiah Coxe, were very concerned about maintaining unity with their paedobaptist brothers. He quotes from the Appendix of the 2LCF where they express their desire to maintain good relations regardless of their differences on baptism (*Baptist Covenant Theology*, p. 55).

46. S. Renihan, *From Shadow to Substance*, p. 229-30. Coxe appreciated John Owen's work on the Mosaic Covenant and took what he did with that covenant and applied it to the Abrahamic Covenant.

47. J. Renihan, 'PART I: Nehemiah Coxe,' in *Covenant Theology: From Adam to Christ* (Palmdale, CA: Reformed Baptist Academic Press, 2005), pp. 33-41. This is a reprint of Coxe, *A Discourse of the Covenants*; see also S. Renihan, *From Shadow to Substance*, pp. 231-33.

remnant of lost mankind through the merits of Christ.[48] This plan, or covenant, between the Father and the Son was made known in Genesis 3:15. In the sentence passed on the serpent there was implied a blessed promise of redemption, worked out by the Son of God born of a woman, whereby the promised salvation would be received by faith. This was the Covenant of Grace promised by God to Adam (a stipulated promise) requiring Adam to respond in faith (the restipulation). Although the Covenant of Grace was revealed to Adam, there was no formal covenant established with him. He did not represent anyone because God dealt with Adam alone on the basis of his faith in the grace of God. Based on the Covenant of Works before the Fall, the descendants of Adam receive the imputation of his sin, are under obligation to obey the Law of God, and are condemned because they are not able to keep it. After the Fall, God dealt with Adam as a private person and so the faith he expresssed in God's promises has no benefit to his descendants because he is not acting as their representative.[49]

The Noahic Covenant

Coxe argues that there is only one covenant with Noah even though God's establishment of a covenant with him is mentioned on two separate occasions. The benefits of the covenant is first expressed more generally and then more particularly. This covenant promised the preservation of Noah and all who were with him in the ark and required the response of faith and obedience. It appears that the Noahic Covenant only promised temporal blessings, but the fact that the covenant preserved the line of Eve showed that eternal blessings were also in view because this secured the birth of the promised seed.[50] The Noahic Covenant is not the Covenant of Grace, but it is a foreshadowing of that covenant, and future generations have equal

---

48.   Coxe also argued that this covenant put the control of the government of the world into the hands of the Son of God whereby everything became subservient to the ends of the new creation and the redemption of fallen mankind (J. Renihan, 'PART I: Nehemiah Coxe', p. 54).

49.   J. Renihan, 'PART I: Nehemiah Coxe,' in *Covenant Theology: From Adam to Christ*, pp. 37-38, 54-58 and S. Renihan, *From Shadow to Substance*, pp. 232, 236-38.

50.   Coxe also saw typological references to Christ in the Flood account (J. Renihan, 'PART I: Nehemiah Coxe,' pp. 62-64).

claim to its blessings without any consideration of their immediate parents.[51]

The Covenant of Grace

The next major advance was the revelation of the Covenant of Grace to Abraham in Genesis 12, which surpassed previous and subsequent covenants in its clarity. This covenant was the same in substance as that which was 'darkly revealed' in previous ages.[52] Abraham has a double role in the covenant as both the father of all true believers and the father of the nation of Israel. God entered into a covenant with Abraham for both of these seeds, which must be formally distinguished from each another. These two must not be confounded without grave consequences to the Christian faith. The blessings appropriate to each seed must be conveyed in a way that is agreeable to their particular covenant interest. Thus, Abraham had two seeds that belonged to two distinct covenants.[53] Coxe discusses these two covenants by devoting a secton to the Covenant of Grace as revealed to Abraham, the Covenant of Circumcision given to Abraham, and the relationship between the two.

In the section on 'The Covenant of Grace Revealed to Abraham', Coxe focuses his comments on Galatians 3:6-9, 16, 27, with some attention given to Genesis 12. This is in line with the hermeneutical principle stated earlier in his work that the New Testament takes priority over the Old in understanding the covenants.[54] God revealed the Covenant of Grace to Abraham, the general nature of that covenant, and the seed involved in it. In Genesis 12 God confirmed His covenant with

---

51.   S. Renihan makes the point that Coxe used the same hermeneutic in the Noahic Covenant as he used in the Abrahamic Covenant in his statement that covenant interest is not maintained through parents, but through federal headship (*From Shadow to Substance*, p. 241).

52.   S. Renihan points out that a previous modern reprint of Coxe's *A Discourse of the Covenants* (perhaps referring to J. Renihan, 'PART I: Nehemiah Coxe', p. 71) states erroneously that the Covenant of Grace was *not* the same in substance (*From Shadow to Substance*, p. 242, n. 65).

53.   J. Renihan, 'PART I: Nehemiah Coxe,' in *Covenant Theology: From Adam to Christ*, pp. 71-73, and S. Renihan, *From Shadow to Substance*, p. 242.

54.   Coxe states that '... the best interpreter of the Old Testament is the Holy Spirit speaking to us in the new' (J. Renihan, 'PART I: Nehemiah Coxe', in *Covenant Theology: From Adam to Christ*, pp. 33).

Abraham, although the word 'covenant' is not used until Genesis 15. The sum and substance of all spiritual and eternal blessings are included in the promises to Abraham in Genesis 12. The gospel is proclaimed to Abraham and the promise of justification of the heathen through faith is expressed in the statement that all the nations will be blessed in Abraham (Gal. 3:8). The promise of a believing seed that would with him inherit the blessings of the Covenant of Grace was confirmed to Abraham in Genesis 15 (Rom. 4:3, 18). Abraham has a special place as 'father', but Christ is the 'first head' of the covenant through whom the promises are ratified as He is the surety of the covenant. Thus, all who believe are Abraham's children because they emulate his faith.[55]

The Covenant of Circumcision

This covenant deals with the promises to Abraham relative to his natural offspring. These promises were not made to Abraham all at one time, nor was the covenant perfected by one transaction, but was given to Abraham in stages and sealed in the Covenant of Circumcision in Genesis 17. In addition to the spiritual promises of the Covenant of Grace, God also gave an earthly promise to Abraham concerning the multiplication of his offspring (Gen. 12:2). God adds the promise of land in which the offspring would dwell in Genesis 13:14-17. In Genesis 15 the promises to Abraham concerning his carnal seed and inheritance are further explained and expanded after Abraham believed God (15:6). Genesis 17 completed God's covenant with Abraham concerning his natural seed. In this covenant, circumcision was a sign that required a response (restipulation) of obedience. A strict and entire obedience was the condition of this covenant in order to inherit the blessings of the covenant.[56]

The focus in Genesis 17 on obedience, and that failure to comply with the command of circumcision resulted in disinheritance, made this

---

55. J. Renihan, 'PART I: Nehemiah Coxe,' in *Covenant Theology: From Adam to Christ*, pp. 73-76, and S. Renihan, *From Shadow to Substance*, p. 243. Coxe argues that Christ is the true seed of Abraham and only those united to Him by faith receive the blessings of the covenant, which is not available to the infant seed of believers.

56. J. Renihan, 'PART I: Nehemiah Coxe,' in *Covenant Theology: From Adam to Christ*, pp. 90-96, and S. Renihan, *From Shadow to Substance*, pp. 248-51.

covenant a Covenant of Works.[57] A connection was made to the Mosaic Covenant which also operated on the same principle that obedience was necessary to inherit the covenant blessings ('do this and live'). Thus, the Covenant of Circumcision was foundational to the Mosaic Covenant. Yet, this did not impede the Covenant of Grace because in the Covenant of Circumcision there was confirmation of one of the great promises of the Covenant of Grace given earlier to Abraham, 'A father of many nations I have made you' (17:4-5 CSB, NIV, NKJV). This promise should be understood in reference to the believing seed who are called out of all the nations (Rom. 4:17). The Covenant of Circumcision was thus subservient to the Covenant of Grace and in a typological way pointed to spiritual blessings which were figuratively implied in it. For example, the numerous offspring through Isaac, which refers to Israel after the flesh, typified that Abraham would become the father of a multitude of believers.[58] The Covenant of Grace, however, was not fully revealed and its promises were not accomplished until after the covenant with Israel according to the flesh. The only way to avoid confusion in these matters is to make clear distinctions between Abraham's spiritual and carnal seed and of the respective promises belonging to each. There is no reason to assign a covenant interest in the typified spiritual blessings to the carnal seed, just as one would not want to convey temporal blessings to the spiritual seed. Thus, the carnal seed of Abraham could not claim a right in the spiritual and eternal blessings of the New Covenant because of their interest in the Covenant of Circumcision.[59]

Coxe argues that the mediate and remote seed in the Covenant of Circumcision were as fully included in the covenant as the immediate

---

57.   S. Renihan makes the point that it is not the presence of obedience that makes it a Covenant of Works but that any covenant that disinherits its members for disobedience is a formal Covenant of Works (*From Shadow to Substance*, p. 248).

58.   The typological connection between the covenants meant that circumcision was a seal of the earthly promises to the earthly seed, but it also confirmed to Abraham that God would keep his promise to give Abraham the spiritual offspring typified in the earthly offspring. Circumcision became a seal of the righteousness of faith to Abraham, but this privilege pertained to Abraham alone (S. Renihan, *From Shadow to Substance*, pp. 250).

59.   J. Renihan, 'PART I: Nehemiah Coxe,' in *Covenant Theology: From Adam to Christ*, pp. 83-89, and S. Renihan, *From Shadow to Substance*, pp. 246-48; see also Denault, *Baptist Covenant Theology*, pp. 119-25.

seed based on their relationship to Abraham as the federal head of the covenant. In other words, disobedient Jews were disinherited from the land of Canaan, but their children were not. This demonstrates the connection of the children to Abraham and not to their parents. God's later covenant dealings with Israel were founded on His covenant made with them in Abraham, which in the New Testament is the old and carnal covenant as distinguished from the gospel covenant (Jer. 31:31-34; Heb. 8:8-13).[60]

Coxe also argued that from the beginning some of the immediate seed were excluded from the covenant even though they received the sign of circumcision. Both Ishmael and Esau were circumcised, but they were not parties to the covenant, and to suppose an interest in the covenant without a right to its promises is mere fancy. The promises of the covenant were not made good to them because they did not belong to them. They were only circumcised in obedience to the command of God. Circumcision was a seal of the covenant on all, but not to all. In other words, no one can have a claim to the covenant without a claim to its promises. Thus, children should not be seen as being in the Covenant of Grace without being a recipient of the covenant promises. A parent who claimed a right to the promises of Abraham's covenant today could not assume it would include all of their children because this was not so even in Abraham's day. This fact questions the principle that believers and their children are included in the covenant.[61]

Throughout his work on the covenant Coxe had emphasized the intermixture and the mutual relationship of the promises related to the spiritual and the carnal seed of Abraham. The mutual relationship of the promises means that there is a typical relationship between them. The promises to Israel after the flesh, which included the people, their worship, and their inheritance, were all typical of the spiritual promises, but their privilege did not reach to an interest in the gospel blessings or the New Covenant except by faith.[62] There are many implications of the typical

---

60.   J. Renihan, 'PART I: Nehemiah Coxe,' in *Covenant Theology: From Adam to Christ*, pp. 97-101, and S. Renihan, *From Shadow to Substance*, pp. 252-53.

61.   J. Renihan, 'PART I: Nehemiah Coxe,' in *Covenant Theology: From Adam to Christ*, pp. 102-06, and S. Renihan, *From Shadow to Substance*, pp. 253-56.

62.   J. Renihan, 'PART I: Nehemiah Coxe,' in *Covenant Theology: From Adam to Christ*, pp. 122-26, and S. Renihan, *From Shadow to Substance*, pp. 259-60; see also Denault, *Baptist Covenant Theology*, pp. 125-28.

relationship between the carnal and the spiritual promises. Just because the promise 'to be a God to you and your offspring after you' occurs in the Covenant of Circumcision does not mean that the blessings of the New Covenant are expressed by these words, even though the same promise occurs in Jeremiah 31 and Hebrews 8. The Covenant of Circumcision has to do with carnal promises to the carnal seed of Abraham and this is what the promise in Genesis 17 has in view.[63] However, the Covenant of Circumcision was typical of the Covenant of Grace so that some of the earthly offspring of Abraham were members of both covenants at the same time. None were justified by the Old Covenant, but they could be justified living under the Old Covenant if they believed in the promise to which the Covenant of Circumcision was a handmaid. For believing Jews, the Law of Moses did not condemn them but was a pedagogue to train them until Christ. The Old Covenant was subservient to the Covenant of Grace but it was not directly a covenant of spiritual blessings. The Covenant of Circumcision could not lead to the salvation of Abraham's offspring because it could not give any infant or adult a right of membership in the gospel church.[64] Circumcision related to Israel after the flesh, was an ordinance of the Old Covenant and so pertained to the law, which bound its subjects to legal obedience.[65] Baptism is an ordinance of the gospel, obliges its subjects to gospel obedience, and is opposed to circumcision. It should not be substituted for circumcision.[66]

Coxe and other Particular Baptists reformulated the character of the Covenant of Grace from 'one covenant under two administrations'

---

63. Coxe argues that just because the promise 'I will be your God' occurs in the Covenant of Grace does not mean that everywhere it occurs it takes on the same nature. The meaning is limited by the covenant to which it belongs (J. Renihan, 'PART I: Nehemiah Coxe,' in *Covenant Theology: From Adam to Christ*, p. 112).

64. J. Renihan, 'PART I: Nehemiah Coxe,' in *Covenant Theology: From Adam to Christ*, pp. 118-21, and S. Renihan, *From Shadow to Substance*, pp. 255-56.

65. Negative texts in the New Testament (Acts 5:10; Gal. 5:3, 13) show that circumcision does not belong to the gospel and is utterly useless to the gospel church. Romans 4:11 relates circumcision as a seal of the righteousness of faith that Abraham had while uncircumcised so that he might be the father of those who believe while in uncircumcision, that is, the Gentiles (J. Renihan, 'PART I: Nehemiah Coxe,' in *Covenant Theology: From Adam to Christ*, pp. 134-39).

66. J. Renihan, 'PART I: Nehemiah Coxe,' in *Covenant Theology: From Adam to Christ*, pp. 131-40, and S. Renihan, *From Shadow to Substance*, pp. 259-62.

to 'one covenant revealed progressively and concluded formally under the New Covenant'.[67] The Covenant of Grace was materially revealed to Abraham and 'made' with him and his spiritual seed, but it was not formally esablished.[68] The New Testament brings the full revelation of the Covenant of Grace because the New Covenant brings about its accomplishment. The Covenant of Grace revealed to Adam, and then to Abraham, was also the promise of the New Covenant. The Abrahamic, Mosaic, and Davidic Covenants were not the Covenant of Grace, nor administrations of it, but it was revealed under each of these covenants. Baptist ecclesiology rested on a different covenant theology that had implications for Baptist ecclesiology and practice. The visible church is not made up of believers and their children. In other words, there is not an external administration of the Covenant of Grace for the non-elect. Only those who had a credible confession of faith made up the visible church, and if anyone became an apostate, he was considered never to have been a member of the covenant (1 John 2:19). Thus, the Covenant of Grace was unconditional because it was limited to the regenerate elect.[69]

The Mosaic Covenant

Coxe did not write on the Mosaic Covenant because he thought it was unnecessary and superfluous in light of John Owen's treatment of it in which he found the very arguments and principles that the Baptists themselves had argued. He referred the reader to Owen and left it at that, but then he 'took all of Owen's tools' and applied them to the Abrahamic Covenant.[70] The Old and New Covenants were not two administrations of the same covenant because they differed in substance. The Mosaic Covenant was a progression of the Covenant of Circumcision that focused on the physical posterity of Abraham and the promises related to their inheritance of the land of Canaan. The Old Covenant was a Covenant of Works for life in the land of Canaan. It revived the original Covenant of Works and directed sinners to the Covenant of Grace.

---

67. Denault, *Baptist Covenant Theology*, p. 63.
68. S. Renihan, *From Shadow to Substance*, p. 262.
69. Denault, *Baptist Covenant Theology*, pp. 63-64, 71, 87, 95. Paedobaptists saw apostates as transgressors of the covenant.
70. S. Renihan, *From Shadow to Substance*, p. 230.

The Old Covenant was distinct from the Covenant of Works and the Covenant of Grace, yet it was related to them.[71]

Owen argued that analysis of a covenant must be based on its promises, which was the basis for distinguishing between the Old and New Covenants in Hebrews 8:6. He classified the Old Covenant as formally based on law and works, whereas the Covenant of Grace was made known through the promises of the gospel. Believers were saved under the Old Covenant but not by it. The Mosaic Covenant republished the Covenant of Works, but it was not the Covenant of Works formally because it did not offer eternal life. It was also subservient to the gospel by showing the impossibility of establishing peace with God except by the promise of God. Therefore, there are two distinct covenants and not two administrations of the same covenant. Through typology the Old Covenant portrayed salvation in Jesus Christ but it did not offer salvation in Jesus Christ in and of itself. This idea is based on the argument of Hebrews that animal sacrifices could not forgive sins, which means the Old Covenant could not perfect its members. Although the Old Covenant and the New Covenant were closely connected through typology, they were not the same in substance and their differences could not be reduced to external administrational changes.[72] The terminology of the WCF 7.2, 4, which speaks of the first covenant and the second covenant, referring to the Covenant of Works and the Covenant of Grace, is ambiguous because the New Testament contrasts the Old and New Covenants (Heb. 8–9). The Old/New Covenant distinction fits with the law/grace antithesis where law would refer to the Covenant

---

71. J. Renihan, 'PART I: Nehemiah Coxe,' in *Covenant Theology: From Adam to Christ*, p. 141, and S. Renihan, *From Shadow to Substance*, pp. 196-97, 261-62. S. Renihan argues that the excitement among Particular Baptists with Owen's view of the Mosaic Covenant is not that they are new ideas, but that they are held by a person of such prominence so that if Owen held these views it would be hard to criticize the Particular Baptists for the very same views. Owen's views were published in his commentary on Hebrews 8:6-13, reprinted in J. Renihan, *Covenant Theology: From Adam to Christ*. See also Mark Jones, 'The "Old" Covenant' in *Drawn into Controversie: Reformed Theological Diversity and Debates Within Seventeenth Century British Puritanism*, ed. Nigel M. de S. Cameron (Edinburgh, 1993), pp. 183-203.

72. J. Renihan, 'PART II: John Owen,' in *Covenant Theology: From Adam to Christ*, pp. 210-11, and S. Renihan, *From Shadow to Substance*, pp. 207-08, 210-11.

of Works (2LCF 7.2), but law can also refer to the Old Covenant. Thus, the Covenant of Works and the old, Mosaic Covenant are very similar to each other. The major distinction among the covenants is primarily between the Old and New Covenants instead of between the Covenant of Works and the Covenant of Grace.[73]

The goal of the Old Covenant was to preserve both the messianic lineage and the Covenant of Grace, to point typologically toward Christ, and to imprison everything under sin in order that the means of salvation would come only through faith in Christ (Gal. 3:19-24). The Old Covenant specifically led to Christ by its condemnation of sin because it shows the need for a perfect mediator to fulfill the law on our behalf. In this way God reaffirmed the Covenant of Works because a righteous person would be needed to substitute for sinners. The Old Covenant was given with a view to the accomplishment of the Covenant of Grace.[74]

The New Covenant

The New Covenant is different from the Old Covenant because it offers more than just the promise of the forgiveness of sins. The coming of Christ fulfills all the promises of the Covenant of Grace and makes them a reality in the lives of those who believe in Him. Until the blood of Christ was shed, the New Covenant was not formally established or sanctioned. The New Covenant is a completely different type of covenant from the Old Covenant, not a renovation of it nor a new administration of it.[75] According to Jeremiah 31:31, the Old Covenant was able to be broken while the New Covenant is not breakable. The New Covenant is new because it is unconditional, which was not true for any covenant that came before it. Thus, the Scriptures do not provide any possibilities of being visibly in the New Covenant without participating effectively in its substance.[76]

---

73. Pascal Denault, 'By Farther Steps: A Seventeenth-Century Particular Baptist Covenant Theology,' in *Recovering a Covenantal Heritage: Essays in Baptist Covenant Theology*, ed. Richard C. Barcellos (Palmdale, CA: RBAP, 2014) pp. 73-74.

74. Denault, *Baptist Covenant Theology*, pp. 130, 133, 140-41.

75. J. Renihan, 'PART II: John Owen', in *Covenant Theology: From Adam to Christ*, pp. 200-06, and S. Renihan, *From Shadow to Substance*, pp. 212-13.

76. Denault, *Baptist Covenant Theology*, pp. 147-48, 152-53.

Comparison and Evaluation of the Views of Confessional Baptists

There are differences among the views of the Confessional Baptists, particularly concerning the nature of the Abrahamic and Mosaic Covenants. Some recent works on covenant theology follow the views of Nehemiah Coxe concerning the two seeds of Abraham and the nature of the covenant in Genesis 17 and the Mosaic Covenant as a Covenant of Works.[77] The differences within the covenants are emphasized in the term 'covenantal dichotomism'.[78] The term 'dichotomism' refers to the importance of the Covenant of Works and the Covenant of Grace in redemptive history as two dichotomous parts within God's singular plan of redemption. But more specifically, it refers to the dual nature of the Abrahamic Covenant.[79]

The Abrahamic Covenant: One Covenant or Two?

Both groups of Baptists described in this chapter, the confessional Reformed and Historic Baptists, agree on the unity of the Covenant of Grace. They are also unified in the view that the administration of the covenant is different in the New Covenant because the principle of believers and their children is not part of the New Covenant, which is based on individual faith in Christ. They differ, however, in their views on the nature of the Abrahamic and Mosaic Covenants. Although covenantal Baptists recognize both the spiritual and earthly aspect of the Abrahamic Covenant, many reject dividing the Abrahamic Covenant into two covenants. Kingdon writes, 'we do not

---

77. Phillip D. R. Griffiths, *Covenant Theology: A Reformed Baptist Perspective* (Eugene OR: Wipf & Stock, 2016); Jeffrey D. Johnson, *The Fatal Flaw of the Theology Behind Infant Baptism* (Free Grace Press, 2010). For full disclosure, my father, Richard P. Belcher, is thanked in the 'Acknowledgments' of Johnson's book as reading the manuscript and making helpful suggestions (p. ix). My father and I have the same name and it is easy to confuse us! Johnson has also written *The Kingdom of God: A Baptist Expression of Covenant and Biblical Theology* (Conway, AR: Free Grace Press, 2014). He expresses appreciation for the renewed interest in the 2LCF (p. 14).

78. Johnson, *Fatal Flaw of Infant Baptism*. The second section of the book which is devoted to a systematic presentation of the divine covenants is titled, 'Covenantal Dichotomism: Continuity and Discontinuity of the Divine Covenants.'

79. Johnson, *Fatal Flaw of Infant Baptism*, p. 207.

divide the Abrahamic Covenant into two or more covenants in the interests of demonstrating that it has a carnal element.' He goes on to ask why one covenant could not embrace both aspects.[80] Waldron argues for the organic unity between the Abrahamic Covenant and the Mosaic Covenant so that it is impossible to call the Abrahamic Covenant a Covenant of Grace and the Mosaic Covenant a Covenant of Works.[81]

Other Confessional Baptists follow the teaching of the Historic Baptists. Griffiths argues that the essential source of division between the Baptists and the paedobaptists can be traced back to different understandings of the Abrahamic Covenant.[82] The conditional covenant of Genesis 17 was made with Abraham and his physical seeds (plural). This covenant was not a Covenant of Grace, but a Covenant of Works (Gen. 17:2), and is essentially the same as the Mosaic Covenant, inherited by the physical seed.[83] A few years before Genesis 17, God revealed to Abraham the *promise* of the unconditional New Covenant, which alluded to Abraham's seed (singular), which is a reference to Christ (Gal. 3:16). Abraham believed this promise and his faith was imputed to him as righteousness (Gen. 15:6). Thus, there are two separate, yet related covenants. One is made with Abraham's carnal seed, the Jews, and the other is the promise of the New Covenant that would be ratified in his 'seed', the Messiah.[84] These two covenants must not be confused or confounded because the Covenant of Circumcision

---

80. Kingdon, *Children of Abraham*, p. 32.

81. Waldron, *The 1689 Confession of Faith*, p. 108. Chantry also denies that the Mosaic Covenant is a Covenant of Works ('Covenants of Works and of Grace', p. 106).

82. Griffiths, *Covenant Theology*, p. 43; Johnson argues the same thing by saying that the key to understanding the continuity and discontinuity between the Old and New Covenants is found in a proper understanding of the Abrahamic Covenant (*Fatal Flaw of Infant Baptism*, p. 209).

83. Johnson, *The Kingdom of God*, pp. 183, 185. In reference to the Abrahamic Covenant he states that 'God republished the covenant of works with the family of His choosing' (p. 183) and 'Abraham broke the covenant of works' (p. 187).

84. Griffiths, *Covenant Theology*, pp. 55-56. Johnson argues that the Abrahamic Covenant is unconditional for the spiritual seed who inherit the spiritual realities, but it is conditional for the physical seed who inherit the temporal blessings in the land (*Fatal Flaw of Infant Baptism*, pp. 210-12). The reality of the spiritual seed is argued on the basis of New Testament passages.

made with Abraham's carnal seed did not impede or fringe upon the Covenant of Grace made with Abraham's spiritual seed.[85]

Galatians 4:22-31 shows that two covenants came from Abraham.[86] The Covenant of Circumcision, connected with Hagar, corresponds to the Old Covenant, and it is a Covenant of Works established with the physical posterity of Abraham. The covenant of the promise, connected to Sarah, corresponds to the New Covenant, and it is the Covenant of Grace revealed to Abraham and concluded with Christ and the spiritual posterity of Abraham (Gal. 3:29). The spiritual and physical seed of Abraham were all together in Abraham's household, but were always ontologically distinct.[87]

Circumcision takes on the same dichotomous character as the Abrahamic Covenant.[88] It was a covenantal sign and initiatory rite that separated Abraham and his posterity from the rest of mankind. As opposed to the promise of the Covenant of Grace, the Covenant of Circumcision had conditions that had to be kept; otherwise, judgment would fall on the covenant breaker (Gen. 17:14). Abraham had physical descendants through the patriarchs, who were circumcised in their physical bodies, and who inherited the physical promises of becoming a nation and taking the land. Abraham also had spiritual descendants through the Messiah who are circumcised in heart. Jesus' spiritual seed have all been circumcised with a circumcision made without hands. Physical circumcision symbolized spiritual circumcision, but many of the physical descendants of Abraham never had faith.[89] Not all those who were physically circumcised inherited the promises. Ishmael was not an heir to the promises because he and his mother were cast out. Circumcision did not signify the same thing for Ishmael as it did for Isaac who inherited the promises. It is hard to see how Ishmael could

---

85. Johnson, *Fatal Flaw of Infant Baptism*, p. 218.

86. Coxe also discusses Galatians 4:21-31 (J. Renihan, 'PART I: Nehemiah Coxe,' pp. 130-31).

87. Denault, 'Covenant Theology,' pp. 95-97; see also Johnson, *Fatal Flaw of Infant Baptism*, pp. 83-94.

88. Johnson, *The Fatal Flaw of Infant Baptism*, pp. 190-93.

89. Nichols, *Covenant Theology*, pp. 169-72. Griffiths (*Covenant Theology*, pp. 64-65) and Johnson (*The Kingdom of God*, p. 32) also affirm that there was an inward and spiritual significance to circumcision.

have received circumcision as a seal because he remained uncircumcised in heart.[90]

Several things can be said in response to viewing the Abrahamic Covenant as two covenants. The two covenant dichotomy is hard to establish from the texts of Genesis because it is not easy to separate the spiritual promises from the physical promises. They are given to Abraham as a unit. The promises of Genesis 12 include the land of Canaan, that Abraham will be a great nation, that his name will be great, and that he will be a blessing to all the families of the earth. The promises of Genesis 15 contain the physical promise of land (15:7, 17), as well as the promise that his descendants will be as numerous as the stars of heaven (15:5). The promises of the 'conditional' covenant in Genesis 17 include making Abraham the father of a multitude of nations and giving his descendants the land. The one promise at the heart of the other covenants is also emphasized: 'to be God to you and to your offspring after you' (17:7). The 'physical' and 'spiritual' aspects of these promises are intermingled so that the Covenant of Grace revealed in Genesis 12 and the conditional covenant in Genesis 17 have the same promises.[91] If Genesis 15 is an unconditional covenant because only God passes through the slain animals, then the 'unconditional' covenant of Genesis 15 and the conditional covenant of Genesis 17 also contain the same promises. God does more in Genesis 15 than just reveal the Covenant of Grace to Abraham. The unconditional nature of the covenant ceremony establishes the Covenant of Grace with Abraham, which has the same unconditional character as the New Covenant. God Himself will fulfill the promises of the covenant (Heb. 6:13-20).[92]

The fact that circumcision is viewed as applying only to Israel after the flesh[93] leads to confusion concerning the import of circumcision.

---

90. Griffiths, *Covenant Theology*, pp. 68-69, 71.

91. Thomas R. Schreiner, *Covenant and God's Purpose for the World* (Wheaton, IL: Crossway, 2017), p. 49. Schreiner, a Baptist, argues for one covenant with Abraham because the promises in Genesis 12, 15, and 17 are the same.

92. See Chapter 5 in this book on the Abrahamic Covenant that argues on the basis of the terminology that Genesis 15 is the establishment of the covenant with Abraham and that Genesis 17 is the confirmation of those promises to Abraham.

93. J. Renihan, 'PART I: Nehemiah Coxe,' in *Covenant Theology: From Adam to Christ*, pp. 134-39.

It is true that not all who were physically circumcised inherited the promises, but that does not mean that circumcision did not signify the same thing for Ishmael as it did for Isaac, who inherited the promises. Someone can receive circumcision as a seal and never respond in faith because a seal guarantees that if a person responds properly in faith, that person will receive the blessings of the promises.[94] It is erroneous to argue that Ishmael and Esau were not parties to the covenant. Abraham and Rebekah are told beforehand by God that Ishmael and Esau are not going to be participants in the covenant blessings, but in both of these situations the parents were given information that is not normally available because it is on the level of the decree of God's election (Rom. 9:6-13). Circumcision promises God's covenant blessings if one responds in faith to God's promises, and it promises judgment if one rejects the covenant promises. Genesis 17 cannot be a Covenant of Works because it is given in the context of Abraham being declared righteous in Genesis 15 and being exhorted to walk in a manner that demonstrates sanctification in Genesis 17:1. The command of circumcision can be a blessing or it can be a means of judgment, similar to the Law of God which can be third use or second use, depending on one's relationship to God.

Although Coxe recognizes a typical relationship between the earthly promises and the spiritual promises so that the gospel promises of the New Covenant are located within the earthly legal covenants made with Israel, the two sets of promises are still kept separate. The earthly promises are only for the carnal seed of Abraham. The New Testament, however, sees the earthly promises as having relevance today for Gentile believers. The promise of land is a foreshadowing of the new heavens and new earth, a promise that has meaning to anyone who is a child of Abraham today. Abraham by faith went to the land of promise because he was looking forward to the city whose builder is God (Heb. 11:9-10). In the next verses the promise of descendants as numerous as the stars of heaven is mentioned (Heb. 11:11-12). The New Testament does not separate the physical promises from the spiritual

---

94. Griffiths asks the question about circumcision as a seal (*Covenant Theology*, pp. 68-69, 71).

promises but understands both promises as having relevance for God's people today.

Galatians 4:21-31 is used to argue for distinctions within the covenant relationship with Abraham. There are several problems in using this passage for this purpose. First, Paul is answering those who argue that a believer in Christ must also be circumcised in order to receive salvation. It would be helpful if the exact argument of Paul's opponents was known to see how they used Abraham to support their view. Paul clearly says that he is interpreting Hagar and Sarah, and their two sons, in a symbolic way. His use of the verb *allegoreō* should give one pause in drawing conclusions about the nature of the Abrahamic Covenant. Whether he is interpreting Sarah and Hagar in an allegorical or in a symbolic way (typology), he is drawing out principles that are in the text to apply to the argument of his opponents. Paul specifically says that Hagar and Sarah represent two covenants. Hagar is an example of trying to bring about the promises of God by works and represents Mt. Sinai that corresponds to the present Jerusalem. Paul describes Hagar's situation through the lens of the Mosaic Covenant, but that does not mean the covenant of Genesis 17 is a Covenant of Works, or that there are two covenants that God made with Abraham.[95]

The Mosaic Covenant as a Covenant of Works

The Historic Baptist position understands the Mosaic Covenant not as a Covenant of Grace or part of the Covenant of Grace, but as a Covenant of Works because the blessings and curses of the covenant are dependent on the obedience or disobedience of its members.[96] The Covenant of Works already had a role in redemptive history in the conditional covenant of Genesis 17 made with Abraham's physical posterity. This covenant connected the natural side of the Abrahamic Covenant to the physical

---

95. Denault discusses Galatians 4:22-31 to show that Baptists from the past have used this passage to argue for two covenants in Abraham, but then he goes on to say that this does not mean they saw two formal covenants with Abraham. He states this on the basis that they did not believe the Covenant of Grace in Genesis 12 was established before the New Covenant ('Covenant Theology', pp. 95-96). Yet Paul argues for two covenants in Galatians 4. Johnson uses Galatians 4 to argue for a distinction between the Old Covenant and the Covenant of Grace (*The Fatal Flaw of Infant Baptism*, pp. 83-87).

96. Denault, 'Covenant Theology,' p. 99.

seed but did not continue the spiritual side of the covenant related to the spiritual seed.[97] A principle of works, expressed in Leviticus 18:5 ('do this and live'), was embedded in the Mosaic Covenant, but this principle had a different end than the Covenant of Works with Adam because it was not designed to procure eternal life through obedience. Perfect obedience was demanded by both, but was not possible in the Mosaic Covenant because of sin, which leads to condemnation.[98] The promises and threatenings of this covenant were of an earthly nature, and if it did speak of life, it was not spiritual and eternal life, but a long earthly life. None were saved as a result of it. The redemption from Egypt was not a true spiritual redemption, but only a temporal type of redemption, and Israel was not the true people of God.[99]

The character of the Mosaic Covenant as a Covenant of Works among Historic Baptists impacts its relationship to the Covenant of Grace relative to whether the latter covenant has conditions. The Mosaic Covenant as a Covenant of Works is a different type of covenant than the Covenant of Grace. The latter is unconditional and the former is not.[100] The charge is made that paedobaptists view the Old and New Covenants as essentially the same covenant, which causes them to view the New Covenant through the eyes of the Old Covenant. This imposes on the New Covenant conditions and the existence of covenant breakers within it. Thus, the Covenant of Grace becomes like the Covenant of Works and is a covenant that can be broken. The problem with the paedobaptist view is that faith alone is not the condition of the Mosaic Covenant because it is a Covenant of Works. The result is that paedobaptists make every law-based condition of the Mosaic Covenant to refer to persevering faith. Rather, the condition of the Old Covenant was complete obedience

---

97.   Johnson, *Fatal Flaw of Infant Baptism*, pp. 224-26. He also affirms that there was a remnant according to grace among the descendants of Abraham under the Mosaic Covenant that did become part of the spiritual seed of Abraham by faith.

98.   Denault, 'Covenant Theology,' pp. 98-99. The Covenant of Works did not provide a substitute to satisfy its righteousness when it was broken. The righteous substitute awaited the New Covenant (Denault, 'Covenant Theology', pp. 103-104).

99.   Griffiths, *Covenant Theology*, pp. 59, 86-87.

100.   The first view discussed in this chapter, the confessional Reformed Baptist view, is more nuanced on this question because they see the Mosaic Covenant as a part of the Covenant of Grace.

(Deut. 27:26). If the Mosaic Covenant is part of the Covenant of Grace (in form or in essence), how does this coincide with the fact that Israel as a whole, and the Israelites as individuals, were unable to perform the conditions of the covenant? Seeing animals sacrificed did not put Israelites into the Covenant of Grace. The few among Israel who were saved by God looked back in faith to the gospel given to Abraham and looked forward in faith to the promised Messiah. Those who individually embraced the gospel were part of the Covenant of Grace.[101]

When the Mosaic Covenant is understood as a Covenant of Works and not part of the Covenant of Grace, even though differences between the Covenant of Works with Adam and the Mosaic Covenant are recognized, the Mosaic Covenant is viewed almost exclusively in negative terms. First, the possibility of salvation in the Mosaic Covenant is downplayed, or even denied.[102] Although some recognize mercy in the sacrificial system, the sacrifices further the negative function of the Mosaic Covenant because they could not accomplish the righteousness of the law. Instead, they remind Israel that the requirements of the law have not been satisfied.[103] But there is another side to the sacrifices. Although it is true that the blood of bulls and goats cannot remove sin, the smoke of the sacrifices was a pleasing aroma to God (Lev. 1:9, 13, 17). The sacrifice and the worshiper who brought the sacrifice were accepted by God. Thus, the sacrificial system was not totally negative and was meant to bring comfort to an Israelite who brought a sacrifice as the right approach to a holy God.

Second, the negative function of the law is emphasized almost to the exclusion of any positive use of the law. The law's main function is to condemn and restrain sinners. Grace comes through the Abrahamic Covenant but the Mosaic Covenant gives us the law. Law and grace are not the same.[104] Again, there is another side to the law. Without a third

---

101. Johnson, *Fatal Flaw of Infant Baptism*, pp. 95-108.

102. Johnson (*The Kingdom of God*, p. 83) quotes Horton approvingly: 'There is no mercy in the Sinaitic covenant itself' (*God of Promise*, p. 50) and he himself states, 'although the old covenant did not *establish* the gospel, it *expected*, *predicted*, and *pointed* to the gospel' (*The Kingdom of God*, p. 124, emphasis original).

103. Denault, 'Covenant Theology,' p. 102.

104. Johnson, *The Kingdom of God*, p. 61.

use of the law there is no positive function of the law in sanctification. Most of the references to the law in the Psalms are postiive. The law brings fruitfulness to the lives of those who meditate on it (Ps. 1), it changes the lives of those who seek it (Ps. 19:7-11), and it is a benefit to those who keep it (Ps. 119). As the psalmist proclaims, 'Oh how I love your law! It is my meditation all the day' (Ps. 119:97). The law furthers the sanctification of God's people. Without a positive role of the law in the Mosaic Covenant, there is no doctrine of the believer's life in the Old Testament. The New Testament is balanced toward the law in recognizing two things: the law condemns those who try to keep it for salvation (Rom. 2:1-11) and it is a blessing to those who respond to God by faith (Rom. 13:8-10). Both the Old and New Testaments affirm the second and third uses of the law.[105]

The dichotomous nature of the Abrahamic Covenant whereby the physical and spiritual seeds are separated, with the Mosaic Covenant dealing with the physical seed, leads to the view that only true believers are part of the Covenant of Grace in the Old Testament. In other words, only the elect are members of the Covenant of Grace. Circumcised descendants of Abraham were not born into the Covenant of Grace but were born as sinners into the Covenant of Works. Although they were given the gospel in the promise to Abraham, they were placed under the legal obligation to obey God by the requirement of circumcision of the Abrahamic Covenant and the law of the Mosaic Covenant.[106] Griffiths argues that when Paul refers to the promise in Galatians he does not have in mind the Abrahamic or Mosaic Covenants, but he has in view what was said to Abraham in Genesis 15 that caused him to believe.[107] The implication is that there is no promise of salvation in the Abrahamic or Mosaic Covenants because the descendants of Abraham were born into the Covenant of Works. This view of these two covenants is too

---

105. Robert J. Cara, 'The Use of the Old Testament in the New: Trusting the New Testament's Hermeneutic,' in *A Biblical-Theological Introduction to the New Testament*, ed. Michael J. Kruger (Wheaton, IL: Crossway, 2016), pp. 595, n. 8. He gives examples of how the New Testament uses one of the Ten Commandments for first, second, or third uses of the law.

106. Johnson, *The Kingdom of God*, pp. 96, 117.

107. Griffiths, *Covenant Theology*, p. 55. In a later chapter he argues that the Old Testament believer was a member of the New Covenant (p. 135).

negative. The continuing obligation to keep perfectly the Law of God continues, but that is different from saying that the Covenant of Works continues as a covenant.[108] The Mosaic Covenant was necessary for the continuation of the promises of the Abrahamic Covenant, including the spiritual promises. These promises are taken up by each of the covenants and advanced in the progress of redemptive history.[109] If the Abrahamic Covenant has two aspects to it, then so do the Mosaic and the Davidic Covenants because the same promises are found in those covenants and there are conditional elements in them. Rather, each of the covenants advance the one plan of God for salvation and those who are descendants of Abraham in the Old Testament are born into the Covenant of Grace.[110] One must distinguish between the Covenant of Grace made with the elect and the historical administration of it that includes everyone one who is circumcised. Some within the Reformed Baptist view, the first view discussed in this chapter, acknowledge that there were people in the Covenant of Grace in the Old Testament who were not true believers.[111]

This section has tried to interact with some of the distinctives of the Confessional Baptists. The Reformed Baptists are much closer to the views of the WCF than the Historic Baptists. They affirm one Covenant of Grace with each individual covenant being related to the ongoing

---

108.   The chart that Johnson uses has the Covenant of Works in a solid black box below the Covenant of Grace in a solid gray box to show that they coexist (*Fatal Flaw of Infant Baptism*, pp. 247-48). In a class that I teach with my colleague, Dr Robert J. Cara, he draws a chart that represents the Covenant of Grace and the Covenant of Works as two overarching covenants, but the Covenant of Works is presented as a dotted line to show that the covenant itself has come to an end but the requirement to keep the law continues.

109.   See Chapter 6 for arguments on the unity of the covenants that includes the Mosaic Covenant.

110.   Of course, this does not deny that everyone is born a sinner in need of God's grace for salvation.

111.   Waldron states the following in commenting on the required response in the divine covenants: 'It is, of course true, that some individuals *in that covenant*, because of their disobedience, would not enjoy its blessing and fruition' (*The 1689 Baptist Confession*, p. 119, emphasis supplied). Blackburn states, 'One could be a true member in good standing of any of the administrations of the Old Covenant, but still not be a recipient of God's grace and salvation' ('Covenant Theology Simplified,' p. 60). He also says that this is not the case in the New Covenant.

progression of the Covenant of Grace. They do not see as many divisions within the individual covenants that the Historic Baptists do. They also discuss the administration of the New Covenant, but it is on different terms than the Old Covenant and is administered only to those who believe. Both Baptist groups would affirm that only believers are in the New Covenant and so only believers should be baptized.

Baptists who adhere to the 2LCF have much in common with Presbyterians who adhere to the WCF. Both affirm a bi-covenantal framework to Scripture between the Covenant of Works and the Covenant of Grace. Both affirm the traditional view of justification by faith and the imputation of Adam's sin and Christ's righteousness. Both affirm the revelation of the Covenant of Grace in redemptive history starting in Genesis 3. Most Confessional Baptists agree with conservative Presbyterians on the role of the moral law and the continuing relevance of the Christian Sabbath because the 2LCF (19.3-5; 22.7-8) and the WCF (19.3-5; 21.7-8) agree on these questions.[112] Agreement on these major theological questions is significant and is something Baptists and Presbyterians can be thankful for, even while they disagree on other important issues. The Baptists covered in the next chapter will not agree on the role of the moral law and the Sabbath.[113] There are other issues that could be discussed here, but many of these will be discussed in the next chapter (the New Covenant in Jeremiah 31, circumcision, and baptism).

---

112. Works on the law from this perspective include Walter J. Chantry, *God's Righteous Kingdom* (Carlisle, PA: The Banner of Truth Trust, 1980) and Richard C. Barcellos, *In Defense of the Decalogue: A Critique of New Covenant Theology* (Winepress Publishing, 2001). Works on the Sabbath include Walter J. Chantry, *Call the Sabbath a Delight* (Carlisle, PA: The Banner of Truth Trust, 1991) and Richard C. Barcellos, *Getting the Garden Right: Adam's Work and God's Rest in Light of Christ* (Cape Coral, FL: Founders Press, 2017), pp. 81-273.

113. Works on the law from this perspective include John G. Reisinger, *Tablets of Stone* (Southbridge, MA: Crowne Publications, 1989); Tom Wells and Fred Zaspel, *New Covenant Theology* (Frederick, MD: New Covenant Media, 2002); and Stephen J. Wellum, 'Progressive Covenantalism and the Doing of Ethics,' in *Progressive Covenantalism*, pp. 215-33. For an analysis of the Sabbath question, see D. A. Carson, ed., *From Sabbath to Lord's Day: A Biblical, Historical, and Theological Investigation* (Grand Rapids: Zondervan, 1982) and Thomas R. Schreiner, 'Good-bye and Hello: The Sabbath Command for New Covenant Believers,' in *Progressive Covenantalism*, pp. 159-88.

CHAPTER 13

Progressive Covenantalism

❀ ❀ ❀

Introduction

JUST as among the Presbyterian and Reformed churches there are several different approaches to covenant theology, so the Baptists are not monolithic in their views. The last chapter covered the Confessional Reformed Baptists who are the closest to the covenant theology of the WCF. Although Baptists agree on believer's baptism and questions related to ecclesiology, there are differences on other issues, such as the role of the moral law and the continuing relevance of the fourth commandment. The Confessional Baptists differ from New Covenant Theology (hereafter NCT)[1] and Progressive Covenantalism (hereafter PC) on the moral law. The views of PC are fairly recent, expressed in the magesterial work, *Kingdom Through Covenant* (hereafter *KTC*).[2] There is significant overlap in the views of NCT and PC in

---

1. Books written from the perspective of new covenant theology include John G. Reisinger, *Tablets of Stone* (Southbridge, MA: Crowne, 1989); Tom Wells and Fred Zaspel, *New Covenant Theology: Description, Definition, Defense* (Frederick, MD: New Covenant Media, 2002); and Blake White, *What is New Covenant Theology? An Introduction* (Frederick, MD: New Covenant Media, 2012).

2. Peter J. Gentry and Stephen J. Wellum, *Kingdom through Covenant: A Biblical-Theological Understanding of the Covenants* (Wheaton, IL: Crossway, 2018).

the area of the law and the nature of the New Covenant, but PC has distinguished itself from some who are NCT in certain areas, such as a covenant at creation, the active obedience of Christ, and imputation.[3] The book *KTC* will be the major work examined in this chapter to understand the views of PC, but there will be references to other works that are relevant to the discussion.[4] The goal will be to highlight the distinctives of their approach and the areas of disagreement with covenant theology.[5]

Progressive covenantalism seeks a middle way (*via media*) between covenant theology and dispensationalism because they believe that both approaches have problems in certain areas of their systems.[6] A covenant is the expression of a relationship with God, the universal king, who establishes His rule in the lives of His people through His faithfulness and loyal love (hence kingdom through covenant).[7] The term 'progressive' underscores the unfolding nature of God's revelation over time and the term 'covenantalism' emphasizes that God's plan unfolds

---

3. Steve Lehrer, *New Covenant Theology: Questions Answered* [n.p.: Steve Lehrer, 2006) is one such work that differs from *KTC* in these areas. For a comparison of similarities and differences between NCT and PC, see Scott R. Swain, 'New Covenant Theologies,' in *Covenant Theology*, eds. Guy P. Waters, J. Nicholas Reid, and John Muether (Crossway November 2020). NCT and PC share a common theological foundation, a common theological method, and common theological conclusions.

4. The book, *KTC*, is not an easy book to summarize and review. It is almost 900 pages with the Appendices, and is written by two authors, one an Old Testament scholar and the other a New Testament scholar. Each author covers similar ground so that there is not one discussion of the covenants, but at least two, and although these discussions agree on the basic issues, the two discussions are at times very different from each other. The book could have been considerably shorter if the discussions of the covenants had been combined and the disagreements with covenant theology and dispensationalism had not been repeated over and over again.

5. Covenant theology is not easy to define because authors take different views on a variety of issues. This author understands covenant theology from the perspective of the WCF. This book has been written to try to explain covenant theology from that perspective.

6. The major problem with dispensationalism is the way they handle the promise of land and the major problem with covenant theology is the way they handle the genealogical principle in Genesis 17.

7. *KTC*, 650-51. A covenant also includes obligations between the parties of the covenant. A sharp distinction should not be made between the treaty and royal grant because an OT covenant may have features of both (*KTC*, pp. 165-67).

through the covenants.[8] The Bible presents a plurality of covenants that progressively reveal God's *one* redemptive plan for His *one* people, which is fulfilled in Christ in the New Covenant.[9] The purpose of this approach is to demonstrate

'... how central and foundational the concept of *covenant* is to the Bible's narrative plot structure and, second, how a number of crucial theological differences within Christian theology, and the resolution of those differences, are directly tied to one's understanding of how the biblical covenants unfold and relate to each other.'[10]

The major covenants in the Bible include the covenant with creation (Gen. 1–3), the covenant with Noah (Gen. 6–9), the covenant with Abraham (Gen. 12/15/17), the Mosaic Covenant (Exod. 19:3b-8/20–24), the covenant with David (2 Samuel 7/Psalm 89), and the New Covenant (Jer. 31-34; Ezek. 33:29–39:29).[11]

The Noahic Covenant

The first covenant examined by *KTC* is the Noahic Covenant because this is the first time that the word 'covenant' occurs in Scripture. Genesis 6 and 9 refer back to a covenant established at creation. This is based on the fact that the normal construction for initiating a covenant is not used in Genesis 6 and 9 (*kārat bᵉrît*), but one that refers to a covenant previously initiated (*hēq'm bᵉrît*). All the blessings and ordinances that God gave to Adam and Eve are now to be made with Noah and his descendants.[12] The Noahic Covenant includes Noah, his descendants, and all of creation with the promise never again to destroy

---

8.   Stephen J. Wellum and Brent E. Parker, eds., *Progressive Covenantalism* (Nashville, TN: B&H Academic, 2016). p. 2. This work includes various chapters that discuss some of the distinctives of PC (the law, circumcision, the Sabbath, ecclesiology, etc.)

9.   *KTC*, p. 34-35 (emphasis original). There is an acknowledgement of a fundamental unity in God's plan of salvation through the covenants even if there is a reluctance to use the term Covenant of Grace (Swain, 'New Covenant Theologies' in *Covenant Theology* (November 2020).

10.   *KTC*, p. 21.

11.   Ibid., pp. 166-67.

12.   Ibid., pp. 188, 195-201. This claim is supported by looking at the Flood narrative as a new creation and by drawing parallels between Adam and Noah.

the earth with a flood. This covenant allows God to work out His plan of redemption and points to the coming deliverance in Christ.[13]

The Creation Covenant

KTC affirms that there is a covenant with creation in Genesis 1–3. Besides the argument that the term 'covenant' does not have to be present for there to be a covenant, the exegesis of Genesis 1:26-28 substantiates the existence of a covenant.[14] The fact that human beings are created in God's image shows that they have a relationship to God as sons and a relationship to creation as servant kings. In the ancient Near East, family relationships and kingly relationships are covenantal, requiring loyal love, obedience, and trust.[15] This covenant relationship is not completely captured by the term 'Covenant of Works' because it was not an impersonal relationship between contracting parties, but a gracious relationship to be lived out and fully enjoyed. It also creates too sharp a distinction between creation and the subsequent covenants. It is better to view the subequent covenants more in continuity with the creation covenant and not as a foil to them. However, it is acknowledged that Adam was required to render perfect obedience and that a fully obedient Adam would have been granted eternal life on the basis of his obedience.[16] Later, in a chapter on theological implications for Christology and the Christian life, there is a fuller discussion of the active obedience of Christ and the imputation of His righteousness is affirmed as the basis for justification by faith.[17]

---

13. Ibid., pp. 174-75. Schreiner calls the Noahic Covenant the 'covenant of preservation instituted by God to preserve human beings from destruction' (*Covenant and God's Purpose for the World*, p. 31).

14. Ibid., pp. 213-15. Gentry contends that Williamson's definition of a covenant (see Chapter 9) prejudices the question against a covenant at creation because he argues that rather than establishing a divine-human relationship, a covenant seals or formalizes it (*Sealed with an Oath*, pp. 75-76). He also thinks that Williamson's assertions of God's universal purpose in creation and of God's intentions, through Noah, to fulfill His original creative intent (*Sealed with an Oath*, pp. 51, 75) are in reality backdoor references to the (covenantal) commitment of the Creator to His creation.

15. *KTC*, 254. Gentry also argues that Hosea 6:7 and Jeremiah 33:19-26 refer back to a creation covenant.

16. Ibid., pp. 675-76.

17. Ibid., pp. 775-82.

The Abrahamic Covenant

The Abrahamic Covenant is set in the plot structure of Genesis with God making a new start with Abraham. The promises of God are given in Genesis 12 and they are ratified in a covenant in Genesis 15.[18] The covenant in Genesis 15 is confirmed in Genesis 17. Abraham did not demonstrate full integrity before God, so God emphasized to Abraham the need to walk before Him in obedience (17:2) as He confirmed His covenant promises. Genesis 17 emphasizes more the international significance of Abraham in becoming a multitude of nations. Also, circumcision is given as a physical sign of the covenant signifying membership in the covenant community (17:14). Negatively, if a person was not circumcised he would be cut off from the community. Postively, circumcision symbolized complete devotion to the service of God.[19] There are several aspects to the seed of Abraham. The natural, biological seed includes every person biologically descended from Abraham (Ishmael, Isaac, the sons of Keturah) who received the sign of circumcision. The natural (biological) special seed was the line through which God worked out His covenant purposes (Isaac, Jacob, and Israel), culminating in the nation of Israel. The ultimate seed of Abraham refers to the true, unique seed, Christ Himself (Gal. 3:16), who is the fulfillment of the promise to Abraham, rooted in Genesis 3:15. Finally, all believers, regardless of nationality, are the spiritual seed of Abraham in the New Covenant, consisting of those who are circumcised of heart and united to Christ by faith.[20]

KTC argues against Williamson's view that Genesis 15 and 17 are two covenants (see Williamson's views discussed in Chapter 9). The phrase used in Genesis 17 is 'to confirm a covenant' (*hēq'm b^{e}rît*) rather than to 'cut a covenant' (*kārat b^{e}rît*), which is normally used to initiate a covenant relationship. Williamson also does not discuss Genesis 15 and 17 in the plot line of the Abraham narratives as a whole. Abraham grew in faith, obedience, and understanding in relationship to

---

18. Ibid., pp. 284-93. There is a lengthy discussion whether the covenant ceremony of Genesis 15 was a self-maledictory oath. Gentry concludes it was and the fact that only God passed through the slain animals showed that the promise depended on Him alone.

19. Ibid., p. 311.

20. Ibid., pp. 691-92.

God's commands, promises, and revelations. This explains the thirteen year gap between Genesis 15 and 17 during which Abraham and Sarah sought to fulfill God's promise by their own efforts (Genesis 16). It is arbitrary to call the covenant in Genesis 15 a temporal covenant and the one in Genesis 17 an eternal covenant. In Genesis 15 the covenant grants 'land' to Abraham (15:18-21) and in Genesis 17 this is called an eternal possession (17:8). Later texts in both Old and New Testaments never refer to God's dealings with Abraham as 'covenants' (plural).[21] Thus, there is only one covenant between God and Abraham.[22]

The Mosaic Covenant

The Mosaic Covenant is found in both the book of Exodus and Deuteronomy.[23] This covenant is significant because all denominational differences ultimately derive from different understandings of the relation of the Mosaic Covenant to God's people today. The promises of God to Abraham focused on descendants and land. In Exodus to Deuteronomy there was the anticipation of the fulfillment of these promises. The Mosaic Covenant was given to administer the fulfillment of the divine promises to Abraham and to the nation as a whole, and through them to the entire world.[24]

The Mosaic or Old Covenant is based on grace and, as in the New Covenant, grace motivates the keeping of the covenant. The Old Covenant is not like the New Covenant because the keeping of the covenant depends on Israel's promise to obey.[25] The Ten Words[26]

---

21. Ibid., pp. 275-80.

22. Ibid., pp. 312-16; see also Schreiner who argues for one covenant with conditional and unconditional elements (*Covenant and God's Purpose for the World*, pp. 51-56).

23. Since Scripture usually names a covenant according to the human partner, and Exodus 34:27 states that this covenant is made with Moses and Israel, it is best to call this the Mosaic Covenant or the Israelite Covenant. It is never called the Sinai Covenant in Scripture (*KTC*, p. 343).

24. Ibid., pp. 339, 342.

25. Ibid., p. 350.

26. *KTC* makes the point that the precise expression the 'Ten Commandments' does not occur in the OT (Ibid., 365); rather, the commands that form the basis of the covenant are called the 'Ten Words' (Exod. 34:28; Deut. 4:13, 10:4). The word 'commandments' is used in the NT to refer to these ten laws (Matt. 5; 19:17; Mark 10:19; Luke 18:20; Rom. 7:7-8; 13:9).

demonstrate how a relationship with God is lived out. On the other hand, the tension in the plot structure of Deuteronomy, particularly chapters 29–30, is the tension between the blessing and cursing sections (30:15-20) and the fact that Yahweh had not given the people a circumcised heart.[27] This relates to the purpose of the law to reveal and intensify sin in preparation for the coming of Christ. God held out the promise of life to an obedient covenant partner (Lev. 18:5), but due to sin this is impossible; rather, the law brings greater condemnation.[28]

Although there is a clear distinction between the Ten Words and the covenant judgments,[29] it is inappropriate to see the former as eternal and the latter as temporal because both constitute the covenant made between God and Israel.[30] Also, the moral, ceremonial, and civil distinction is foreign to the laws of the Old Testament and is imposed on it. The different categories of the law are all mixed together. Even the Ten Words have ceremonially elements. The problem with this distinction is that it is used by those who want to say the ceremonial and civil laws no longer apply but the moral law is eternal. But Jesus has fulfilled both the Ten Words and the judgments (Matt. 5:17). Hebrews also declares that these laws are made obsolete by the New Covenant (Heb. 8:13). However, the righteousness of God, codified and encapsulated in the Old Covenant, has not changed; in fact, this same righteousness is now codified and enshrined in the New Covenant. Thus, as a code, the Ten Words do not apply today but the righteousness contained in the code is the same as that in the New Covenant.[31]

An important text that has implications for how descendants are included in the making of a covenant is Deuteronomy 5:1-6. The covenant that God made 'with us at Horeb' (5:2) refers to the covenant at Sinai in Exodus 19–24. Moses states that this covenant was not made

---

27. Ibid., pp. 430-33.

28. Ibid., pp. 695, 698-99.

29. The Ten Words are different from the covenant judgments in the following ways: they are presented as absolute commands or prohibitions (usually in the second-person singular), they are not related to a specific social situation, and there are no fines or punishments associated with them (Ibid., p. 344).

30. Ibid., p. 393. The covenant is one package and so it is inappropriate to accept the Ten Words and reject the judgements.

31. Ibid., p. 394, n. 112.

with our fathers (5:3), a reference to Abraham, Isaac, and Jacob. The language at the end of 5:3, that this covenant was made with us who are alive here today, is a rhetorical device where Moses seeks to connect the people at Moab with the covenant at Sinai, even though they were children at that time. Deuteronomy is a renewal of the covenant because the previous generation broke the covenant and died in the wilderness because of unbelief. Thus, the covenant is made not only with those who are present, but also with all future generations of Israel so that the chidren cannot argue that the covenant at Sinai was made with their parents but not with them.[32]

The New Covenant of Jeremiah 31[33]

In the examination of the New Covenant in Jeremiah 31, the nature of the New Covenant community is discussed. Based on the statement: 'And no longer shall each one teach his neighbor and each his brother, saying, "Know the LORD, for they shall all know me, from the least of them to the greatest, declares the LORD" (31:34 NKJV)', *KTC* argues that all members of the New Covenant are believers. In the Old Covenant, people became members of the covenant by being born into the community. Not all were believers, which led to a situation where some members could urge other members to know the Lord. In the New Covenant a person does not become a member by physical birth but by spiritual birth through faith. The only members of the New Covenant are true believers: 'all *members* are *believers*, and *only* believers are members.'[34] Therefore, in the New Covenant community there will no longer be members who urge other members to know the Lord. There are no unregenerate members in this community. All are believers and all know the Lord because all have experienced the forgiveness of sins.

The later edition of *KTC* (2018) answers several objections concerning their view of the New Covenant in the earlier edition (2012), particularly

---

32. Ibid., pp. 437-38.

33. Although the Davidic Covenant is very important, there is nothing unusually distinct in the discussion of that covenant (see *KTC*, pp. 443-486 and Schreiner, *Covenant and God's Purpose for the World*, pp. 73-88).

34. Ibid., p. 555 (emphasis original).

their rejection of understanding the promises of Jeremiah 31:31-34 in an 'already, not yet' way. First, they argue that this distinction is a confusion of the kingdom of God and the New Covenant. Although the kingdom of God is here in an 'already, not yet' way, the apostles do not speak of the New Covenant in this way. Hebrews 8 cites all of Jeremiah 31 and affirms it is here in its fullness now.

Second, based on a discussion of 1 John 1:5–2:2, the forgiveness of sins cannot be understood in an 'already, not yet' way. Believers in Jesus Christ experience the full forgiveness of sins because moment-by-moment, when and if a believer sins, Jesus Christ as high priest is already presenting the merits of His finished work on the believer's behalf. Although it is important to confess our sin, God does not wait for us to confess our sin to apply the atoning work of Christ. So, we now have full forgiveness of sins. The final judgment will only confirm what believers already possess.

Third, the parable of the sower (Matt. 13:1-23) should not be used to argue that the New Covenant community is a community made up of believers and unbelievers. In the church, believers experience the blessings of the New Covenant which do not apply to the unregenerate. The only blessings the unregenerate receive are those given in the covenant with creation to all human beings.

Finally, *KTC* makes clear that the law written on the heart of the believer in Jeremiah 31:31-34 is not the Ten Commandments.[35] New Covenant believers are not bound by the Ten Commandments as a code. They do not apply to believers today because our relationship with God is determined by the New Covenant. However, the righteousness of God demonstrated in the Ten Commandments is enshrined in the New Covenant. New Covenant divine instruction calls believers to love their neighbors so that it is clear that adultery, murder, and stealing are still covenant violations. Thus, there is no evidence that the church is a transformed people in a 'now, not yet' way. The church has been transferred from Adam to Christ, individually and corporately, and

---

35. The role of the moral law in the New Covenant is not examined in this chapter; for a grounding of the moral law in creation and anthropology as a basis for seeing the relevance of the moral law for the New Covenant, see Swain, 'New Covenant Theologies' in *Covenant Theology* (November 2020).

has become participants in the age to come. At present we enjoy what it means to be God's new people.[36]

The strongest evidence that the church at present includes unbelievers are the warning passages in the book of Hebrews. *KTC* eventually recognizes that there may be in the church professed believers who were baptized and accepted as part of the New Covenant community, who are not really part of the community. But this does not prove that the New Covenant community is a mixed community of believers and unbelievers because unbelievers do not receive the blessings of being in Christ, even in a partial sense. The fact that the New Covenant cannot be broken is also important because if the New Covenant is meant to remedy apostate covenant members, how can it be possible for New Covenant members to apostasize? Otherwise, the New Covenant will be like the Old Covenant. In conclusion, the best way to understand the warning passages within a transformed, regenerative view of the church is to see them as a means of salvation.[37]

The Genealogical Principle

The way the genealogical principle in Genesis 17:7 is understood is also important for how one understands of the nature of the New Covenant community. Covenant theology needs to give more attention to the typological nature of this principle in relationship to Christ. Even though Christ is recognized as the true Israel, a quick move is made from Israel to the church without contemplating the ecclesiological implications of Christ as the antitype of Israel. Under the New Covenant, the order is not Christ, then the believer, then the children, but it is Christ as head of all those He represents, who are believers only. The genealogical principle does not remain unchanged in the New Testament because the church is seen as something new in relationship to Christ her head.[38]

The church is now identified as the spiritual, believing seed of Abraham, the new people of God from every nation (Eph. 2:11; Rev. 5:9),

---

36. Ibid., pp. 559-62, 808.

37. Ibid., pp. 803, 811-12. They argue that only by assuming that a professed believer is a New Covenant member could someone conclude that the New Covenant is partially fulfilled.

38. Ibid., pp. 152, 660-62.

who are regenerate. To be a member of the church is to be united to Christ and to have the Spirit. Everyone within the New Covenant community is given the Spirit as a seal, a down payment, and guarantee of the promised inheritance (Eph 1:13-14). The New Testament knows nothing of one who is in Christ but who is also not regenerate and awaiting glorification.[39]

A proper view of the genealogical principle goes hand-in-hand with the nature of the New Covenant community and the understanding of baptism as a sign given only to those who have faith. The fundamental meaning of baptism is that it signifies a believer's union with Christ, which is received by grace through faith, and all the benefits included in that union. Circumcision, on the other hand, as the sign of the Abrahamic Covenant does not carry the same meaning as baptism in the New Covenant. Rather, it marks out a national people to set them apart as a kingdom of priests and a holy nation (Gen. 17:9-13). Although circumcision began to point forward to the need of an internal circumcision of the heart, the genealogical principle was transformed with the coming of Christ where spiritual adoption, not natural descent, became the mark of the New Covenant community. Colossians 2:11-13 does not make the connection between circumcision of the flesh and baptism, as if the latter replaced the former, but between circumcision of the heart and baptism. Circumcision of the flesh and baptism are different because in baptism the objective realities of having died to sin and being made alive to Christ have actually taken place. Baptism communicates the grace of God to those who have faith, something that could not be said about circumcision of the flesh.[40]

Evaluation of Progressive Covenantalism (PC)

The differences between progressive covenantalism and covenant theology are significant not only because they involve the interpretation of Scripture, but also because they impact church practice. Both of these are important, but the differences in church practice hits people where they live, particularly the question of who should be baptized.

---

39. Ibid., pp. 660, 751, 755.
40. Ibid., pp. 816-17, 821-24.

The goal of this section is to give some perspective on the arguments of PC, recognizing that those who are firm in their beliefs will not likely change their minds. It is beyond the scope of this section to give detailed, exegetical arguments concerning the different views.[41]

The Nature of the New Covenant Community

One of the main emphases of PC is that the New Covenant community is not a mixed community made up of believers and unbelievers. This is based on the promise of Jeremiah 31:34, that 'they shall all know me', which is understood as an absolute statement. This view is set over against covenant theology that views the New Covenant community as a mixed community, partly based on infant baptism, but also based on the fact that all the promises of the Old Testament partake of a 'now, but not yet' character. Sometimes the view of covenant theology is presented as if the mixed community of the church is understood *in the same way* as the mixed community of ancient Israel in its structure and nature, as if there is there is no difference between Israel and the church,[42] and as if there is contentment with the *status quo* of having unbelievers as part of the covenant community.[43] The church is not the same in structure and nature as Israel. The church is not seeking to establish a theocracy because it is spiritual in nature, engaged in fighting spiritual battles, and not trying to advance through physical warfare (Eph. 6:10-20).[44]

The existential reality in all churches is that there are unbelievers who are part of the church, including churches that practice believer's baptism. It is easy to become confused with the terminology used in *KTC* to explain Jeremiah 31:34. Absolute statements are made that only true believers make up the New Covenant and the New

---

41. The focus will be on *KTC* which has been called the defining document of progressive covenantalism (Jason C. Meyer, 'The Mosaic Law, Theological Systems, and the Glory of Christ,' in *Progressive Covenantalism*, p. 73), with reference or limited interaction with other works.

42. *KTC*, 810 (see also pp. 90 and 97).

43. Berkhof comments concerning children in the covenant that it is incumbent on them to accept their covenant responsibilities voluntarily by a true confession of faith (*Systematic Theology*, pp. 287-88).

44. Both PC and covenant theology recognize unity between Israel and the church on some level.

Covenant community. There is no distinction in the use of the terms New Covenant, New Covenant community, or covenant community. They are used interchangeabley and many times are not qualified in any way.[45] Later in the book the term 'profession of faith' is used to describe those whose profession may not have been genuine.[46] If these 'believers' were baptized and accepted as part of the New Covenant community, but were not really true believers, this raises the question whether everyone in the New Covenant community is a true believer. The response is that this does not prove that the New Covenant community is a mixed community of believers and unbelievers because unbelievers do not receive the blessings of Christ. Plus, Jeremiah 31:32 implies that the New Covenant cannot be broken. This confuses election and covenant. It is true that the New Covenant cannot be broken for those who are *true* members of the New Covenant (the elect), but not everyone who professes faith in Christ and is baptized as a believer is a true member of the New Covenant, yet they are members of the New Covenant community. So much rides on their view that the New Covenant community is not a mixed community that it feels like special pleading to argue that there are professed believers, who may not be true believers, in the New Covenant community, but that does not make it a mixed community. Yet not everyone who professes faith in Christ and is baptized is truly united to Christ. Some who profess faith turn out to be unbelievers. The evidence for this may not happen for years or even decades, but they were part of the New Covenant community during that time. We do not know fully who is a true believer and who is not; otherwise the warning passages and church discipline, including excommunication, would not be needed.[47]

---

45. See *KTC*, pp. 554-56 (this is Gentry's discussion of the New Covenant).

46. *KTC*, pp. 803, 811 (this is Wellum's discussion of the New Covenant community).

47. James R. White also argues that all those in the New Covenant are true believers based on Jeremiah 31:34, but he distinguishes between the New Covenant and the visible church, which contains both true and false covenant members. There can be no apostasy from the New Covenant, but there can be apostasy from a false profession of faith in Christ from someone who is a member of the visible church ('The Newness of the New Covenant: Better Covenant, Better Mediator, Better Sacrifice, Better Ministry, Better Hope, Better Promises (Part Two)' in *Recovering a Covenantal Heritage*, ed. Richard C. Barcellos (Palmdale, CA: RBAP, 2014). However, White argues against

Paedobaptists recognize that, while everyone who is a true member of the New Covenant will not fall away from the faith (the elect), there will be those who are not true members of the New Covenant because their profession of faith is false. Yet, from a human standpoint they are received as part of the New Covenant, and thus as part of the New Covenant community (the church). They receive the benefits of being part of the community, including the Lord's Supper, but this results in a mixed covenant community. God knows if the profession of faith is a true profession because God knows the elect. Church leaders do not have infallible insight into a person's heart, so anyone who makes a credible profession of faith is baptized. If such persons fall away from the faith it is evidence that they were not really part of the New Covenant. Even with adult baptism, many Baptists are hesitant to acknowledge that the non-elect who profess faith are part of the New Covenant based on Jeremiah 31:34. Yet, the book of Hebrews draws a parallel between the Old Covenant and the New Covenant based on the reality that, in both, people can break the covenant. If there was judgment in the Old Covenant on someone who set aside the Law of Moses (that is, broke the covenant), how much worse punishment is there for those in the New Covenant who profane the blood of the covenant (Heb. 10:28-29). The parallel between the two covenants is striking.[48] Would it then at least be appropriate to say that it appears from a human standpoint that someone today who professes faith is in the New Covenant? It would clear up some confusion in the discussion if Baptists at least distinguished between the New Covenant and the New Covenant community. In other words, a distinction should be made between God's establishment of the New Covenant with true believers, the elect, and the existence of the New Covenant community, the church, where there are professed believers who are part of the New Covenant community. Cowan recognizes this distinction in the following statements:

Richard Pratt's view that the New Covenant is not yet here in its fullness ('Infant Baptism in the New Covenant,' in *The Case for Covenantal Infant Baptism*, ed. Gregg Strawbridge [Phillipsburg, NJ: P&R, 2003], pp. 156-75).

48.   Pratt, 'Infant Baptism in the New Covenant,' p. 170. He writes, 'Judgment was and is possible for both the old and new covenant communities and judgment flows from covenant breaking that leads to that judgment.'

I do not believe genuine apostasy is possible for New Covenant members, given the nature of the New Covenant according to NT authors. Therefore, those who formally affiliate with the New Covenant community and subsequently depart from the faith experience *phenomological* apostasy. They are examples of 1 John 2:19, demonstrating that they were never actually covenant members in whom the promises of Jer. 31:31-34 had been fulfilled.[49]

Baptists should be able to recognize that there is a category of professing adults who are in the covenant legally without the guarantee that every one who professes faith is a true believer, and without having to affirm infant baptism. The goal could be a regenerate community without having to say that every believer is a true believer, or without denying that there are some who are received as members of the New Covenant who may not be true believers. This would allow the visible church, the New Covenant community, to be a mixed community where some who profess faith are not true believers.

The Warning Passages and the 'Already, Not Yet' Character of Salvation

Cowan argues that the warning passages are a means of salvation intended to ensure the perseverance of the saints. This view is well argued and has merit, epecially if the warning passages are directed to both true believers and professed believers in the church.[50] He argues that exhortations to persevere in order to obtain eternal life are not a denial that Christians now possess eternal life. Rather, it is

---

49. Christopher W. Cowan, 'The Warning Passages of Hebrews and the New Covenant Community', in *Progressive Covenantalism*, eds. Stephen J. Wellum and Brent E. Parker (Nashville, TN: B&H Academic, 2016) p. 197, n. 38.

50. There seems to be hesitancy to include professed believers in the warnings because the warnings are not viewed as retrospective declarations that certain individuals were never Christians in the first place. The statement is made that the author of Hebrews warns believers (not pseudo-believers) to avoid apostasy. But then it is recognized that those who separate themselves from the covenant community demonstrate that they were never true believers (Cowan, 'Warning Passages', pp. 201-03). Since we do not absolutely know those who are true believers and those who are not, the warning passages legitimately apply to both. Even if the main purpose of the warning passages is prospective so that readers will heed the warnings and escape the consequences threatened, the result is to show that some professed believers were not true believers.

an acknowledgement of the 'already, not yet' character of salvation. Concerning the book of Hebrews, salvation is primarily presented as a future reward, but it also clearly reflects the inaugurated eschatology of the rest of the New Testament. Although the apostles present a variety of metaphors to describe eschatological life in the kingdom of God, all of them have present and future dimensions because salvation has been inaugurated, but not yet consummated. The redemptive work of Christ is the objective basis of salvation, and the individual exercise of faith in Christ is the subjective means of salvation. The author of Hebrews can consistently speak of the once-for-all sacrifice of Christ and the corresponding realization of the covenant promises in the heart of believers (Heb. 8:7-12; 10:10-17, 22).[51] This view properly recognizes the completed accomplishment of salvation by Christ and the ongoing application of salvation to believers.[52] Perhaps more agreement between both sides can be achieved based on the distinction between the completed work of Christ and the ongoing application of salvation (the latter containing an 'already, not yet' aspect) and a determination to be more careful on the use of the terms 'New Covenant' and 'New Covenant community'. There is significant overlap between the two, but they are not identical because there are professing believers who are members of the church who are not part of the elect because their faith is not genuine. Thus, it is not possible for true believers, the elect, who are part of the New Covenant, to apostasize. It is possible, however, for a professing believer, who is received as a member of the New Covenant and is part of the New Covenant community (the church), to apostasize because he or she is not a true believer.

The Administration of the Covenant

Progressive covenantalism does not discuss very much the administration of the New Covenant. The terms of a covenant have to be administered

---

51. Cowan, 'The Warning Passages,' pp. 200-03.

52. *KTC* recognizes the 'already, not yet' nature of the kingdom of God inaugurated by Christ (pp. 736-38) and they argue that 'God's long-awaited kingdom is inaugurated in this world *through* the new covenant', as in 'kingdom through covenant' (p. 653; emphasis original), but they also argue that the New Covenant should not be seen as being 'now, but not yet' (p. 557). It is unclear how the kingdom can have this quality, and the New Covenant does not, when it is the kingdom that comes through covenant.

because we live in a fallen world and people are not always truthful or faithful. Jesus speaks of a branch that is 'in me' that does not bear fruit (John 15:2). There can be someone connected to Jesus, or associated with Him as a disciple, who is not a true believer, such as Judas Iscariot. If such a branch does not bear fruit it is removed.[53] Paul comments on the administration of the covenant in Romans 11:16-24 where he affirms the unity between Israel and the church by means of an olive tree. The root of the tree represents the Old Testament foundation, including its promises, that paved the way for the coming of Christ and the inclusion of Gentiles. Paul makes the point in verse 16 that, if the root is holy, so are the branches. Branches that are part of the olive tree are holy. There is no distinction in verse 16 concerning the spiritual condition of these branches. They are holy by virtue of being connected to the olive tree whose root is holy. Paul then makes the point that some of these branches were broken off so that the Gentiles, although wild olive shoots, could be grafted into the olive tree to share its nourishment. The branches broken off were removed because of their unbelief (v. 20).[54] Paul then warns the Gentiles who have been grafted into the olive tree that the same thing could happen to them (vv. 21-22). They too are considered part of the olive tree, and are thus holy, but they can also be cut off from the tree. In other words, it is possible for a branch to be considered holy because it is connected to the olive tree even though that branch is removed because of unbelief. There is a status of holiness that comes by being part of the covenant that is separate from the inward holiness that is the result of the Spirit's work in the life of a believer. This status of holiness refers to the legal aspect of the covenant.[55]

Marriage, for example, is a covenant where promises and vows are sealed with oaths and the exchange of rings. Marriage as a covenant

53. Strawbridge, 'The Polemics of Anabaptism from the Reformation Onward,' in *The Case for Covenantal Infant Baptism*, p. 282. He comments that regenerate people cannot be broken off which means that not all who are members of the New Covenant are regenerate.

54. Paul does not have spiritual Israel in view because the branches that manifest unbelief were part of the covenant.

55. For more on the legal aspect of the covenant, see Berkhof, *Systematic Theology*, pp. 286-89, Kline, *Kingdom Prologue*, pp. 362-64, and Vos, *Reformed Dogmatics*, pp. 2:104-05.

has a wonderful, personal side to it, but there is also a legal side to it. Both sides are important. The personal side enhances the marriage relationship, but it is incomplete without the legal side. Someone can be legally married and have less than a desirous personal relationship. The covenant we have with God has both a personal and a legal relationship to it.[56] This explains how someone can make a profession of faith, become legally part of the New Covenant, and be received into the New Covenant community when in reality they are not true believers. As members of the church, they have all the benefits that come with membership, including worship, the preaching of the Word, fellowship, partaking of the Lord's Supper, and spiritual oversight from the leaders of the church. For most members of the church the personal and the legal sides are a blessing, but for some who depart from the faith or begin to live a life of sin, the responsibilities related to the legal aspects of the covenant become important. Church discipline is for the restoration of the offender but sometimes it may end in excommunication. Without the legal administration of the covenant, there is no category for a professed believer who is not really a true believer, and there is no way to deal with such a person when they go astray. Both Presbyterian and Baptist churches desire a pure church and both of them need church discipline to help make it possible.[57]

The Genealogical Principle

Another difference between covenant theology and PC is the way the genealogical principle is understood (Gen. 17:7). The charge is made that covenant theology treats the genealogical principle in relationship to Israel but not in relationship to Christ. This is important because there are ecclesiological implications if this principle is treated typologically

---

56. Vos speaks of a relationship that is legal and a relationship that expresses fellowship (*Reformed Dogmatics*, p. 2:105).

57. It is inaccurate to argue that infants who are baptized are received into the church, or New Covenant, as full members (*KTC*, p. 97 and Jason S. DeRouchie, 'Father of a Multitude of Nations: New Covenant Ecclesiology in OT Perspective,' in *Progressive Covenantalism*, p. 23). Only those who accept Federal Vision teaching would affirm this view. Among the major conservative Presbyterian churches, baptized children are not allowed to partake of the Lord's Supper apart from being examined by the elders as to their faith in Christ (based on 1 Corinthians 11:28-30).

in relationship to Christ as the antitype of Israel. Then the church is seen as something new in relationship to Christ with Christ as head of those who are believers, but not believers and their children.[58] Thus, the legitimate recipients of baptism in the New Covenant community are believers only.

Several things can be mentioned to give some perspective to this question. First, there is a typological relationship between Israel and Christ because both are firstborn sons (Exod. 4:22; Matt. 2:15). In fact, Matthew presents Christ as recapitulating the early history of Israel as the true son who will fulfill all righteousness.[59] Israel had a special relationship with God, but Christ's relationship was even greater because of His special divine status.

Second, the principle of Genesis 17:7 is embedded in the Old Testament and has a special role in relationship to covenants. The way covenants work reinforce certain principles that aid the outworking of redemptive history. A covenant is administered through the representative principle whereby covenants include the descendants of the representative.[60] Every major covenant of the Old Testament includes the descendants as part of the very nature of the covenant (Gen. 9:8; 15:7; 17:7; Deut. 5:1-5; 2 Sam. 7:12-14).[61] Deuteronomy 5 is particularly interesting because most of the people Moses was speaking to were either children or were not even born when the covenant at Sinai was made, and yet Moses could say, 'The LORD spoke with you face to face at the mountain.'[62] The administration of the covenant also included blessings for faithfulness and judgment

---

58.   KTC, pp. 152, 660-62.

59.   Vern Poythress, *The Shadow of Christ in the Law of Moses* (Phillipsburg, NJ: P&R Publishing, 1991), pp. 252-55.

60.   Bryan Chapell, 'A Pastoral View of Infant Baptism,' in *The Case for Covenantal Infant Baptism*, pp. 13-14. He makes the point that the representative principle explains how women were included in the covenant even though they were not circumcised.

61.   Sinclair Ferguson, 'Infant Baptism View,' in *Baptism: Three Views*, ed. David F. Wright (Downers Grove, IL: IVP Academic, 2009), p. 102. He notes that the phrase 'and their seed' was part of the definition of a covenant.

62.   KTC recognizes this principle in its discussion of Deuteronomy 5:1-5 in the following statement, 'And this time the covenant is made not only with the Israel present but with all future generations of Israel so that the children cannot argue that the covenant at Sinai was with their parents and not with them' (p. 439).

for breaking it. The principle 'I will be your God and you will be my people' stresses the relationship that should develop in the covenant, but many times that relationship was broken. When covenant regulations were broken, the legal side to the covenant is demonstrated in covenant judgment.

God's covenant with Abraham promised numerous descendants who will be a blessing to the nations. Circumcision is the sign of the covenant given to all those who were of his household (Gen. 17:23-27). Not everyone who received the sign of circumcision followed Abraham's God and they were removed from the covenant community and the blessings of the covenant (Ishmael and Esau). Others were grafted into the covenant by faith (Rahab and Ruth) and lived as faithful members of the covenant (the child born to Ruth and Boaz even became part of the Davidic line). Circumcision should not be limited to a national covenant because the Abrahamic Covenant was intended by God to fulfill a spiritual purpose. Circumcision is an outward sign pointing to an inward, spiritual need.[63] The covenants develop in relationship to each other in an organic way, each taking up the promises of the covenants that have gone before. It is better to see one line that develops in redemptive history than to argue for different seeds of Abraham.[64] Paul describes Israel in the Old Testament as one olive tree from which natural branches are being broken off because of unbelief and wild olive shoots are being grafted in through faith (Rom. 11:16-24).

Because these principles are built into the administration of covenants, including the New Covenant, a typological understanding of the genealogical principle does not do justice to how the principle continues to operate in the New Covenant (Rom. 11:16-24). When Peter proclaims on the day of Pentecost that 'the promise is for you and your children and for all who are far off, everyone whom the Lord our God calls to himself,' he is using terminology that would be familiar to the audience he is addressing. Several times the audience is

---

63. Guy M. Richard, *Baptism: Answers to Common Questions* (Sanford, FL: Reformation Trust, 2019), pp. 44-49.

64. As in *KTC*, pp. 691-692 and John G. Reisinger, *Abraham's Four Seeds: A Biblical Examination of the Presuppositions of Covenant Theology and Dispensationalism* (Frederick, MD: New Covenant Media, 1998); see also Chapter 12 on Confessional Baptists.

identified as men (Acts 2:5, 14, 22) or brothers (Acts 2:29, 37).[65] These would be Jewish men who were heads of their households so that when Peter mentions 'you and your children' they would naturally think of the representative principle. The very fact that children are mentioned is significant in light of the way covenants operate.[66] Acts 2:39 uses a covenant formula based on Genesis 17:7 to include children in the promise.[67] This principle is exhibited in the household baptisms in the book of Acts, which include the households of Cornelius (10:48; 11:14), Lydia (16:15), and the Philippian jailer (16:31-34). These are examples of the gospel going to the Gentiles, those who are far off, and the pattern is the same as in Acts 2:39: the promise is to you and your children. Some may argue that the evidence from these incidents does not really prove that infants were baptized. In Cornelius' situation, baptism came after the Holy Spirit fell on them. In the case of the Philippian jailor, they spoke the Word of the Lord to him and to all who were in his house. But even in those situations, if there were infants in the household, they would not be included in receiving the Holy Spirit or in receiving the Word of the Lord. It is hard to conceive of Luke using the term 'household' if he meant to restrict

---

65.   Jamin Hübner, 'Acts 2:39 in its Context [Part 1]: An Exegetical Summary of Acts 2:39 and Paedobaptism,' in *Recovering a Covenantal Heritage*, p. 389. He highlights that Peter is talking primarily to Jewish men.

66.   A common argument is that the last phrase, 'everyone whom the Lord our God calls to himself,' is a phrase that limits the promise to those who are called (Jewett, *Infant Baptism*, p. 121). But the Jewish men to whom Peter is speaking would understand 'you and your children' in light of the covenant promise to Abraham. The astonishing thing is that this promise now goes out to a wider audience who are not aware of this promise and will have the opportunity to respond to it. Plus, when *hosos* is used with *an* it makes the expression more general, as in Matthew 22:9; Luke 9:5, and not more restrictive (*BDAG*, p. 729).

67.   Joel R. Beeke and Ray B. Lanning, 'Unto You, and to Your Children,' in *The Case for Covenantal Infant Baptism*, p. 56. Both Presbyterians (Simon J. Kistemaker, *Exposition of the Acts of the Apostles* [Grand Rapids: Baker, 1990], p. 106) and Baptists (Darrell L. Bock, *Acts* [BECNT; Grand Rapids: Baker Academic, 2007], p. 144) argue that the promise refers to the Holy Spirit. Although it is possible that Peter is thinking of Diaspora Jews and God-fearers, the development of this idea in Luke includes Gentiles (Bock, *Acts*, p. 145). David Peterson (*The Acts of the Apostles* [PNTC; Grand Rapids: Eerdmans, 2009], p. 156) argues that generally God's promise in Acts refers to his covenant commitment to Abraham (3:26; 7:17; 26:6).

baptism to adults.[68] Plus, the representative principle is evident in the statement to the head of the household, 'you will be saved, you and your household' (Acts 11:14; 16:31). The summary of the account of the Philippian jailor notes that he rejoiced along with his entire household that *he* had believed in God. The household rejoiced in the faith of the head of the household.[69]

Two other factors are important for this discussion. The first is that children are considered holy because they are part of the covenant whether or not they have believed. This corresponds to the legal side of the covenant in Romans 11:16-21, where branches are called holy because of their connection to the tree even though they are broken off because of unbelief. They were not holy in the experiential sense but in the sense that they were set apart because they were in the covenant. Paul describes something similar in 1 Corinthians 7:12-16 where the husband or wife becomes a Christian and wonders if he or she should stay married to an unbelieving spouse. Paul counsels that they should stay married if the unbelieving spouse wants to continue the marriage. Although such a situation can be difficult, part of the reason for staying married is the impact on both the unbelieving spouse and the children. Both are called holy. It would be inappropriate, however, to force an unbelieving spouse to be baptized, but they can be positively impacted by the influence of the believing spouse through godly example, the godly wisdom of the Word of God, and prayers offered for them. The children are also postively influenced because they are no longer unclean, but now they are holy. The word 'unclean' is a strong word that indicates unacceptability in the presence of the holy God (Lev. 10:9-10;

---

68. Jonathan M. Watt, 'The *Oikos* Formula' in *The Case for Covenantal Baptism*, 80-81. It is likely in the Greco-Roman world that infants were included because the make-up of the household was not just the nuclear family.

69. Chapell, 'A Pastoral View of Infant Baptism,' p. 21. There is debate whether 'household' goes with the main verb, in support of the ESV that the man believed, or if it goes with the participle, in support of the NAS 'having believed in God with his whole household.' Jewett offers the literal translation that the jailor 'rejoiced with all his house, himself believing' (*Infant Baptism*, p. 49). If the Presbyterians are accused of assuming infants are part of the household, the other side also makes assumptions, as in the comment about Lydia, 'there must have been other adults in her household ... who were led by her example to confess their faith with her in baptism' (Jewett, *Infant Baptism*, p. 49).

Num. 5:2-3).[70] There is a concept of holiness, used in the sense of being set apart, in connection with the covenant community in the New Testament (Rom. 11:11-26; Heb. 10:29).[71]

The second factor is that there is warrant to include children as part of the covenant because they are addressed as part of the church. Paul writes the letter of Ephesians 'To the saints who are in Ephesus' (1:1 NKJV), and then later in the letter exhorts the children to follow the fifth commandment (6:1-3). There is no qualification that only children who have believed should follow the fifth commandment. Rather, there is an expectation that children are being trained according to the Word of God through the influence of godly parents and other Christians (see also Colossians 1:1 with 3:20). If we teach our children the song, 'Jesus Loves Me,' before they have themselves expressed faith in Christ, then we are treating them as part of the covenant community. We should call them to accept for themselves the blessings of the covenant that have been promised to them in their baptism and to respond by faith in Jesus Christ.[72]

Several factors have been discussed concerning the way God operates through covenants that are also at work in the New Testament.[73] These include the following: the promise continues to be for the children of believers, the household baptisms, the representative principle, the external status of holiness in the sense of being set apart, and the way children are addressed as part of the covenant community. These factors are also important for the discussion of infant baptism as the sign of the New Covenant. A lot has been written on the meaning of circumcision and baptism and their relationship to each other. Only a few things can be touched on here.

Circumcision is the sign of the Abrahamic Covenant, placed on male infants, to show they are part of the covenant and that they are

---

70. Richard L. Pratt, Jr., 'Infant Baptism in the New Covenant,' p. 172. Jewett explains the children as being holy in the sense that they are not contaminated with the taint of illegitimacy (*Infant Baptism*, p. 133), a rather weak view of holy.

71. Contra Jewett who calls such use highly exceptional (*Infant Baptism*, p. 126).

72. Mark E. Ross, 'Baptism and Circumcision as Signs and Seals,' in *The Case for Covenantal Baptism*, p. 98.

73. The New Testament basis for these factors answers the charge that Presbyterians are merely reading the Old Testament into the New Testament because the New Testament itself teaches that the covenant continues to have these elements.

consecrated to God.[74] It promises that those who respond in faith and accept their covenant responsibilities will receive the removal of the uncleanness of their flesh in the circumcising of their hearts in order to love God. If the uncircumcised heart is a heart polluted by sin (Lev. 26:41; Isa. 52:1), then a circumcised heart is a heart that has been cleansed and seeks to follow God (Deut. 30:6). In Romans 4:11 circumcision is a sign and seal of the righteousness that Abraham had by faith. It sealed the promise of God and guaranteed that righteousness will be given on the basis of faith.[75] On the other side, circumcision also promised that those who break the covenant would experience God's judgment of being cut off from Him and the people. This is represented in the act of cutting off the foreskin of the flesh (Gen. 17:14).[76]

Colossians 2:11-12 teaches that the Colossians were circumcised with a circumcision made without hands. This refers to a spiritual circumcision that corresponds to the circumcision of the heart in the Old Testament. The phrase 'circumcision without hands' is qualified by two phrases that explain the impact of spiritual circumcision (both phrases begin with *en tē*). The result 'by putting off the body of the flesh' refers to cleansing from the pollution of sin.[77] The statement 'by the circumcision of Christ' can be understood in different ways. It can refer to the circumcision that comes from Christ, that is, the circumcision that Christ performs. He is the one who gives us a new heart (a circumcision of the heart).[78] It could also refer to the circumcision that Christ Himself experienced when He was cut off, or put to death, through crucifixion. Instead of the covenant breaker being cut off, Christ Himself was

---

74. Ross, 'Baptism and Circumcision,' p. 100. Consecration means that the person is claimed by God as His own and is bound in duty to serve God through obedience and service.

75. Ibid., p. 101, 89-93. Ross argues against the idea that circumcision was merely a sign of Abraham's faith or of inward spiritual transformation. Circumcision as a seal guarantees that righteousness will be given to his descendants on the basis of faith.

76. Ibid., p. 95.

77. Ross, 'Baptism and Circumcision,' p. 101 and Richard C. Barcellos, 'An Exegetical Appraisal of Colossians 2:11-12,' in *Recovering a Covenantal Heritage*, p. 456. Barcellos takes flesh in a spiritual, moral sense as referring to the sinful natures of the Colossians.

78. Ross, 'Baptism and Circumcision,' p. 101 and Barcellos, 'An Exegetical Appraisal of Colossians 2:11-12,' p. 458. This understands the genitive as a subjective genitive.

cut off so that those who have broken the covenant might be saved.[79] A third option is to understand 'the circumcision of Christ' as Christ's circumcision, or Christian conversion pictured as a 'circumcision' performed on us by Christ.[80] Whatever view is taken (the first and third options are very close in meaning), physical circumcision no longer has the function of the sign of the covenant (Gal. 2:3); rather, baptism is the sign and seal of the New Covenant and it points to the salvation we have from God by faith. It is a seal of the righteousness that is given on the basis of faith. It represents cleansing (Acts 22:16), the forgiveness of sins (Acts 2:38), and union with Christ on the basis of the washing of regeneration (Rom. 6:3-6; WCF 28.1).

Covenant theologians can agree with the definition of baptism given in *KTC*: 'it signifies a believer's union with Christ, by grace through faith, and all the benefits that are entailed by that union.'[81] The difference is that PC argues that baptism should be given only to those who have expressed faith in Christ and thus have received all the benefits that come with union with Christ. This cannot be said about those who were circumcised, or infants who are baptized. On this basis, *KTC* argues that baptism and circumcision of the flesh are not speaking about the same things.[82] But there is no guarantee that everyone who is baptized on the basis of faith has genuine faith.[83] The sign can be given in anticipation of

---

79. Peter T. O'Brien, *Colossians, Philemon* (WBC; Waco, TX: Word Books Publisher, 1982), pp. 117-18, and G. K. Beale, *Colossians and Philemon* (BECNT; Grand Rapids: Baker, 2019), pp. 188-90. This would take the phrase as an objective genitive as the circumcision performed on Christ.

80. Douglas J. Moo, *The Letters to the Colossians and to Philemon* (PNTC; Grand Rapids: Eerdmans, 2008), pp. 124-26. He calls the genitive a possessive genitive. See also Petr Pokorny, *Colossians* (Peabody, M: Hendriksen Publishers, 1991), pp. 124-25. He calls the genitive a genitive of quality. This view was suggested to me by my New Testament colleague Dr Robert J. Cara.

81. *KTC*, p. 818.

82. Ibid., pp. 823-24.

83. Although in evangelistic settings the sequence is faith, then baptism, to ground the validity of baptism in something within the recipient is a departure from the *soli deo gloria* of Reformed theology. Paul can exhort believers to lifelong faithfulness on the basis of their baptism (Rom. 6:3-14) because its validity is not based on something found within the recipient but is based on the promise of God (James R. Payton, Jr., 'Infant Baptism and the Covenant of Grace: A Review Article', *WTJ* p. 42.2 [1980]: pp. 416-17).

true faith. Covenant theology agrees with the statement that 'Baptism communicates the grace of God to those who have faith',[84] but faith and baptism do not have to occur together.[85] This is true even for someone who is baptized on a profession of faith but does not have true faith until after his baptism.[86] Such a person is outwardly in the covenant, and so part of the covenant community, but he is not inwardly part of the covenant until he comes to true faith in Christ.[87]

The proper subjects of baptism is one of the most difficult questions for people to decide. Both Baptists and Presbyterians are trying to be faithful to Scripture. As a paedobaptist, I believe the New Testament affirms infant baptism because it affirms the continuing administration of the covenant, the representative principle, and the category of holiness not related to inward transformation. These are important concepts that are rooted in the Old Testament, but the New Testament also teaches them. Although there are differences between Baptists and Presbyterians on baptism and ecclesiology, I am thankful for my Baptist brethren who are faithful to the gospel of Jesus Christ, including imputation and justification by faith.

---

84. *KTC*, pp. 823-24.

85. WCF 28.6 states, 'The efficacy of baptism is not tied to that moment of time wherein it is administered.'

86. Charles Hodge argued that the child of Christian parents, as well as the adult who makes a profession of faith, were members of the church on the same basis of presumptive membership in the invisible church. They are not considered regenerate or true members of Christ's body, but they are considered members of Christ's church (Lewis Bevins Schenk, *The Presbyterian Doctrine of Children in the Covenant* [Eugene, OR: Wipf & Stock, orig. Yale University Press, 1940], pp. 99, 129-30). He is quoting Hodge from several editions of *Biblical Repertory and Princeton Review*, 'The General Assembly' (1859, 1861, 1863).

87. Vos, *Reformed Dogmatics*, pp. 2:106-10.

CHAPTER 14

The Benefits of Covenant Theology: Legal, Personal, and Corporate

A Review of the Covenants

Covenant theology provides a substantive framework for understanding the plan of God's salvation worked out in redemptive history. God is a faithful God who fulfills the promises He has made to His people. He assures the fulfillment of those promises by entering into covenant relationships that bind Him to His people and to the promises He has made. Salvation has personal, legal, and corporate aspects that are expressed by way of covenant which allows for a fullness of salvation encompassing every aspect of life.[1] A brief review of the covenants will highlight the wonderful plan of salvation that God accomplishes for His people.

The Covenant of Works in the context of creation shows God's beneficence as He provides everything that Adam needs to live a full and abundant life. He prepares a special place for Adam in the garden, gives him a companion in Eve to help him fulfill his calling, and enters into communion and fellowship with the ones created in His image

---

1. Robert J. Cara, NT professor and colleague at Reformed Theological Seminary in Charlotte, uses the terms legal, existential, and corporate to explain covenants in the lecture, 'Covenant Theology', in the course 'Hermeneutics', which we teach together.

(personal). The legal side of this covenant is seen in the probationary test whereby God gave Adam a law with a penalty attached to it if that law is disobeyed. If death is the result of disobedience, then a greater level of life would have resulted from obedience.

The disobedience of Adam has far-reaching consequences. It impacts all his relationships, including his relationship with God. He hides from God when He comes into the garden, blames his wife for his sin, and tries to cover his nakedness on his own. He is spiritually dead, and physical death will follow. God must act to confront Adam with his sin and to cover his nakedness. Adam is banished from the garden. The corporate side of the covenant is seen in the results of sin being passed on to his descendants even as the requirement to obey God perfectly continues. The devastating results of sin in Adam's immediate family are manifested in Genesis 4, and the impact of sin for Adam's descendants are demonstrated in Genesis 6. Disobedience and death are the major problems that confront the human race. The covenant headship of Adam lays the groundwork for the work of the second Adam where imputation and the necessity of obedience are foundational for justification by faith. God takes seriously disobedience to His law because it diminishes His blessings, ignores His goodness, and rejects His authority even after God has demonstrated His goodness.

The promise of hope in the midst of death and alienation is given in Genesis 3:15 where the Covenant of Grace is initiated. Even though Adam failed to keep the Covenant of Works, God did not respond with judgment alone, but also with grace. Even in the pronouncement of judgment, the mandate that God gave to Adam still continues (marriage, work, dominion). God Himself covers Adam and Eve's nakedness with animal skins, a foreshadowing of the sacrificial system and the death of the mediator. The seed of the woman will one day defeat the seed of the serpent. Adam responds in faith that the promises of God will be fulfilled by naming his wife Eve, the mother of all living. Once again, the covenant is forward-looking, including future descendants.

Both the Covenant of Works and the Covenant of Grace have the goal of eternal life which is procured by someone's obedience to the Law of God. Adam's disobedience led to the imputation of his sin to his descendants, making it impossible for any natural descendant of Adam to keep perfectly the Law of God. The second Adam must fulfill this obligation as part of His defeat of the seed of the serpent. The multifaceted work of the coming Redeemer is developed progressively in redemptive history through the types and shadows of the Covenant of Grace as manifested in the covenants of the Old Testament and then fulfilled in the New Covenant established by Christ.

The Noahic Covenant was instituted by God after the judgment of the Flood to ensure that history would continue so that God's plan of salvation could be carried out. This covenant has both common grace and redemptive elements. It was made with Noah and his family, with Noah's descendants, and with the animals as a guarantee that all life on earth will never again be destroyed by a flood. The focus of this covenant is God's commitment to what He has created, including human beings and animals, regardless of whether they recognize Him as their Creator. In other words, there is a covenant relationship without the necessity of a personal relationship between God and those who are part of the covenant. This is an aspect of God's common grace. God does have a relationship with Noah, the mediator of this covenant, through whom the redemptive elements of the covenant are manifested. The legal and corporate aspects of the covenant are seen in the continuation of the mandate that God had given to Adam, in God's commitment to keep the covenant in the sign of the rainbow, and in the inclusion of descendants, not only in the making of the covenant itself, but also when Noah pronounces judgment on Canaan, the descendant of Ham, for his dishonoring of his father.

Sin continues after the Flood as people try to make a name for themselves in the Tower of Babel. God chooses an individual to continue His redemptive plans. He makes promises to Abram concerning a land, descendants, and that He will make his name great. Abram leaves his own land to go to the land that God promised to give to his descendants, the land of Canaan. Although Abram struggles with the promise of an heir (Gen. 15:1-6), this promise is confirmed by God and he responds with faith. God then demonstrates His commitment to His servant by establishing a covenant where He takes on the obligation to fulfill His covenant promises. In Genesis 15 God is the only party that passes through the slain animals. God not only has a personal relationship with

Abram, but He is willing to bind Himself legally to the fulfillment of His promises. Confirmation of the promise of an heir comes in Genesis 17 with the institution of circumcision, the sign of the covenant, given to Abram (now Abraham) and his children (corporate). Although God will bring about the covenant promises, Abraham and his descendants must be faithful to God and keep their covenant obligations, including circumcision. As the sign of the Abrahamic Covenant, circumcision symbolizes judgment on those who fail to keep it, but it also points to a spiritual relationship with God by those who have the faith of Abraham leading to a circumcision of the heart. The legal side of the covenant is evident in those who are circumcised but who do not have a personal relationship with God (as in Ishmael).

The promises of the Abrahamic Covenant are remembered by God when God's people are in Egypt and they cry out to Him for deliverance (Exod. 3:7). God demonstrates His faithfulness by bringing Israel out of Egypt in a display of His power and glory over Pharaoh and the gods of Egypt. The Mosaic Covenant is a development of the Covenant of Grace and is necessary for the promises to Abraham to be fulfilled. At Mt. Sinai God enters into a covenant to make Israel into a nation so she can fulfill her mission of being a kingdom of priests and a holy nation (Exod. 19:5-6). The people commit themselves to do everything that God has commanded them and the covenant is confirmed by the blood of the covenant being thrown on them (Exod. 24:7-8). The distinct nature of the Mosaic Covenant is the law God gave to His people making clear to them what obedience looked like. The context of the giving of the law (Exod. 20:2) is redemption (third use of the law). The form of the covenant is a treaty covenant that has stipulations and sanctions which lay out the blessings for obedience and the curses for disobedience (second use). In order for Israel to fulfill her mission and to enjoy covenant blessings, including inheritance of the land, she must be faithful to the covenant by obeying the Law of God. This legal aspect of the covenant also has a corporate aspect that includes future generations (Deut. 5:1-5; chaps. 27–30). The intent of the Mosaic Covenant is not just legal, but it includes a personal relationship where the law is written on the heart (Deut. 6:6; 11:18; 30:14). The law in the Mosaic Covenant has many functions. Although the Mosaic Covenant is not a republication of the Covenant of Works, there is a works principle in the law that shows the continuing obligation to keep the law perfectly. Paul argues that Moses wrote about the righteousness that is based on the law from the statement in Leviticus 18:5 that the person who does the commandments shall live by them (Rom. 10:5). But there is also in the Mosaic Covenant a righteousness based on faith where Paul refers to Deuteronomy 30:11-15 (Rom. 10:6-9). The law can function as second use to condemn any who break it and show the need for someone to keep it on our behalf (justification by faith), but it can also function as third use to guide those who have faith on how to live faithful lives (sanctification). Paul is able to use the same law as either second or third use.

The Davidic Covenant is an advancement of the redemptive purposes of God that brings together the promises of the previous covenants and sets the stage for the future fulfillment of those promises. Instead of David building a house (temple) for God, God promises to build a house (dynasty) for David. The Davidic Covenant ensures that a descendant of David will sit on the throne. Although the focus in 2 Samuel 7 is on David's immediate successor, the covenant emphasizes that each son of David should have a personal relationship with God, but even more, a father-son relationship. This relationship heightens the status of the king who acts as representative of the people (corporate). If the king does not obey God, then he will be disciplined (conditional nature of the covenant), but God will not take the dynasty and kingdom away from David as he did with Saul (unconditional nature of the covenant). The reign of a righteous king has great opportunity to bring blessing to God's people (Psalm 72) and to impact the nations. The early reign of Solomon is presented as a fulfillment of God's promises in prior covenants and a temporary fulfillment of Israel's mission to the nations as queens and kings come to see the great things God has accomplished through Solomon in Israel. Sadly, these blessings did not last long as Solomon's heart was turned from God by his foreign wives (1 Kings 11) and the kingdom was divided after his death. But the stage is set for a son of David to come in fulfillment of the promises to David that his throne will be established forever.

The New Covenant is the fulfillment of all the covenant promises of the Old Covenant in Jesus Christ. Some promises are full and complete, as when we are regenerated and declared righteous, but most of the promises are not fully experienced yet, particularly the outworking of our salvation in sanctification. The fulfillment of these promises takes on the character of the kingdom that Jesus came to establish. It is a spiritual kingdom that is in existence now, but it is not yet here in its fullness. The complete manifestation of that kingdom will become a reality when Jesus comes again, defeats all His enemies, and brings His people into the new heavens and earth. At that time, creation will be restored and believers will receive the fullness of their salvation encompassing spiritual and material blessings. A misunderstanding of the present nature of the kingdom and the not yet character of the fulfillment of the promises can lead to false conclusions.

The specific promises of the New Covenant are set forth in Jeremiah 31:31-34, but the whole section of Jeremiah 30–33 emphasizes the many promises of the previous covenants, including restoration to the land, security, repentance and forgiveness, and the reign of a coming king. Each of these promises have been initially fulfilled, but there still remains a future fulfillment to bring God's people into the fullness of salvation. We have received a down payment of our inheritance, but not the full inheritance (Eph. 2:13-14). Abraham was heir of the land of Canaan, but now he and his descendants are heirs of the world (Rom. 4:13) because our mission is to take the gospel to the nations (Matt. 28:19-20). The completion of that mission awaits the coming of our King. We are secure in Christ but we still face many trials that discourage us. We wait for our full security in the new heavens and earth. The King has come and He now reigns at the right hand of the Father, but we wait for the demonstration of His reign to the whole world, which will include our vindication. The promises of the covenants in the Old Testament are experienced by all who believe, but we will not experience the fullness of those promises until Christ comes again. The law is now written on the hearts of those who believe, but obedience to the law is not yet perfected. This is why we still need to seek forgiveness regularly until the day we no longer sin. The covenant relationship with God has been established by Christ ('I will be your God and you will be my people'), but we grow in this relationship by dying unto sin and living unto righteousness, by receiving the discipline of our heavenly Father, and by heeding the warnings about not falling away from Christ and from what we believe. God's people are still in the wilderness on our way to our eternal destination. It is clear that the church continues to struggle with those who make false professions of faith and teach false doctrine that leads people astray. Not everyone in the New Covenant community 'knows the Lord' because not every profession of faith is genuine. Leaders must be diligent to watch over the flock and when necessary to protect the flock from false teaching and to ensure the purity of God's people. Church discipline is needed until we receive the fullness of our salvation when everyone in glory will know the Lord.

The New Covenant also continues the personal, legal, and corporate aspects of the older covenants. The legal aspects of the New Covenant are seen in a number of ways. There is a righteousness based on the law to the person who fulfills the law (Lev. 18:5), but the problem is no one can fulfill the law (second use), showing the need for faith in One who has fulfilled the law. The law functions to show us our need of Christ's righteousness in justification and to show us how we are to live as God's people in sanctification. Christ as the second Adam fulfilled all righteousness in His life and death whereby His righteousness can be imputed to those who believe in Him (Rom. 5:12-21). The administration of the New Covenant also has legal aspects for those who are members of the covenant. Paul shows that there is a holy status related to being part of the covenant even if one does not have a personal relationship with God (Rom. 11:17-24). The root of the tree is holy which makes the branches holy, but some of the natural branches (Jewish people) were broken off because of unbelief. Gentiles who have been grafted into the tree can also be cut off from the tree through unbelief. The same principles of covenant administration work for Jewish and Gentile branches. There is a legal covenant relationship and a personal covenant relationship, but these do not always exist at the same time. The goal is for every member of the covenant to have a personal relationship with God and to grow in the faith. Once we are declared righteous by faith in what Christ has done for us, the process of sanctification begins whereby 'we are renewed in the whole man after the image of God, and are enabled more and more to die unto sin, and live unto righteousness' (WSC 35). The personal, existential element is prominent in sanctification, but this process is not an individualistic and autonomous effort because the corporate church aids the process by facilitating growth through the reading and preaching of the Word, prayer, fellowship, and the administration of the sacraments (Acts 2:42). If a personal relationship does not develop through faith, the person could be cut off from the covenant. The covenant community is a mixed community which supports the notion of a visible/invisible church. Not every profession of faith is genuine, but this shows the necessity of church discipline to maintain the purity of God's corporate people.

A Brief Evaluation of the Different Views of Covenant Theology

An evaluation of the different approaches to covenant theology shows how important the legal, personal, and corporate aspects are in understanding our salvation. Some emphasize the personal aspects of the covenant over the legal aspects which leads to an emphasis on the third use of the law and sanctification. The result is usually a denial of the Covenant of Works. Unless the legal aspect of the covenant is acknowledged in some other way, the tendency is to define righteousness and justification in relational terms instead of legal terms. For many, the result is a weakening of the traditional view of justification by faith and a loss of the clear distinction between justification and sanctification. For others, legal aspects are recognized in the law/gospel distinction (see Chapter 9). Some are firm in their view of justification by faith, but do not recognize a continuing administration of the covenant that has both personal and legal aspects to it. If one overemphasizes the personal aspect of the covenant, then everyone who is baptized (either as infants or as believers) partakes of all the benefits of the covenant. For those who believe in infant baptism, this means that the infant who is baptized receives all the benefits of being united to Christ. This has implications for the understanding of baptism and who can partake of the Lord's Supper. For those who argue for believer's baptism, it has implications for the nature of the covenant and the distinction between the visible and invisible church. The legal aspect of the New Covenant is important for when a profession of faith turns out to be a false profession and church discipline is needed.

Others emphasize the legal aspects of the covenants. Kline is very strong here as he defines the covenant in legal terms and has good discussions on the administration of the covenant. He affirms the Covenant of Works and understands its foundational nature to justification by faith. There is a law that Adam failed to keep which impacted his descendants as his sin was imputed to them. There is a continuing obligation for people to keep the law and condemnation results when it is not kept. Christ came to keep the law and to die on the cross in the place of condemned sinners so that they might be declared righteous through faith (imputation). Kline also emphasizes the works principle in the Mosaic Covenant. Although it continues the Covenant of Grace on its foundational level, where individuals receive salvation through faith, there is also a typological level, a secondary level, where the principle of works operates in the earthly provisional kingdom. If Israel breaks the covenant she will lose her inheritance. Thus, the Mosaic Covenant is seen as a republication of the Covenant of Works. Although Kline would affirm the personal relationship of the covenants and the third use of the law, the emphasis is on the legal side of the covenants and the second use of the law.

The Fullness of Salvation

God dispenses His salvation through covenants that have legal, personal, and corporate aspects to them. In order to fully comprehend the fullness of the benefits we receive from God we need to understand the importance of these different aspects of the covenant. The legal aspect is important for understanding the work of Christ, including His death on the cross, as the basis for our justification. Here God is our Judge and we stand condemned because we have broken His law (second use) and we need someone to fulfill the law for us and take the penalty that we deserve so we can be declared righteous (imputation). The legal aspect is also important for understanding the administration of the covenant (see the discussion in Chapter 8) where even Gentiles who have been engrafted into the tree can be cut off through unbelief. The legal aspect emphasizes our responsibilities in the covenant relationship and is the basis for church discipline if we begin to believe or behave in ways that are contrary to Scripture.

267

The personal aspect of the covenant is important because we are brought into a relationship with God as our heavenly Father through faith in Christ. We are transformed by the power of the Spirit and are to work out our salvation through the process of sanctification. This is not an easy process as we face trials and tribulations in this life. We might even face the loving discipline of our heavenly Father, but it is for our good and to help us grow in our relationship with Him. We have all the privileges that come with being united to Christ, including the certain hope of eternal life so that nothing in this life can separate us from the love of God our Father. Even though we continue to sin, we are by God's grace able to do the works that God has prepared for us to do and thus live in a way that reflects His righteousness. These works are not the basis of our salvation but are the evidence that God is at work in us.

The corporate aspect of the covenant is seen in that we are not only united to Christ, but we are also united to His body and enjoy the fellowship of believers, the prayers of the saints, the encouragement of the sacraments, and participation in the mission of the church. The sacraments also show both legal and personal aspects of our salvation. We are invited to the Lord's table as those who have faith in Jesus Christ, not just a personal faith, but also a public confession of our faith whereby we are members of a local body of believers. As we partake of the Lord's Supper, we experience communion with Christ. In baptism, we become members of the covenant with the goal of developing a personal relationship with God through faith in Christ (infant baptism), or furthering that relationship expressed by faith (credo-baptism). The assurance of our salvation is also aided by the various aspects of the covenant. We are assured of our salvation because we recognize that it does not depend on our works but on the work of Christ, whose righteousness has been imputed to us (legal). We are assured by the evidence of the work of the Spirit in our lives as we grow in our sanctification. We are assured by the fellowship of believers who recognize God's work in our lives, admonish us when we need it, and encourage us to persevere in the faith.[2]

2. Ligon Duncan, 'Recent Objections to Covenant Theology: A Description, Evaluation and Response,' in *The Westminster Confession of Faith into the 21ˢᵗ Century,*

Covenant theology shows us that God has made full provision for our salvation. His plan is not hit-and-miss, but has been planned before the foundation of the world. God's plan cannot be thwarted because He has the power to defeat all our enemies (sin, death, and Satan). This plan is worked out in redemptive history. Covenant theology gives unity to redemptive history and the plan of salvation which culminates in Christ. All the Old Testament covenants point us to the person and work of Christ. He establishes the New Covenant where all the covenant promises of God are fulfilled in Him. He sits at the right hand of the Father directing the course of history for the benefit of His people. Nothing can hinder His work on our behalf and we have the assurance that we are His. One day we will experience the full benefits of our salvation, to which all the different aspects of the covenant point, when He comes to establish the fullness of His kingdom. Even so, come quickly, Lord.

Volume Three, ed. Ligon Duncan (Ross-shire: Christian Focus, 2009). He lists the benefits of covenant theology as deepening our understanding of the atonement (the death of Christ), assurance (the basis of our confidence of communion with God and the enjoyment of his promises), the sacraments (what they are and how they work), and the continuity of redemptive history (the unity of God's plan of salvation).

Appendix 1

Covenants in the Context of the Ancient Near East

Discoveries from the ancient Near East have been important in the discussion of the nature and origin of the covenant in Scripture. The evidence, however, is difficult to evaluate. A scholar's general approach to Scripture is important when they evaluate the ancient Near Eastern material. Presuppositions concerning the history of Israel and the dates of certain books have played a major role in their conclusions. Critical scholars tend to operate with Wellhausen's view that the prophets represent the high point of Israel's history with the law and priestly elements developing after the prophets. Most of the Pentateuch comes after the exile.[1] Wellhausen saw the covenant developing through the work of the prophets where their ethical concerns inspired the idea that the relationship between God and Israel was bounded by conditions. The prophets represent the creative force of biblical monotheism and so any references to the covenant in earlier works are insertions of later views.[2]

Another development took place with G. E. Mendenhall's view that some parts of the biblical text showed the form of the Hittite vassal treaty of the second millennium that combined history with covenant. This combination is particularly seen in the Decalogue (Exodus 20) and the covenant at Shechem (Joshua 24). These texts must have a second

---

1. Julius Wellhausen, *Prolegomena to the History of Israel* (Atlanta: Scholars Press, 1994 [reprint 1885]), pp. 411-24; Ernest W. Nicholson, *God and His People: Covenant and Theology in the Old Testament* (Oxford: Clarendon Press, 1986), pp. 3-7.

2. Noel Weeks, *Admonition and Curse: The Ancient Near Eastern Treaty/Covenant Form as a Problem in Inter-Cultural Relationships* (New York: T&T Clark, 2004), pp. 160, 162.

millennium origin. The book of Deuteronomy, which also combines the pedagogic use of history and the covenant, was not dated earlier by Mendenhall because he saw it as a revival of older ideas.[3] It would have been too radical to date Deuteronomy in the second millennium because Deuteronomy was associated with the reform of Josiah in 621 B.C. Assyrian treaties were discovered from the first millennium that also used history so that many believed the seventh century view of Deuteronomy was supported by this evidence. Most critical scholars rejected Mendenhall's appeal to the second millennium Hittite treaties and returned to the older position that the covenant was late in the history of Israel and that earlier covenants were retrojections from the first millennium.[4]

Other scholars saw differences between the second millennium Hittite treaties and the first millennium Assyrian treaties with Deuteronomy matching the second millennium Hittite treaties.[5] Of course, this view went against the critical consensus that Deuteronomy originated in conjunction with Josiah's reform and supported the possibility of Mosaic origin of Deuteronomy.[6]

Weeks raises questions concerning the presuppositions of critical scholars, who are not open to a second millennium date for Deuteronomy. He also raises questions concerning the methodological principles in analyzing ancient Near Eastern documents. For example, one should not assume that a ritual in one culture connected to a treaty means the same in another culture. There are problems when defining

---

3. G. E. Mendenhall, *Law and Covenant in Israel and the Ancient Near East* (Pittsburgh: Board of Colportage of W. Penn., 1955), p. 36.

4. Weeks, *Admonition and Curse*, pp. 135-36.

5. For arguments that Deuteronomy fits the Hittite treaties of the second millennium rather than the Assyrian treaties of the first millennium, see the discussions in Joshua Berman, 'CTH 133 and the Hittite Provenance of Deuteronomy 13,' *JBL* 130.1 (2011): pp. 25-44, 'Histories Twice Told: Deuteronomy 1-3 and the Hittite Treaty Prologue Tradition,' *JBL* 132.2 (2013): pp. 229-50, and Markus Zehender, 'Building on Stone? Deuteronomy and Esarhaddon's Loyalty Oaths (Part 1): Some Preliminary Observations,' *BBR* 19.3 (2009) pp. 341-74; 'Building on Stone? Deuteronomy and Esarhaddon's Loyalty Oaths (Part 2): Some Additional Observations,' *BBR* 19.4 (2009) pp. 511-35.

6. Meredith Kline, *Treaty of the Great King* (Grand Rapids: Eerdmans, 1963), pp. 21, 42-44.

general characteristics of early treaties and later treaties because of the assumption that there is a uniform development for the whole ancient Near East. This approach fails to consider each culture on its own merits. As more complex treaties are being discovered it is less likely that there was one fixed form of treaty in the ancient Near East.[7] Although templates for a standard treaty existed, a set of concepts that deal with relationships was more basic and modified treaty formats came into existence to secure the goals of the relationship. Deuteronomy seeks to secure Israel's relationship with God based on treaties in the ancient Near East. The basic elements of a treaty are found in the same order in Deuteronomy and the Hittite treaties.[8] These include the use of history, the combination of elements such as the historical prologue, stipulations with blessings and curses, and the provision for depositing the treaty text with each party. But instead of arguing that Israel borrowed the treaty form it is better to allow for the possibility of independent development of a basic common inheritance. In other words, covenants developed within Israel to meet the goals of a certain type of relationship between covenant partners. In this development there will be factors that are distinctive to the covenants in Israel but also factors that are comparable to covenants in the ancient Near East. The fact that there are no ancient Near Eastern covenants with the deity as a covenant partner is not a problem and neither is it a problem when a covenant does not include all of the typical elements. Not even the covenants outside the Bible are uniform in their treaty form. The appeal in Deuteronomy to history may not be due to the practice of ancient Near Eastern treaties but it may be a development within Israel of the importance of history and God's actions in history.[9]

Comparisons have also been made between the Abrahamic and Davidic Covenants and ancient Near Eastern royal grant covenants.

---

7. Weeks, *Admonition and Curse*, p. 152.

8. Weeks shows that the prophets used the threats of Deuteronomy in their oracles of judgment that leads to the fairly obvious conclusion that Wellhausen is wrong in his view that the covenant developed later than the prophets (*Admonition and Curse*, pp. 156, 160, 165).

9. Weeks comments that the 'pedagogic use of history is more congruent with some political-social orders than with others and hence the Bible and the Hittites use treaties in analogous ways' (*Admonition and Curse*, pp. 169-70, 173).

M. Weinfeld argues that there are two types of covenant in the Old Testament. The obligatory type is exemplified in the covenant of God with Israel and the promissory type is reflected in the Abrahamic and Davidic Covenants. Both types of covenants share an historical introduction, border delineations, stipulations, witnesses, and blessings and curses, but these two types of covenants operate differently. The grant is an obligation of the master to his servant and the curse in the grant protects the rights of the servant as it is directed toward anyone who will violate the rights of the covenant partner. The grant is a reward to the servant for loyalty and good deeds already performed.[10]

Weinfeld's comparisons between the Abrahamic and Davidic Covenants have been questioned on methodological grounds. Gary N. Knoppers argues that the structure, form, and content of the royal grants are more complicated than Weinfeld's comparisons allow. A typical structure for royal land grants is difficult to establish. The evidence for the language parallels between the Davidic Covenant and ancient Near Eastern land grants is problematic. The Davidic promises vary in the account of different biblical authors and do not exhibit a consistent structure, form, or content. One would not expect dynastic succession to occur in the Davidic Covenant if it was a land grant because dynastic succession occurs in vassal treaties, not in land grants. Also, land grants were predominantly conditional in their nature and function. Unconditional language, including clauses that disallow a rebellious son to forfeit the inheritance, comes from a variety of documents and is not peculiar to any one form. This should cause one to hesitate in associating the Davidic Covenant with a certain form or genre.[11]

The way forward in understanding the covenant in Scripture in the context of the ancient Near East is to recognize that the situation is

---

10. M. Weinfeld, 'Covenant Grant in the Old Testament and the Ancient Near East,' *JAOS* 90 (1970): pp. 184-85. He contrasts the grant with the treaty where in the latter the obligation is of the vassal to the master, the curse is directed against the vassal if he violates the terms of the treaty, the treaty protects the rights of the master, and the treaty is an inducement for future loyalty.

11. Gary N. Knoppers, 'Ancient Near Eastern Royal Grants and the Davidic Covenant: A Parallel?' *JAOS* 116.4 (1996): pp. 673-74, 676, 684-85. The argument that some Biblical covenants are royal grants and some are treaties does not take into account the complexity of the Biblical covenants.

complex and that simple comparisons between cultures should not be drawn. There is no fixed treaty form, even within one society at one particular time. Instead, there is clustering around typical patterns. The fluidity of form derives from the particular kind of relationship that is in view in the covenant related to the loyalty due the suzerain and the beneficence he bestows. Although Israel shares a common inheritance with the ancient Near East, covenants take on distinctive emphases within Israel because of the nature of Israel's God and the view of history related to Him. Both monotheism and a distinctive view of history are there from the beginning. The covenants in Israel are best explained as developing internally within Israel. Each covenant should be examined on its own to see how obligation, loyalty, benefits, conditions, and curse function in the covenant relationship. Designating some covenants as conditional and some as unconditional seems to be too simplistic to explain the biblical evidence. Although different covenants will have distinctive characteristics, the covenants will build on each other with later covenants assuming the content of earlier covenants.[12]

---

12. Robertson, *Christ of the Covenants*, pp. 27-52.

Appendix 2

The Question of 'Testament' in Hebrews 9:16-17

There is debate whether Hebrews 9:16-17 refers to a 'covenant' or a 'testament'. The Greek word *diathēkē* is the word commonly used to translate the Hebrew word *bᵉrîṯ*. It can refer to the same kind of a relationship to which a covenant refers, but it can also be used to refer to a last will and testament.[1] The difference between covenant and testament can be seen in how they function in relationship to death. Death stands at the beginning of a covenant relationship, but in a testament death stands at the end of the relationship. Death is presented as an option in a covenant if the stipulations of the covenant are broken but death in a testament is what actualizes the inheritance.[2]

Some argue that *diathēkē* in Hebrews 9:16-17 should be understood as 'testament' and not covenant.[3] The reason for this is that some things

---

1. The word *sunthēkē* is not used very often in the Greek Old Testament (Isa. 28:15; 30:1; Dan. 11:6; 11:17). It is used when the parties are mutual and *diathēkē* is used when one party is superior to the other (J. Lust, E. Eynikel, and K. Hauspie, *A Greek-English Lexicon of the Septuagint; Part II* [Stuttgart: Deutsche Bibelgesellschaft, 1996], 458). Based on this information it makes sense that *diathēkē* would be the more common word to translate the Hebrew word for covenant.

2. Robertson, *Christ of the Covenants*, pp. 11-14. He lists more differences between covenant and testament and argues against the idea of a testament in explaining the death of Christ because substitution for another has no place in the making of a last will and testament, but it does in a covenant.

3. It seems that WCF 7.4 argues for testament: 'The covenant of grace is frequently set forth in Scripture by the name of a testament, in reference to the death of Jesus Christ the Testator, and to the everlasting inheritance, with all things belonging to it, therein

are said in 9:16-17 that do not fit well with how covenants operate. Hebrews 9:16 states that where there is a *diathēkē*, the death of the one who made it is necessary. Hebrews 9:17 states that a *diathēkē* takes effect at death and is not in force as long as the maker of the covenant is alive. In a covenant, death occurs when the covenant is broken, not when the covenant is made. The argument is that the term *diathēkē* in 9:15 refers to the New Covenant of chapter 8 and focuses on the results of the establishment of the covenant brought about by the death of Christ. Christ's death is mentioned in anticipation of verses 16-17.[4] In verses 16-17 the author switches from a religious setting to a legal argument and introduces the concept of a last will which becomes valid on the death of the person who made it. Christ's death validates the last will and testament so that believers may receive the promised eternal inheritance.[5] The discussion of verses 18-22 clearly refers to the Old Covenant so that the idea of a testament has disappeared in these verses.[6] Thus only verses 16-17 refer to a testament.

There are questions related to this view. If the author of Hebrews consistently uses *diathēkē* to refer to a covenant and the context of 9:15-22 uses *diathēkē* as covenant, there would have to be strong evidence to understand 9:16-17 as testament. Hahn states:

> It would be a priori unlikely for the author of Hebrews, in the midst of this tightly knit argument, to use *diathēkē* in vv. 16-17 in a sense entirely different from its meaning in the rest of the passage; and unlikely or not, it would seriously damage the logical coherence of the whole argument.[7]

---

bequeathed.' WCF 7.4 also references Hebrews 9:22, Luke 22:20, and 1 Cor. 11:25 as supporting the idea of testament. Chad Van Dixhoorn comments, 'On one level … the members of the Westminster assembly are avoiding contention over words … The gospel can be described in the dialect of covenant theology, or in the language of the last will and testament' (Carlisle, PA: The Banner of Truth Trust, 2014), p. 101.

4. Paul Ellingworth, *The Epistle to the Hebrews: A Commentary on the Greek Text* (Grand Rapids: Eerdmans, 1993), p. 459.

5. William Hendriksen and Simon J. Kistemaker, *Exposition of Thessalonians, the Pastorals, and Hebrews*, NTC (Grand Rapids: Baker, 1996), pp. 256-57.

6. Ellingworth, *Hebrews*, p. 466.

7. S. W. Hahn, 'A Broken Covenant and the Curse of Death: A Study of Hebrews 9:15-22,' *CBQ* 66 (2004): p. 421. He offers an extensive critique of the testament view, including legal issues, grammatical issues, lexical issues syntactical issues, and contextual issues.

There is also the question whether 9:16-17 refers to any known legal Hellenistic practice of that day. Was a will made valid at death or when it was written down, witnessed, and deposited?[8] Others argue that *diathēkē* in Hebrews 9:15-17 should be understood as a covenant and not a testament. Several reasons are given for this view. First, the word *diathēkē* in 9:15 and 9:18-21 means 'covenant'.[9] In 9:15 the death of Christ is required for the ratification of the New Covenant. As mediator of the covenant He died in the place of those who had broken the first covenant, and He guarantees that all of God's promises will be kept. In 9:18-21 the inauguration of the Mosaic Covenant (the first covenant) is described. The point made about covenants in general is applied to the New Covenant.[10] If *diathēkē* means 'covenant' in verses 15 and 18-21, it seems likely that it would mean 'covenant' in verses 16-17.

Second, the content of verses 16-17 bears this out. These verses explain why Christ had to die to become mediator of the New Covenant. In the ratification of the covenant, the ratifying party invokes a curse on himself, so that if he does not comply with the terms of the covenant, he will experience the covenant curse (represented by the disembodied bodies of the sacrificial animals).[11]

Third, the role of death operates differently in a covenant than in a testament. The death of the covenant maker appears in two stages: in the symbolic representation of the curse anticipating possible covenant violation and if there is a violation of the covenant the one who violates the covenant experiences death. Also, substitutionary death is central to the work of Christ, but a testament has no provision for substitutionary death. Death activates a testament but inaugurates and vindicates a covenant.[12]

Fourth, the most difficult problem for the consistent translation of *diathēkē* as covenant throughout Hebrews 9 is the last phrase of

8. Hahn, 'Broken Covenant,' p. 418. He also notes that the distribution of the estate could occur when the testator was still living.

9. Robertson, *Christ of the Covenants*, p. 141.

10. William L. Lane, *Hebrews 9–13* (WBC; Dallas: Word Books, 1991), pp. 241-44.

11. Lane, *Hebrews 9–13*, pp. 242-43.

12. Robertson, *Christ of the Covenants*, p. 139.

verse 17.[13] Lane translates verse 17b as 'since it [a covenant] is never valid while the ratifier lives.'[14] In context verse 17a refers to a covenant that is made firm over dead bodies. The making strong of the covenant in verse 17b refers to the same principle. Multiple dead bodies are required for the inauguration of a covenant but only one body is required for the activation of a testament. A covenant does not become strong while the ratifier lives because the making of the covenant must include the symbolic death of the covenant maker.[15] The difficulty of this view is that it requires the death to be symbolic rather than actual, but the problem can be solved by assuming a violated covenant would bring actual death. The context of the inauguration of the covenant requires the death to be symbolic.[16]

Questions are also raised concerning this view. First, not all covenants were ratified by the ritual slaughter of animals. In some situations, the oath establishes the covenant. Second, the actual death of the covenant maker makes better sense of the passage than a symbolic or figurative interpretation of his death.[17]

A third view argues that in Hebrews 9:16-17 *diathēkē* does not refer to a covenant in general but to the broken covenant at Sinai. This explains why death was necessary for the remission of sins under the first covenant (9:15). A broken covenant demands the curse of death so that the death of the covenant maker 'must be borne' (9:16).[18] This expression does not specify that the covenant maker must die but that a death in relation to the covenant maker must be endured. Someone other than the covenant maker could die, such as Christ, who endured death on behalf of covenant breakers. This fits the overall teaching of Hebrews that the first covenant brought the curse of death on those who broke it (2:2; 10:28) and that Christ takes that curse upon Himself to free them from that curse (2:9, 14-15; 9:15; 10:14).[19] Hebrews 9:17

---

13. Robertson, *Christ of the Covenants*, pp. 143-44.
14. Lane, *Hebrews 9–13*, p. 229.
15. Lane, *Hebrews 9–13*, p. 243, Robertson, *Christ of the Covenants*, pp. 143-44.
16. Robertson, *Christ of the Covenants*, pp. 143-44.
17. Hahn, 'Broken Covenant,' pp. 430-31.
18. Hahn, 'Broken Covenant,' p. 432.
19. Hahn, 'Broken Covenant,' p. 435. Hahn also discusses connections between Hebrews 9:17 and Isaiah 53, including the use of the word 'bear' (*pherō*) and that

elaborates on the necessity of death by mentioning the death of the sacrificial animals by which covenants were ratified as exemplified in the Sinai Covenant in particular (vv. 18-22).[20] The phrase 'since it is not in force as long as the one who made it is alive' (v. 17b) means that for the covenant maker to remain alive after breaking the covenant indicates that the covenant has no binding force. A covenant is not *in force* if it is not *enforced*.[21]

The meaning of *diathēkē* in Hebrews 9:16-17 is a difficult question. Several who have followed Hahn have made minor adjustments to his view. Rather than identifying the corpses with Israel they identify them with the slain animals in covenant ceremonies where self-maledictory oaths were enacted. Hebrews 9:17 makes the point in general that someone had to bear the necessary death penalty for transgressing the covenant which is reflected in the death of the sacrificial animals. Then 9:18-22 illustrates this point with the Sinai Covenant in particular.[22] The overall thrust of the passage is not greatly impacted by which view of *diathēkē* one adopts. All views would emphasize the necessity of the death of Christ in order for us to receive the promised eternal inheritance.

---

the victim undergoes a vicarious death on behalf of the many and then receives his inheritance.

20. This view understands the word *nekroi* as 'dead bodies', and Hahn identifies them with the people of Israel who have broken the covenant ('Broken Covenant,' p. 434).

21. Hahn, 'Broken Covenant,' p. 434.

22. Williamson, *Sealed with an Oath*, pp. 205-06; see also Peter T. O'Brien, *The Letter to the Hebrews* (PNTC; Grand Rapids: Eerdmans, 2010), pp. 326-27. Both Williamson and O'Brien give helpful summaries of the different arguments.

Selected Bibliography

This bibliography is limited to books that specifically deal with the covenant, or related matters, and does not include every work that is cited in the text, particularly commentaries.

Alexander, T. Desmond. 'Messianic Ideology in the Book of Genesis' (pp. 19-40 in *The Lord's Anointed: Interpretation of Old Testament Messianic Texts*. Eds. Philip E. Satterthwaite, Richard S. Hess, and Gordon J. Wenham. Grand Rapids, MI: Baker Books, 1995).

Barcellos, Richard C. *In Defense of the Decalogue: A Critique of New Covenant Theology*. Winepress Publishing, 2001.

_____. 'An Exegetical Appraisal of Colossians 2:11-12' (pp. 449-74 in *Recovering a Covenantal Heritage*. Ed. Richard C. Barcellos. Palmdale, CA: RBAP, 2014).

_____. *The Covenant of Works: Its Confessional and Scriptural Basis*. Palmdale, CA: pp. Reformed Baptist Academic Press, 2016.

_____. *Getting the Garden Right: Adam's Work and God's Rest in Light of Christ*. Cape Coral, FL: Founders Press, 2017.

Bartholomew, Craig G. 'Covenant and Creation: Covenant Overload or Covenantal Deconstruction?' *CTJ* 30 (1995): pp. 11-33.

Beale, G. K. *A New Testament Biblical Theology: The Unfolding of the Old Testament in the New*. Grand Rapids: Baker Academic, 2011.

Beeke, Joel R. and Ray B. Lanning. 'Unto You, and to Your Children' (pp. 49-69 in *The Case for Covenantal Infant Baptism*. Ed. Gregg Strawbridge. Phillipsburg, NJ: P&R Publishing, 2003).

Beisner, E. Calvin, ed., *The Auburn Avenue Theology, Pros & Cons: Debating the Federal Vision*. Fort Lauderdale, FL: Knox Theological Seminary, 2004.

Berkhof, Louis. *Systematic Theology*. Grand Rapids: Eerdmans, 1941.

Berman, Joshua. 'CTH 133 and the Hittite Provenance of Deuteronomy 13', *JBL* 130.1 (2011): pp. 25-44.

_____. 'Histories Twice Told: Deuteronomy 1-3 and the Hittite Treaty Prologue Tradition', *JBL* 132.2 (2013): pp. 229-250.

Blackburn, Earl M., ed. *Covenant Theology: A Baptist Distinctive*. Birmingham, AL: Solid Ground Christian Books, 2013.

_____. 'Covenant Theology Simplified' (pp. 17-62 in *Covenant Theology: A Baptist Distinctive*. Ed. Earl M. Blackburn. Birmingham, AL: Solid Ground Christian Books, 2013).

Bolt, John 'Why the Covenant of Works is a Necessary Doctrine' (pp. 171-90 in *By Faith Alone: Answering the Challenges to the Doctrine of Justification*. Eds. Gary L. W. Johnson and Guy P. Waters. Wheaton, IL: Crossway, 2006).

Bozak, Barbara. *Life 'Anew': A Literary Theological Study of Jeremiah 30–31*. Rome: Pontifical Biblical Institute, 1991.

Brown, Michael and Zach Keele. *Sacred Bond: Covenant Theology Explored*. Grandville, MI: Reformed Fellowship, Inc., 2012.

Cara, Robert J. 'The Use of the Old Testament in the New: Trusting the New Testament's Hermeneutic' (pp. 593-602 in *A Biblical-Theological Introduction to the New Testament*. Ed. Michael J. Kruger. Wheaton, IL: Crossway, 2016).

_____. *Cracking the Foundation of the New Perspective on Paul*. Ross-shire: Christian Focus, 2017.

Carson, D. A., ed. *From Sabbath to Lord's Day: A Biblical, Historical, and Theological Investigation.* Grand Rapids: Zondervan, 1982.

Chalmers, Aaron. 'The Importance of the Noahic Covenant to Biblical Theology', *TynBul* 60.2 (2009): pp. 207-16.

Chantry, Walther J. *God's Righteous Kingdom.* Carlisle, PA: The Banner of Truth Trust, 1980.

_____. *Call the Sabbath a Delight.* Carlisle, PA: The Banner of Truth Trust, 1991.

_____. 'The Covenants of Works and of Grace' (pp. 89-110 in *Covenant Theology: A Baptist Distinctive.* Birmingham, AL: Solid Ground Christian Books, 2013).

_____. 'Imputation of Righteousness & Covenant Theology (An overview of Romans 5:12-21)' (pp. 111-24 in *Covenant Theology: A Baptist Distinctive.* Birmingham, AL: Solid Ground Christian Books, 2013).

Chapell, Bryan. 'A Pastoral View of Infant Baptism' (pp. 9-29 in *The Case for Covenantal Infant Baptism.* Ed. Gregg Strawbridge. Phillipsburg, NJ: P&R Publishing, 2003).

Collins, C. John. 'A Syntactical Note on Genesis 3:15: Is the Woman's Seed Singular or Plural?' *TynBul* 48.1 (1997): pp. 141-48.

Coppes, Leonard J. קוּם (*qûm*), *TWOT*, 2:793.

Cowan, Christopher W. 'The Warning Passages of Hebrews and the New Covenant Community' (pp. 189-214 in *Progressive Covenantalism.* Eds. Stephen J. Wellum and Brent E. Parker. Nashville, TN: B&H Academic, 2016).

Coxe, Nehemiah. 'A Discourse of the Covenants that God Made with men before the Law (pp. 7-142 in *Covenant Theology: From Adam to Christ.* Ed. James M. Renihan. Palmdale, CA: Reformed Baptist Academic Press, 2005).

Craigie, Peter. *Deuteronomy.* NICOT. Grand Rapids: Eerdmans, 1976.

Curtis, Bryon G. 'Hosea 6:7 and Covenant-Breaking Like/At Adam' (pp. 170-209 in *The Law is not of Faith: Essays on Works and Grace in the Mosaic Covenant*. Eds. Bryan D. Estell, J. V. Fesko, and David VanDrunen. Phillipsburg, NJ: P&R, 2009).

Denault, Pascal. *The Distinctiveness of Baptist Covenant Theology: A Comparison between Seventeenth-Century Particular Baptist and Paedobaptist Federalism*. Birmingham, AL: Solid Ground Christian Books, 2013.

Derouchie, Jason S. 'The Heart of YHWH and His Chosen One in 1 Samuel 13:14', *BBR* 24.4 (2014): pp. 467-90.

_____. 'Father of a Multitude of Nations: New Covenant Ecclesiology in OT Perspective' (pp. 7-38 in *Progressive Covenantalism*. Nashville, TN: B&H Academic, 2016).

Dumbrell, W. J. *Covenant and Creation*. Nashville: Thomas Nelson Publishers, 1984.

Duncan, J. Ligon. 'The Covenant Idea in Ante-Nicene Theology,' PhD Dissertation, University of Edinburgh, 1995.

_____. 'Recent Objections to Covenant Theology: A Description, Evaluation and Response' (pp. 467-500 in *The Westminster Confession of Faith into the 21st Century, Volume Three*. Ed. Ligon Duncan. Ross-shire: Christian Focus, 2009).

Dutcher-Walls, Patricia. 'The Circumscription of the King: Deuteronomy 17:16-17 in its Ancient Social Context', *JBL* 121.4 (2002): 601-616.

Elam, Andrew M., Robert C. Van Kooten, and Randall A. Bergquist, eds. *Merit and Moses: A Critique of the Klinean Doctrine of Republication*. Eugene, OR: Wipf & Stock, 2014.

Estelle, Bryan D., J. V. Fesko, and David VanDrunen, eds. *The Law is Not of Faith: Essays on Works and Grace in the Mosaic Covenant*. Phillipsburg, NJ: P&R, 2009.

Ferguson, Sinclair. 'Infant Baptism View' (pp. 77-112 in *Baptism: Three Views*. Ed. David F. Wright. Downers Grove, IL: IVP Academic, 2009).

Ferry, Brenton C. 'Works in the Mosaic Covenant: A Reformed Taxonomy' (pp. 76-108 in *The Law is Not of Faith*. Eds. Bryan D. Estelle, J. V. Fesko, and David VanDrunen. Phillipsburg, NJ: P&R, 2009).

Fesko, J. V. *The Trinity and the Covenant of Redemption*. Ross-shire: Christian Focus, 2016.

Ferguson, Sinclair B. *John Owen on the Christian Life*. Carlisle, PA: Banner of Truth Trust, 1987.

Firth, David G. 'Speech Acts and Covenant in 2 Samuel 7:1-17' (pp. 79-99 in *The God of the Covenant: Biblical, Theological, and Contemporary Perspectives*. Eds. Jamie A. Grant and Alistair I. Wilson. Downers Grove: Inter-Varsity Press, 2005).

Fox, Michael V. 'The Sign of the Covenant: Circumcision in the Light of the Priestly *'ôt* Etiologies', *RB* 81.4 (October 1974): pp. 557-96.

Fryer, Ken. 'Covenant Theology in Baptist Life' (pp. 145-59 in *Covenant Theology: A Baptist Distinctive*. Ed. Earl M. Blackburn. Birmingham, AL: Solid Ground Christian Books, 2013).

Gentry, Peter J. and Stephen J. Wellum. *Kingdom through Covenant: A Biblical-Theological Understanding of the Covenants*. Wheaton: Crossway, 2018.

Girardeau, John L. *The Federal Theology: Its Import and Its Regulative Influence*. Greenville, SC: Reformed Academic Press, 1994.

Golding, Peter. *Covenant Theology: The Key of Theology in Reformed Thought and Tradition*. Ross-shire: Christian Focus, 2004.

Griffith, Howard and John R. Muether, eds. *Creator, Redeemer, Consummator: A Festschrift for Meredith G. Kline*. Greenville, SC: Reformed Academic Press, 2000.

Griffiths, Phillip D. R. *Covenant Theology: A Reformed Baptist Perspective*. Eugene OR: Wipf & Stock, 2016.

Haas, Gene. 'Calvin, Natural Law, and the Two Kingdoms' (pp. 33-64 in *Kingdoms Apart: Engaging the Two Kingdoms Perspective*. Phillipsburg, NJ: P&R, 2012).

Hahn, S. W. 'A Broken Covenant and the Curse of Death: A Study of Hebrews 9:15-22,' *CBQ* 66 (2004): pp. 416-36.

Helm, Paul. 'Calvin and the Covenant: Unity and Continuity,' *EQ* 55 (1983): pp. 65-82.

Hillers, Delbert R. *Covenant: The History of Biblical Idea*. Baltimore: John Hopkins, 1969.

Hoekema, Anthony A. 'Calvin's Doctrine of the Covenant of Grace', *Reformed Review* 15.4 (1962): pp. 1-12.

Horton, Michael. *God of Promise: Introducing Covenant Theology*. Grand Rapids: Baker Books, 2006.

Hübner, Jason. 'Acts 2:39 in its Context [Part 1]: An Exegetical Summary of Acts 2:39 and Paedobaptism,' (pp. 383-416 in *Recovering a Covenantal Heritage: Essays in Baptist Covenant Theology*. Ed. Richard C. Barcellos. Palmdale, CA: RBAP, 2014).

Irons, Lee 'Redefining Merit: An Examination of Medieval Presuppositions in Covenant Theology'. (pp. 253-70 in *Creator, Redeemer, Consummator: A Festschrift for Meredith G. Kline*. Eds. Howard Griffith and John R. Muether. Greenville, SC: Reformed Academic Press, 2000).

Jeong, Koo Jeon. *Covenant Theology: John Murray's and Meredith G. Kline's Response to the Historical Development of Federal Theology in Reformed Thought*. Lanham, MD: University of Press America, 1999.

_____. *Covenant Theology and Justification by Faith: The Shepherd Controversy and Its Impacts*. Eugene, OR: Wipf & Stock, 2006.

_____. *Biblical Theology: Covenants and the Kingdom of God in Redemptive History*. Eugene, OR: Wipf & Stock, 2017.

Jewett, Paul K. *Infant Baptism and the Covenant of Grace*. Grand Rapids: Eerdmans, 1978.

Johnson, Jeffrey D. *The Fatal Flaw of the Theology Behind Infant Baptism*. Free Grace Press, 2010.

_____. *The Kingdom of God: A Baptist Expression of Covenant and Biblical Theology*. Conway, AR: Free Grace Press, 2014.

Jones, Mark, 'The "Old" Covenant' (pp. 183-203 in *Drawn into Controversie: Reformed Theological Diversity and Debates Within Seventeenth Century British Puritanism* Ed. Nigel M. de S. Cameron. Edinburgh, 1993).

Jordan, James B. 'Merit Versus Maturity: What Did Jesus Do For Us?' (pp. 151-202 in *The Federal Vision*. Eds. Steve Wilkins and Duane Garner. Monroe, LA: Athanasius Press, 2004).

Kaiser, Jr., Walter C. 'The Blessing of David: The Charter for Humanity' (pp. 298-318 in *The Law and the Prophets*. Ed. John H. Skilton. Nutley, NJ: Presbyterian and Reformed, 1974).

Karlburg, Mark W. *Covenant Theology in Reformed Perspective*. Eugene, OR: Wipf & Stock, 2000.

Kingdon, David. *Children of Abraham: A Reformed Baptist View of Baptism, the Covenant, and Children*. Sussex: Carey Publications, 1973.

Kline, Meredith. 'The Intrusion and the Decalogue', *WTJ* 16 (1953/54): pp. 1-22.

_____. 'Because It Had Not Rained', *WTJ* 20 (1958), pp. 146-57.

_____. *The Treaty of the Great King: The Covenant Structure of Deuteronomy*. Grand Rapids: Eerdmans, 1963.

_____. *By Oath Consigned*. Grand Rapids: Eerdmans, 1968.

_____. *The Structure of Biblical Authority*. Grand Rapids: Eerdmans, 1972.

_____. 'Of Works and Grace', *Presbyterion* 9 (1983): pp. 85-92.

_____. 'Gospel until the Law: Rom. 5:13-14 and the Old Covenant', *JETS* 34 (1991): pp. 433-46.

_____. *Kingdom Prologue: Genesis Foundations for a Covenantal Worldview*. Overland Park, KS: Two Age Press, 2000.

_____. *God, Heaven, and Har Magedon*. Eugene, OR: Wipf & Stock, 2006.

_____. *The Essential Writings of Meredith G. Kline*. Peabody, MA: Hendriksen Publishers, 2017.

Knoppers, Gary N. 'Ancient Near Eastern Royal Grants and the Davidic Covenant: A Parallel?' *JAOS* 116.4 (1996): pp. 670-97.

Lehrer, Steve. *New Covenant Theology: Questions Answered*. n.p.: Steve Lehrer, 2006.

Leithart, Peter J. *The Kingdom and the Power*. Phillipsburg, NJ: P&R Publishing, 1993.

_____. '"Judge Me, O God": Biblical Perspectives on Justification'. (pp. 203-236 in *The Federal Vision*. Eds. Steve Wilkins and Duane Garrett. Monroe, LA: Athanasius Press, 2004).

Lillback, Peter A. 'The Continuing Conundrum: Calvin and the Conditionality of the Covenant', *CTJ* 29 (1994): pp. 42-74.

_____. *The Binding of God: Calvin's Role in the Development of Covenant Theology*. Grand Rapids: Baker, 2001.

Loretz, O. 'The *Perfectum Copulativum* in 2 Sam. 7, 9–11', *CBQ* 23 (1961): pp. 294-96.

Lusk, Rich. 'A Response to "The Biblical Plan of Salvation"' (pp. 118-48 in *The Auburn Avenue Theology: Pros & Cons*. Ed. E. Calvin Beisner. Fort Lauderdale, FL: Knox Theological Seminary, 2004.

Macleod, Donald, 'Covenant Theology' (pp. 214-18 in *Dictionary of Scottish Church History and Theology*. Ed. Nigel M. de S. Cameron. Downers Grove, IL: InterVarsity Press, 1993).

Malone, Fred A. *The Baptism of Disciples Alone: A Covenantal Argument for Credobaptism Versus Paedobaptism.* Cape Coral, FL: Founders Press, 2003.

———. 'Biblical Hermeneutics and Covenant Theology (pp. 63-88 in *Covenant Theology: A Baptist Distinctive.* Birmingham, AL: Solid Ground Christian Books, 2013).

Matthews, A. G., ed. *The Savoy Declaration of Faith and Order 1658.* London: Independent Press, 1959.

McConville, Gordon J. ברית, *NIDOTTE*, 1:748.

McDowell, Mark I. 'Covenant in the Theology of Karl Barth, T. F. & J. B. Torrance' (Forthcoming in *Covenant Theology.* Eds. Guy Waters, J. Nicholas Reid, and John Muether. Wheaton, IL: Crossway, forthcoming November 2020).

McIlhenny, Ryan C. ed., *Kingdoms Apart: Engaging the Two Kingdoms Perspective.* Phillipsburg, NJ: P&R, 2012.

Myers, Stephen. 'Critiquing the Klinean Doctrine of Republication: A Review Article'. *Reformation 21*, March 2015.

Mendenhall, G. E. *Law and Covenant in Israel and the Ancient Near East.* Pittsburgh: Board of Colportage of W. Penn., 1955.

Meyer, Jason C. 'The Mosaic Law, Theological Systems, and the Glory of Christ' (pp. 69-100 in *Progressive Covenantalism.* Nashville, TN: B&H Academic, 2016).

Muller, Richard A. *After Calvin: Studies in the Development of a Theological Tradition.* Oxford: Oxford University Press, 2003.

Murray, John. *The Covenant of Grace.* Phillipsburg, NJ: P&R, 1953/1988.

———. *Redemption Accomplished and Applied.* Grand Rapids: Eerdmans, 1955.

———. 'The Adamic Administration' (pp. 47-59 in the *Collected Writings of John Murray: Volume Two, Select Lectures in Systematic Theology.* Carlisle, PA: The Banner of Truth Trust, 1977).

_____. 'Common Grace' (pp. 93-122 in the *Collected Writings of John Murray, Volume Two: Select Lectures in Systematic Theology*. Carlisle, PA: The Banner of Truth Trust, 1977).

Nichols, Greg. *Covenant Theology: A Reformed and Baptistic Perspective on God's Covenants*. Birmingham, AL: Solid Ground Christian Books, 2011.

Nicholson, Ernest W. *God and His People: Covenant and Theology in the Old Testament*. Oxford: Clarendon Press, 1986.

Packer, J. I., 'Introduction: On Covenant Theology' (n.p. in *The Economy of the Covenants between God and Man*. Herman Witsius. Phillipsburg, NJ: P & R, 1990).

Parler, Branson. 'Two Cities or Two Kingdoms? The Importance of the Ultimate in Reformed Social Thought' (pp. 176-86 in *Kingdoms Apart: Engaging the Two Kingdoms Perspective*. Ed. Ryan C. McIlhenny. Phillipsburg, NJ: P&R, 2012).

Payton, Jr., James R. 'Infant Baptism and the Covenant of Grace: A Review Article', *WTJ* 42.2 (1980): pp. 416-19.

Poythress, Vern S. *The Shadow of Christ in the Law of Moses*. Phillipsburg, NJ: P&R Publishing, 1991.

_____. *Theophany: A Biblical Theology of God's Appearing*. Wheaton, IL: Crossway, 2018.

Pratt, Jr., Richard L. 'Infant Baptism in the New Covenant' (pp. 156-74 in *The Case for Covenantal Baptism*. Ed. Gregg Strawbridge. Phillipsburg, NJ: P&R Publishing, 2003).

Ramsey, D. Patrick. 'In Defense of Moses: A Confessional Critique of Kline and Karlburg'. *WTJ* 66 (2004): pp. 373-400.

Reisinger, John G. *Tablets of Stone*. Southbridge, MA: Crowne Publications, 1989.

_____. *Abraham's Four Seeds: A Biblical Examination of the Presuppositions of Covenant Theology and Dispensationalism*. Frederick, MD: New Covenant Media, 1998.

Renihan, James M., ed. *Covenant Theology: From Adam to Christ*. Palmdale, CA: Reformed Baptist Academic Press, 2005.

_____. 'PART I: Nehemiah Coxe' (pp. 7-142 in *Covenant Theology: From Adam to Christ*. Palmdale, CA: Reformed Baptist Academic Press, 2005).

_____.'PART II: John Owen' (pp. 143-312 in *Covenant Theology: From Adam to Christ*. Palmdale, CA: Reformed Baptist Academic Press, 2005.

_____. 'Introduction' (pp. 13-18 in *Recovering a Covenantal Heritage: Essays in Baptist Covenant Theology*. Ed. Richard C. Barcellos. Palmdale, CA: RBAP, 2014).

_____. 'Covenant Theology in the First and Second London Confessions of Faith' (pp. 45-70 in *Recovering a Covenantal Heritage Essays in Baptist Covenant Theology*. Ed. Richard C. Barcellos. Palmdale, CA: RBAP, 2014).

Renihan, Samuel D. *From Shadow to Substance: The Federal Theology of the English Particular Baptists (1642–1704)*. Oxford: Regent's Park College, 2018.

Rhodes, Jonty. *Covenants Made Simple*. Phillipsburg, NJ: P&R Publishing, 2013.

Richard, Guy M. *Baptism: Answers to Common Questions*. Sanford, FL: Reformation Trust, 2019.

Robertson, O. Palmer. *The Christ of the Covenants*. Phillipsburg, NJ: P&R, 1980.

Rolston III, Holmes. *John Calvin versus the Westminster Confession*. Richmond, VA: John Knox, 1972.

Ross, Mark E. 'Baptism and Circumcision as Signs and Seals' (pp. 85-111 in *The Case for Covenantal Baptism*. Ed. Gregg Strawbridge. Phillipsburg, NJ: P&R Publishing, 2003).

Schaff, Philip. *The Creeds of Christendom*, Volume 3: *The Evangelical Protestant Creeds*. Grand Rapids: Baker Books, 1996.

Schenk, Lewis Bevins. *The Presbyterian Doctrine of Children in the Covenant*. Eugene, OR: Wipf & Stock, 2001; orig. Yale University Press, 1940.

Schreiner, Thomas R. and Shawn D. Wright, eds. *Believer's Baptism: Sign of the New Covenant in Christ*. Nashville: B&H, 2006.

Schreiner, Thomas R. *Faith Alone: The Doctrine of Justification*. Grand Rapids: Zondervan, 2015.

_____. 'Good-bye and Hello: The Sabbath Command for New Covenant Believers' (pp. 159-88 in *Progressive Covenantalism*. Nashville, TN: B&H Academic, 2016).

_____. *Covenant and God's Purpose for the World*. Wheaton: Crossway, 2017.

Schwertley, Brian M. *Auburn Avenue Theology: A Biblical Critique*. Kearney, NE: Morris Publishing, 2005.

Shepherd, Norman. 'Thirty-four Theses on Justification in Relation to Faith, Repentance, and Good Works', presented to the Philadelphia Presbytery of the Orthodox Presbytery of the Orthodox Presbyterian Church, Nov. 18, 1978, Thesis 19.

Smick, Elmer B. ברה, [ברית], *TWOT*, 1:128.

_____. 'The Psalms as Response to God's Covenant Love: Theological Observations' (pp. 77-86 in *Creator, Redeemer, Consummator: A Festschrift for Meredith G. Kline*. Eds. Howard Griffith and John R. Muether. Greenville, SC: Reformed Academic Press, 2000).

Smith, Morton H. 'The Biblical Plan of Salvation with Reference to the Covenant of Works, Imputation, and Justification by Faith' (pp. 96-117 in *The Auburn Avenue Theology Pros and Con: Debating the Federal Vision*. Ed. Calvin E. Beisner. Fort Lauderdale, FL: Knox Theological Seminary, 2004).

_____. 'Federal Theology and the Westminster Standards' (pp. 15-46 in *The Covenant*. Eds. Joseph A. Pipa, Jr. and C. N. Willborn. Taylors, SC: Presbyterian Press, 2005).

Smith, Ralph. *Eternal Covenant: How the Trinity Reshapes Covenant Theology*. Moscow, ID: Canon, 2003.

Stek, John H. '"Covenant" Overload in Reformed Theology', *CTJ* 29 (1994): pp. 12-41.

Swain, Scott R. 'Covenant of Redemption' (pp. 107-25 in *Christian Dogmatics: Reformed Theology for the Church Catholic*. Eds. Michael Allen and Scott R. Swain. Grand Rapids, MI: Baker Academic, 2016).

————. 'New Covenant Theologies' (Forthcoming in *Covenant Theology*. Eds. Guy P. Waters, J. Nicholas Reid, and John Muether. Wheaton, IL: Crossway, November 2020)

Taylor, Justin. 'Was There a Covenant of Works? (pp. 137-45 in *Covenant Theology: A Baptist Distinctive*. Birmingham, AL: Solid Ground Christian Books, 2013).

Torrance, T. F. 'From John Knox to John McLeod Campbell: A Reading of Scottish Theology' (pp. 1-28 in *Disruption to Diversity: Edinburgh Divinity 1846-1996*. Eds. David F. Wright and Gary D. Babcock. Edinburgh: T & T Clark, 1996).

Torrance, J. B. 'Covenant or Contract? A Study of the Theological Background of Worship in Seventeenth-Century Scotland', *SJT*, 23.1 (1970): pp. 51-76.

Turner, Laurence A. 'The Rainbow as a Sign of the Covenant in Genesis ix 11-13', *VT* 43.1 (1993): pp. 119-24.

VanDrunen, David and R. Scott Clark. 'The Covenant before the Covenants' (pp. 167-96 in *Covenant, Justification, and Pastoral Ministry*. Ed. R. Scott Clark. Phillipsburg, NJ: P&R, 2007).

VanDrunen, David. *A Biblical Case for Natural Law*. Grand Rapids: Acton Institute, 2006.

————. 'The Importance of the Penultimate: Reformed Social Thought and the Contemporary Critiques of the Liberal Society', *Journal of Markets and Morality* 9/2 (Fall 2006): pp. 219-49.

_____. 'Natural Law and the Works Principle under Adam and Moses' (pp. 283-314 in *The Law is Not of Faith: Essays on Works and Grace in the Mosaic Covenant.* Phillipsburg, NJ: P&R, 2009).

_____. *Natural Law and the Two Kingdoms: A Study of the Development of Reformed Social Thought.* Grand Rapids: Eerdmans, 2010.

_____. *Living in God's Two Kingdoms: A Biblical Vision for Christianity and Culture.* Wheaton, IL: Crossway, 2010.

_____. *Divine Covenants and Moral Order: A Biblical Theology of Natural Law.* Grand Rapids: Eerdmans, 2014.

Venema, Cornelius P. *Christ and Covenant Theology: Essays on Election, Republication, and the Covenants.* Phillipsburg: P&R, 2017.

Vos, Geerhardus. *Biblical Theology.* Grand Rapids: Eerdmans, 1948.

_____. 'The Doctrine of the Covenant in Reformed Theology' (pp. 234-67 in *Redemptive History and Biblical Interpretation, The Shorter Writings of Geerhardus Vos.* Ed. Richard B. Gaffin, Jr. Phillipsburg, NJ: Presbyterian and Reformed Publishing Co., 1980).

_____. *The Eschatology of the Old Testament.* Ed. James T. Dennison. Phillipsburg, NJ: P&R, 2001.

_____. *Reformed Dogmatics, Volume Two: Anthropology.* Ed. Richard B. Gaffin, Jr. Bellingham, WA: Lexham Press, 2012–2014.

Vos, Johannes G. *The Westminster Larger Catechism: A Commentary.* Ed. G. I. Williamson. Phillipsburg, NJ: P&R, 2002.

Waddington, Jeffrey C. '*Duplex in Homine Regimen.* A Response to David VanDrunen's "The Reformed Two Kingdoms Doctrine: An Explanation and a Defense"', *The Confessional Presbyterian* 8 (2012): pp. 191-96, 286-87.

Waldron, Samuel E. *A Modern Exposition of the 1689 Baptist Confession of Faith.* Darlington, Evangelical Press, 1989.

Walther, C. F. W. *The Proper Distinction Between Law and Gospel.* St. Louis, MO: Concordia Publishing House, 1929 reprint.

Warfield, B.B. 'Hosea 6:7: Adam or Man?' (pp. 116-29 in *Collected Shorter Writings*. Ed. John E. Meeter. 2 vols. Phillipsburg: Presbyterian and Reformed, 2001).

Waters, Guy. *New Perspective on Paul: Review and Response*. Phillipsburg, NJ: P&R Publishing, 2004.

_____. *The Federal Vision and Covenant Theology: A Comparative Analysis*. Phillipsburg, NJ: P&R, 2006.

_____. 'Romans 10:5 and the Covenant of Works' (pp. 210-39 in *The Law is not of Faith: Essays on Works and Grace in the Mosaic Covenant*. Eds. Bryan D. Estelle, J. V. Fesko, and David VanDrunen. Phillipsburg, NJ: P&R, 2009).

Watt, Jonathan M. 'The *Oikos* Formula' (pp. 70-84 in *The Case for Covenantal Baptism*. Ed. Gregg Strawbridge. Phillipsburg, NJ: P&R Publishing, 2003).

Weeks, Noel. *Admonition and Curse: The Ancient Near Eastern Treaty/ Covenant Form as a Problem in Inter-Cultural Relationships*. New York: T&T Clark, 2004.

Weinfeld, M. 'Covenant Grant in the Old Testament and the Ancient Near East', *JAOS* 90 (1970): pp. 184-203.

Wells, Tom and Fred Zaspel. *New Covenant Theology*. Frederick, MD: New Covenant Media, 2002.

Wellum, Stephen. 'Baptism and the Relationship between the Covenants (pp. 97-162 in *Believer's Baptism: Sign of the New Covenant in Christ*. Eds. Thomas R. Schreiner and Shawn D. Wright. Nashville: B&H, 2006).

_____. 'Progressive Covenantalism and the Doing of Ethics' (pp. 215-33 in *Progressive Covenantalism*. Nashville, TN: B&H Academic, 2016).

Wellum, Stephen J. and Brent E. Parker, eds. *Progressive Covenantalism*. Nashville, TN: B&H Academic, 2016.

Westerholm, Stephen. *Perspective Old and New on Paul: The 'Lutheran' Paul and His Critics*. Grand Rapids: Eerdmans, 2004.

White, Blake. *What is New Covenant Theology? An Introduction.* Frederick, MD: New Covenant Media, 2012.

White, James R. 'The Newness of the New Covenant: Better Covenant, Better Mediator, Better Sacrifice, Better Ministry, Better Hopoe, Better Promises (Part Two) (pp. 357-82 in *Recovering a Covenantal Heritage*. Ed. Richard C. Barcellos. Palmdale, CA: RBAP, 2014).

Wilkins, Steve and Duane Garrett, eds. *The Federal Vision.* Monroe, LA: Athanasius Press, 2004.

Williamson, Paul R. *Sealed with an Oath: Covenant in God's Unfolding Purpose.* NSBT. Downers Grove, IL: Inter-Varsity Press, 2007.

_____. 'The "Pactum Salutis": A Scriptural Concept or Scholastic Mythology?', *TynBul* 69.2 (2018): pp. 259-82.

Wilson, Doug. *'Reformed' is not Enough: Recovering the Objectivity of the Covenant.* Moscow, ID: Canon Press, 2010.

Witsius, Herman. *The Economy of the Covenants Between God and Man.* Escondido, CA: The den Dulk Christian Foundation, 1990.

Woolsey, Andrew A. *Unity and Continuity in Covenantal Thought: A Study in the Reformed Tradition to the Westminster Assembly.* Grand Rapids: Reformation Heritage Books, 2012.

Zehender, Markus. 'Building on Stone? Deuteronomy and Esarhaddon's Loyalty Oaths (Part 1): Some Preliminary Observations', *BBR* 19.3 (2009): pp. 341-74.

_____. 'Building on Stone? Deuteronomy and Esarhaddon's Loyalty Oaths (Part 2): Some Additional Observations', *BBR* 19.4 (2009): pp. 511-35.

Scripture Index

Subject Index

O

Also available from Christian Focus Publications...

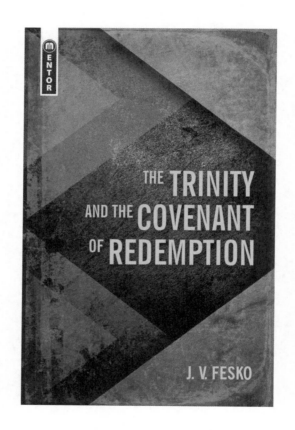

978-1-7819-1765-7

The Trinity And the Covenant of Redemption

J. V. Fesko

When Christians reflect on the gospel, their attention is rightly drawn to the cross and empty tomb. But is this it? Or is there much more to the story? In a ground–breaking work, J. V. Fesko reminds us that the great news of this gospel message is rooted in eternity, whereby a covenant was made between the persons of the Trinity in order to redeem sinners like you and me. J. V. Fesko, in the first of a three part series on covenant theology featuring Redemption, Grace and Works, aims to retrieve and recover classic Reformed covenant theology for the church.

Some books today exegete the shining truths of the Holy Scriptures, others mine the treasures of Reformed orthodoxy, and yet others interact with influential theologians of the modern era. This book is one of the few that does all three, and does them well.

Joel R. Beeke
President, Puritan Reformed Theological Seminary, Grand Rapids, Michigan

... displays the vitality and richness of the covenant of redemption for other doctrines-not least, the Trinity. In both method and substance, this is an exemplary work that will edify as well as inform.

Michael Horton
J. Gresham Machen Professor of Systematic Theology and Apologetics, Westminster Seminary California, Escondido, California

Christian Focus Publications

Our mission statement –

STAYING FAITHFUL

In dependence upon God we seek to impact the world through literature faithful to His infallible Word, the Bible. Our aim is to ensure that the Lord Jesus Christ is presented as the only hope to obtain forgiveness of sin, live a useful life and look forward to heaven with Him.

Our books are published in four imprints:

CHRISTIAN FOCUS

Popular works including biographies, commentaries, basic doctrine and Christian living.

CHRISTIAN HERITAGE

Books representing some of the best material from the rich heritage of the church.

MENTOR

Books written at a level suitable for Bible College and seminary students, pastors, and other serious readers. The imprint includes commentaries, doctrinal studies, examination of current issues and church history.

CF4•K

Children's books for quality Bible teaching and for all age groups: Sunday school curriculum, puzzle and activity books; personal and family devotional titles, biographies and inspirational stories – because you are never too young to know Jesus!

Christian Focus Publications Ltd,
Geanies House, Fearn, Ross-shire,
IV20 1TW, Scotland, United Kingdom.
www.christianfocus.com